R&D Cooperation among Marketplace Competitors

R&D Cooperation among Marketplace Competitors

William J. Murphy

QUORUM BOOKS
NEW YORK • WESTPORT, CONNECTICUT • LONDON

Library of Congress Cataloging-in-Publication Data

Murphy, William J. (William Joseph), 1949–
    R & D cooperation among marketplace competitors / William J.
Murphy.
        p.   cm.
    Includes index.
    ISBN 0–89930–489–3 (lib. bdg. : alk paper)
    1. Cooperative industrial research – United States.   I. Title.
    II. Title: R and D cooperation among marketplace competitors.
    T176.M87   1991
    338.97306 – dc20   90–8919

British Library Cataloguing in Publication Data is available.

Library of Congress Catalog Card Number: 90–8919
ISBN: 0–89930–489–3

First published in 1991

Quorum Books, 88 Post Road West, Westport, CT   06881
An imprint of Greenwood Publishing Group, Inc.

Printed in the United States of America

The paper used in this book complies with the
Permanent Paper Standard issued by the National
Information Standards Organization (Z39.48–1984).

10 9 8 7 6 5 4 3 2 1

Contents

Illustrations

R&D Cooperation among Marketplace Competitors

1

Introduction

Cooperative activities or joint ventures are becoming increasingly popular as instruments of strategic action. Companies, like newly married couples, are entering into strategic alliances full of hope and enthusiasm, but if past experience is any indication of the future, they most likely will experience disillusionment and eventual divorce.[1] Despite this newfound interest in collective ventures, our understanding regarding the strategic management of collective action needs improvement if the hoped-for benefits of cooperation are to be realized. As one authority on joint ventures bluntly put it, "This shortfall in the strategic management literature reflects a serious weakness in what managers know about cooperative strategies."[2] This book examines the management of a specific type of cooperative action, one that has become critically important to company and national competitiveness — the cooperative research venture.

Three forces are at play in the modern economy that make cooperative research ventures attractive. First, marketplace pressures exerted by foreign companies, most notably the Japanese, which have a history of cooperative research activity, often orchestrated by governmental institutions such as MITI (Ministry of International Trade and Industry), have caused domestic corporations to reexamine the prevailing "go it alone" attitude.[3] Second, the amount of resources, both financial and human, necessary to conduct modern-day, high technology research has become so vast that fewer individual companies can tackle these projects as independent entities.[4] And finally, changes in the antitrust prohibitions against certain types of cooperative research have lessened some of the legal uncertainties surrounding joint activities among competing companies.[5]

Figure 1.1
Forces Encouraging Cooperation

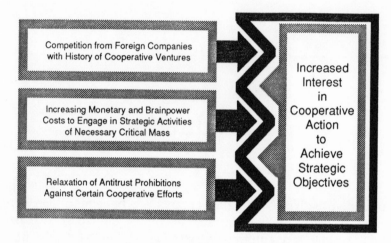

KNOWLEDGE – THE FUEL OF THE INFORMATION SOCIETY

Although much of the underdeveloped world is still struggling with the transformation from an agricultural society to an industrial society, the United States, Japan, and Europe are in the midst of a new transformation, the transformation from industrial to information societies. So many people have written and spoken about this imminent information revolution or the emerging information society over the last decade that often the wrong notion is conjured up of just how such a change might occur. The transformation of society from an industrial-based one to an information-based one will be neither sudden nor especially dramatic as some accounts suggest. In fact, many of the changes will be so small and incremental that it may sometimes be hard to detect any change at all. But, if we raise our plane of perspective high enough so that a larger time span can be taken into account, the importance of the transformation becomes clear.

Perhaps it is better to think not of the transformation from an industrial to information society as some sort of violent revolution but rather as a slow blending as the latter overlays the former. In fact, the various "societies" – agricultural, industrial, and information – are inextricably intertwined. In an agricultural society a majority of the population is involved in farming and related work. For example, it is estimated that 80 percent of the people in the People's Republic of China are employed in the agricultural sector. As an agricultural society evolves toward an industrial one, a smaller and smaller percentage of the population will be involved with food production. This does not mean that industrial activity completely replaces agricultural activity. Elements of the agricultural society that precedes the industrial one will still survive, and may even flourish. In this country, for example, although only 6 percent of the population is involved in the agricultural sector, that 6 percent produces enough food to feed us and much of the world, and it is our industrial progress that has made this agricultural achievement possible.

In an agricultural society one's wealth is based on how much land one owns or controls. In the industrial society one's wealth is based on the capital or other factors of production one owns or controls. In the information society wealth is based on the creation and control of information and knowledge. And, just as the industrial revolution first took hold in those areas of the world that had ready access to the factors of production (water power for the mills, rivers for easy transportation of goods, or cities with cheap and abundant labor), the information society is beginning to grow around the locations that produce the commodities of value: information and knowledge.

The fundamental importance of information and knowledge to the modern economy is reflected in the geographic distribution of today's high-growth businesses. The first manufacturing organizations of the American Industrial Revolution, the early textile companies, began to flourish at sources of water power to run the looms and spinners. Many New England cities, such as Lowell, Massachusetts, or Manchester in New Hampshire were born along the waterfalls and rapids of the area's streams and rivers. As mass production and mass transportation technologies spread throughout the nation in the 1900s, important economic centers flourished around the transportation resources, first the canals and ports, and later the railroads.

In the modern society areas of economic vitality have prospered around new resource centers, those producing information and knowledge. Boston, San Francisco and the Bay Area, Research Triangle in North Carolina, and the Austin area in Texas have all reaped the economic benefits of first-class educational institutions that produce an increasingly valuable competitive resource: brainpower. It is no accident that the once run-down manufacturing area behind MIT has been transformed into "Artificial Intelligence Alley," or that silicon is replacing silage on the prairies surrounding the University of Texas in Austin. Like the Mesabi range or the Texas oilfields of old, educational institutions, research laboratories, and corporate think tanks are providing the essential raw material that is fueling the information society.

Information and knowledge, long important elements in enhancing manufacturing productivity, have become products in and of themselves. Some of the most prosperous sectors of the national economy produce and handle little else. Although the computer software industry is the most obvious illustration, there are others of equal interest. The financial industry is but one example. Today the financial world is a world of information. Rarely does the actual physical transfer of money or its symbolic equivalents take place. Even paper money, itself a basically worthless item except for the information it represents, is becoming rare for all transactions save the small. In sharp contrast to early industrial society in which the wealth of a nation was based on the size of an actual pile of gold bullion stacked in a vault or fortress somewhere, the wealth of today's modern industrial nation is represented by millions of account entries on a network of thousands upon thousands of computers. It is this cumulative information of debts and lendings, earnings and liabilities that makes a nation either wealthy or poor.

As knowledge becomes increasingly important to the success and prosperity of a company, and ultimately a nation, more systematic efforts to encourage and harness new, creative ideas have arisen, and one of the most promising is through interfirm cooperation.

One of the difficulties in trying to gain a better understanding of the management issues involved in cooperative activities stems from the incredible diversity in the types of collective undertakings. Companies are not independent entities but exist in a complex web of external relationships with other companies that range from minimal interaction, as exemplified by short-term contracts with buyers and sellers, to the full integration of mergers and acquisitions. In between these two extremes lie joint or cooperative ventures.[6]

Cooperative ventures also exist along a continuum of interaction. On one hand are the contractual cooperative ventures which, in their simplest form, are merely agreements between two or more companies regarding a specified exchange of performances. At the other extreme are equity cooperative ventures which provide for joint decision-making within the context of a jointly owned enterprise. Even within these broad categories great diversity remains. Many equity

joint ventures undertaken by U.S.-based multinational companies in
the past involved a passive foreign partner in terms of managerial
decision-making.[7] These joint ventures are often the result of foreign
investment legislation and might be deemed "shotgun marriages."
Domestically, passive financial partnerships or joint ventures in such
areas as real estate, oil drilling, and movie making have long been
common. Also common are contractual joint ventures in which two or
more businesses agree to cooperate but do not establish a separate
business entity to carry out the collective action. Even among contractual joint ventures there is a substantial degree of diversity. Cross-licensing and cross-distribution agreements are just two subtypes of
contractual joint ventures that abound in the modern economy.

   Neither contractual nor equity cooperative ventures are new.[8] For

Figure 1.2
Form of Cooperative Activity

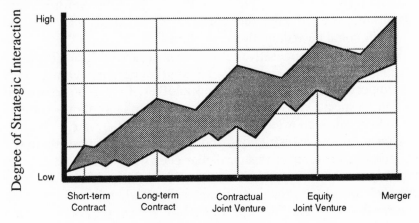

Form of Cooperative Activity

example, the aerospace industry is replete with examples of contractual cooperative ventures. The specialized nature of the work and the
scale of resources required has long fostered cooperation among
individual companies. It is commonplace to find an airframe manufacturer teaming up with a computer or propulsion system manufacturer
to develop an advanced design product. Although contractual cooperative ventures are more likely to be associated with shorter-term
projects than equity cooperative ventures, it is not difficult to find
contractual joint efforts that last for years, or equity joint ventures that
are short-lived.

Examples of equity cooperative ventures can also be found throughout the modern industrial age. Most often an equity cooperative
venture is formed by two or more existing firms to exploit a new
opportunity that is of common interest. Companies involved in natural
resource exploration and exploitation have long seen the benefits of
equity cooperative ventures.[9]

Although the creation, existence, and death of cooperative ventures
has been going on for decades they have received increased attention
lately as more corporations look to collective activity to achieve
strategic objectives. General Motors teams up with its highly successful competitor Toyota to produce a small car in California.[10] IBM,
departing from its "invented here" tradition, forms two strategically
important joint ventures during a six-month period in 1983.[11] Even
Kodak, a company that in the past placed such a high value on
self-sufficiency that it operated its own paper mills and lumber forests,
has embarked on the cooperative venture path by entering the important electronic imaging business through a joint venture with
Matsushita, even though the president of Kodak admits that the
company could have done the work alone.

While all these cooperative activities can be, and often are, included
together under the general rubric of joint or cooperative ventures, they
are importantly different from one another. In this book we will
examine a special class of interorganizational collaboration — cooperation to produce knowledge.

Due to antitrust restrictions and concerns in the past, domestic
cooperative ventures of this particular class were somewhat rare. In
fact, many of the few collective undertakings that could be classified
as involving active, equal, and competing participants were often
vigorously pursued by the Department of Justice or the Federal Trade
Commission as anticompetitive.[12] As a result of changes in the competitive and legal environment, a new breed of cooperative research
venture has emerged.

In the fast-moving electronics field, significant collaborative research efforts are already underway. The Microelectronics and Computer Technology Corporation, or MCC, a collection of twenty-one
competing U.S. computer and component manufacturers headquartered in Austin, Texas, is a prime example of this new breed of
collective activity. MCC, the subject of chapter 5, is widely seen as a
pioneer in cooperative research and is a major part of a worldwide
effort pursuing the "fifth generation" of computers. Sematech, a more
recent example of interfirm cooperation within the computer industry

Figure 1.3
Growth in Domestic Cooperation (1970–1984)

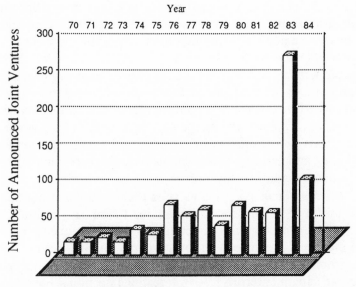

Data source: Announced Joint Ventures per year taken from Table 1–3, Kathryn Rudie Harrigan, *Strategies for Joint Ventures* (Lexington
Books, 1985), pp. 10–11.

that is discussed in more detail in chapter 7, adds an additional twist
with more active government involvement.

The importance of the technology being developed by MCC and
Sematech is well-recognized, not only by the companies directly involved and by companies in associated industries that stand to benefit,
but also by governmental agencies. But common recognition of the
significance of the technology does not necessarily lead to a common
approach regarding its development.

Just as the cooperative venture researchers will be required to
develop new technology, cooperative venture managers will be required to develop new management systems and organizational structures to deal with the unprecedented problems facing a collaborative
effort of this nature. One of the key management tasks is to forge a
consensus among the participants regarding solutions to shared problems. Underlying this book is a general assumption that managing a
cooperative research venture differs in important ways from managing
a single-participant research organization.

My interest in these questions stems from case studies I conducted into cooperative research ventures while a fellow and later a doctoral student at the Harvard Business School[13] and from my earlier experience as an antitrust trial attorney with the Federal Trade Commission. This initial research suggested that the tasks facing the general manager of a collective undertaking are importantly different from those facing the general manager of a single-participant organization. In particular, there was evidence that in cooperative research the essential executive functions of (1) establishing and maintaining a workable communication system among the participants, (2) securing the necessary efforts and resources from them, and most importantly, (3) formulating and defining an acceptable purpose were complicated by the presence of multiple sponsors.[14]

As the number of participants rises there is a corresponding increase in the need for negotiation among them. The multiplicity of participants in a cooperative venture places the general manager under increased pressure to discover and put into operation methods of accommodation, when compared to the general manager of a single-participant enterprise. An interesting question is how this process of accommodation and negotiation undertaken by executives of cooperative ventures expresses itself in (1) the strategy-making process, (2) the organizational structure, (3) the communication and control systems, and (4) the resource allocation process.

To cite an example of how the accommodation requirement is translated by the general manager of a cooperative research venture into the organizational structure, processes, and goals, consider the following. A number of corporations join together in a cooperative venture, such as the Microelectronics and Computer Technology Corporation, to engage in R&D efforts that would be immensely costly if done individually. Because "know-how" is an important component of the "product" produced by the cooperative venture, mechanisms to produce and transfer know-how must be developed. As a result, the executive of the collective enterprise is compelled to design an organizational structure that facilitates active participation and subsequent repatriation of sponsor employees. This brings up a plethora of difficulties for the general manager in that each sponsoring company from whom employees are "borrowed" may have a different compensation system, a different system of work methods and habits, a different cultural milieu, and a different strategic outlook. How does one put together an effective cooperative research enterprise given these particular constraints?

Although all executives must negotiate to one degree or another among conflicting and competing demands generated by both the external and internal environments, the general manager of a cooperative research venture faces a unique situation particularly with regard to strategy-making. By definition, a cooperative venture is composed of more than one strategy-making and -pursuing entity.

As the interaction between two strategy-pursuing entities increases so does the need for strategic coordination. There is little strategic coordination required to successfully execute a short-term contract between a buyer and a seller. On the other hand, a merger of separate businesses is the ultimate in strategic coordination in that only a single legal entity survives. The strategic coordination problems facing a cooperative venture such as MCC pose difficult and unique problems to the general managers of the participating companies as well as to the general manager of the cooperative activity in that the cooperative venture participants retain their individual strategic objectives.

In many ways the strategy-making task facing the general manager of a collective enterprise is similar to that facing the corporate general manager with regard to separate divisional or business strategies, but with one important difference. In the corporate setting, the strategy of the collective entity (the corporation) is expected to take precedence over the strategies of the components (divisions or business units), although this is often not the case in fact. In the cooperative venture, the strategy of the collective entity is expected, at least by the sponsors, to be subordinate to the strategies of the participants. In other words, the general manager of the cooperative venture must develop a unity of purpose with much less control over the constituents.

One of the main problems facing the general manager of a collective effort involves balancing collective costs and benefits against individual costs and benefits. Although the corporate general manager is faced with a similar situation with regard to decisions affecting both the corporation and its sub-unit elements, again, the task confronting the general manager of the cooperative enterprise is complicated by the ultimate independence of the individual participants. The difficulty of the task facing the management of the collective undertaking will depend on how the relative costs and benefits are distributed. For example, if the individual costs are higher than the individual benefits (as in situations where scale economies are such that they cannot be economically achieved by single participants) but the collective costs are less than the collective benefits, then the establishment and maintenance of cooperation should be facilitated. On the other hand, there are situations, such as the training of personnel or conducting basic research that have opportunities for an individual to obtain the collective benefit without bearing any of the costs. The general manager of a cooperative venture designed to produce such collective benefits will have a more difficult time establishing and maintaining cooperation.

From the above examples, one cannot help but note that there are important differences between the management tasks of single-participant organizations and the management tasks of cooperative undertakings. An important focus of this book is to help sort out these differences and discover how the manager of cooperative research ventures involving numerous, equal, active, and competitive participants seeks to resolve the difficulties facing the cooperators.

2

A Review of the Prior Literature on Interfirm Cooperation

A number of theoretical approaches have been used to help explain and understand cooperation between and among firms. Insights regarding such collaborative undertakings can be extracted from a review of the literature in a number of fields such as economics, game theory, organizational theory, legal/political thought, and general management. Each field draws upon separate but often related procedures, conceptual frameworks, algorithms, and models that have been accumulated in an associated body of literature for enlightenment and increased understanding. In each area the theorists and researchers have pursued agendas unique to that particular field, each trying to find the answers to different but related questions through the use of a wide variety of research methodologies.

One of the richest sources of knowledge regarding cooperative activities, at least in terms of scope and volume, is to be found in the legal literature, especially that associated with the antitrust laws and competition policy. This particular body of literature is separately discussed in the next chapter. The legal literature is especially interesting in that it relies heavily upon the other disciplines to help provide an intellectual framework to analyze cooperation. In addition, the legal literature provides data on cooperative action, since it documents real-life business situations. This chapter looks at the areas of literature outside the law, although many of the studies and ideas cited have found their way into the legal literature as part of the ongoing

debate regarding the appropriate policy to be taken toward cooperation in a competitive economic system.

Figure 2.1
Relevant Literature Overview

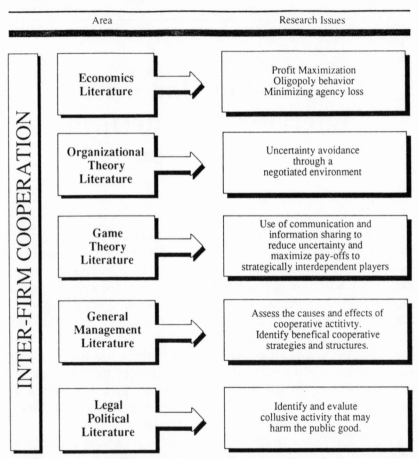

This chapter briefly examines the literature pertaining to interfirm
cooperation that is found in four other fields: economics, organizational theory, game theory, and general management. One cannot help
but note that although each body of literature and research relates in
some important way to interfirm cooperation, each provides only a
partial understanding of the phenomenon. This is partially due to the
fact that a particular field may have a restricted scope of concern that
translates into a limited research focus. This is arguably the case with
regard to the economic and game theory research. On the other hand

the constraining factor to a broader understanding may be lack of research data. Some have suggested this is the case with regard to the general management literature.[15] Figure 2.1 charts each of the five areas of relevant literature regarding interfirm cooperation and lists the primary research focus of each.

THE ECONOMICS LITERATURE

Economists have devoted considerable energy in an effort to explain why business firms might view interfirm cooperation as a profit-maximizing activity. Out of this effort has emerged a number of explanations as to how a corporation might profit from collaboration.[16] Forms of cooperation generally considered harmful to the public interest, such as price-fixing cartels and oligopolistic pricing, have drawn much attention from economists mainly because of their important implications for public policy-making and law enforcement activities. Economic inquiry that focuses on how oligopolistic cooperation might help a firm and its competitors maximize profits forms the basis of much of modern antitrust enforcement.[17] In this light, cooperation becomes the more sinister collusion aimed at shifting benefits from consumers to the "conspirators." This is not to say that more benign or even benevolent forms of interfirm cooperation such as collective standard-setting have been neglected by economists.[18]

The drive to capitalize on scale economies has been advanced by some economists as one explanation for interfirm cooperation.[19] Most scale effects tend to occur at the plant level, therefore collaboration among firms seeking to take advantage of plant-level scale economies tend to be in the form of actions aimed at industry rationalization, whereby plants on a smaller than minimally efficient scale are removed by agreement from the market so that they do not compete with the larger, more economical plants.[20]

More recently, economic analyses relating to principals and agents have begun to examine the phenomenon of institutional cooperation.[21] This body of work differs from prior economic analyses of cooperation in that it focuses on the cooperator–joint venture relationship rather than on the cooperator-cooperator relationship. Under this conceptual framework, a joint venture can be cast in terms of an agent to the sponsoring companies, who are viewed as the principals.[22]

The basic foundation premise of this body of literature is that the principal cannot monitor the actions of the agent without costs. As a consequence, the principal/agent relationship needs to be structured in such a manner so that the agent will have sufficient incentive to act in the principal's interest, even under circumstances where the agent's actions cannot be observed by the principal.[23] Simple contractual relationships between agent and principal are impractical in most situations which require a complex set of performances over time, particularly when the exact nature of the expected task needs to evolve in response to environmental change. Long-term institutional relationships develop in such cases to help reduce contracting and monitoring costs. By building trust and establishing information flows it is argued that the agent can make last-minute decisions on behalf of the principal without the need for lengthy renegotiation and additional contracting.

A joint venture, while capable of conferring the benefits of an agency/principal relationship upon its sponsors, also exposes the sponsors to the risks associated with agency relationships. The wish to avoid contracting and monitoring costs on the part of the principal affords the agent a certain latitude and independence. This downside to the principal/agent relationship is often referred to as "agency loss or agency costs"[24] and tends to be greatest in situations where "the interests or values of the principal and agent diverge substantially, and information monitoring is costly."[25] Although interest among economists in the agency/principal relationship may add an extra dimension to economic analyses once confined to examination of interfirm competition, the literature of the field, constrained by economic paradigms, remains limited in its utility to those wishing to establish and operate some form of collaborative venture.

ORGANIZATIONAL THEORY

For some researchers the search for economic or profit-maximizing explanations for interfirm cooperation has not been wholly satisfying. Cyert and March sought to explain cooperative action in terms of organizational dynamics. Although their attention was directed toward the individual firm, their conceptualization of what constitutes an organization is very broad and ranges outside the actual legal borders of the corporation.[26] To them an organization is composed of coalitions and sub-coalitions. With little difficulty one can consider a joint venture and its sponsors as within the same "organization," as the term is used by Cyert and March, and that the various participants and groups of participants represent coalitions and sub-coalitions.

Using this conceptual framework to examine the organizations, cooperation is seen as "an attempt to avoid uncertainty while obtaining a return that satisfies the profit and other demands of the coalition [and] firms will devise and negotiate an environment so as to eliminate the uncertainty."[27]

For Cyert and March, evidence of "[t]he lack of a profit-maximizing rationale" was suggested by the long-term stability of cooperation in many situations and examples of profitability for cooperation defectors.[28] It was their contention that an organization could enhance the manageability of decision-making through collaboration, by creating a "negotiated environment."[29]

Of particular interest in connection with the study of complex cooperative research ventures such as this is Cyert and March's assessment of the studies conducted regarding organizational objectives that "[a]greement on objectives is usually agreement on highly ambiguous goals. . . . The studies further suggest that behind this agreement on rather vague objectives there is considerable disagreement and uncertainty about subgoals, that organizations appear to be pursuing different goals at the same time."[30]

This is in sharp contrast to the viewpoint that in a successful cooperative undertaking conflict is eliminated through conformity to a common goal or purpose.[31] Rather than describe cooperation as characterized by goal consensus, Cyert and March describe cooperation as a dynamic process of bargaining, learning, and adjustment.[32]

James D. Thompson further developed this notion by arguing that organizations managed the uncertainty associated with the interdependences between a firm and its environment through three degrees of cooperation and commitment: contracting, co-opting and coalescing.[33] Again, like Cyert and March, Thompson was concerned with individual firms, but the concept of the coalition-based organization can be easily expanded to encompass more complex institutions such as interfirm collaborative ventures. Thompson went so far as to prescribe the "appropriate method of coordination" for the type of interdependence.[34]

The conceptualization of coalitions and sub-coalitions competing against and cooperating with one another in pursuit of the individual coalition's or sub-coalition's goals leads one to the next body of literature, namely game theory. This collection of research and theory also grew out of an examination of decision-making underlying economic behavior. Through the application of mathematics and logic, practitioners in this field have endeavored to describe and explain competitive and cooperative actions.

GAME THEORY

The theory of games developed out of an effort some fifty years ago by the famous mathematician John von Neumann and economist Oskar Morgenstern to answer some questions concerning economic behavior. The result of that collaborative effort was a book that forms the foundation of modern-day game theory.[35] Decision-making situations in which chance and other players take an active role are common. Selecting an appropriate strategy to pursue amidst such complexity can be a formidable task. It is the intent of game theorists to develop tools to assist decision-making in these complex situations.

Game theory, using the tools of mathematics and logic, has been useful in identifying certain types of situations such as zero-sum games, non-zero-sum games, The Battle of the Sexes,[36] Colonel Blotto,[37] and The Prisoner's Dilemma.[38] In addition to helping define and understand these types of situations, game theory can suggest potential solutions to decision makers confronting similar circumstances.

Of all game theory terminology, zero-sum and non-zero-sum games are two of the most widely used. Zero-sum games, as the name suggests, are situations in which the gain of one participant inevitably involves a corresponding loss to another participant. These are situations of pure competition: whatever one gains, the gain is at someone else's expense. Non-zero-sum games describe situations in which one participant's gain does not necessarily have to come at the expense of another. In other words, in non-zero-sum games the total payoff to the players can be increased by the actions of the players themselves and is not fixed as in the zero-sum game.

One particular form of non-zero-sum game often mentioned in the literature is that involving pure cooperation. In this game, the goals of the various players are identical. Unfortunately, like the pure conflict zero-sum game, the pure cooperation game is not particularly useful as an analytical tool because so few real-world situations can be classified at either one of these two extremes. As many have recognized, most "games" thrown at us in life lie somewhere in between, in what Thomas Schelling calls bargaining or mutual dependence games.[39] In these situations the players are faced with mixed motives of competition and cooperation.

The game theory literature provides insights into how strategically interdependent individuals or organizations make the decision to compete or cooperate.[40] Underlying game theory analysis is the assumption that organizations and individuals will consciously seek to maximize the cost/benefit trade-offs facing them. In zero-sum games, competition among strategically interdependent players is expected, in that the gain for one is at the expense of another. With non-zero-sum games, cooperation is allowed as individuals and firms seek to explore ways to maximize their joint gains. An important element of many non-zero-sum game situations is the use of communication and information sharing to reduce uncertainty.

One of the main problems with game theory literature and research is that it is often difficult to make useful extrapolations to the real world from the simplified world of games. It can be something of an achievement merely to demonstrate that game theory can accurately describe an authentic situation.

Cooperative R&D Personnel Recruiting and the Prisoner's Dilemma

Of the various representations developed by game theorists to assist in our understanding of such mixed-motive, real-life circumstances, the Prisoner's Dilemma Game offers insight into a variety of everyday situations. The Prisoner's Dilemma was created by Merrill Flood and Melvin Dresher around 1950 and formalized not long after by A. W. Tucker.[41] This game theory classic has been useful in describing situations in which non-cooperative pursuit of self-interest can lead to an unsatisfactory outcome, such as biological systems,[42] vote trading in the U.S. Congress,[43] and oligopolistic competition.[44]

In the simplest form of the Prisoner's Dilemma there are two players each facing two choices: cooperate or defect. The dilemma is that self-interest favors a decision to defect by each player, but mutual defection results in a payoff that is less than the payoff possible under mutual cooperation. In abstract form the game is often depicted as shown in Figure 2.2.

To define a Prisoner's Dilemma situation, one must make reference to the relationships among the various payoffs. Referring to the chart below, there are four potential outcomes for either player: R = the reward for cooperation, T = the temptation to defect, S = the sucker's payoff (so called because the trust of one player is betrayed and taken advantage of by the other), and P = the punishment for mutual defec-

Figure 2.2
The Prisoner's Dilemma (General Case)

	Cooperate	Defect
Cooperate	R, r	S, t
Defect	T, s	P, p

Required conditions $\left\{ \begin{array}{l} (1) \quad T > R > P > S \\ (2) \quad R > (T+S)/2 \end{array} \right.$

tion. If both players choose a cooperative strategy then the payoff will be (R,R) to players A and B, respectively. If player A cooperates and B defects then the payoff will be (S,T), for A and B, respectively. The converse (T,S) will be true if B cooperates and A defects. If both players defect they will receive the punishment for mutual defection (P,P).

The Prisoner's Dilemma is distinguished from other similar situations by the nature of the relationships of R,T,S, and P. Specifically, the following must be true: $T > R > P > S$. Or in plain English, the temptation to defect must be greater than the reward for mutual cooperation, which, in turn, must be greater than the punishment for mutual defection, and all must be greater than the sucker's payoff.

If the Prisoner's Dilemma Game is played over and over again, then one can say that the situation is an iterated Prisoner's Dilemma. The importance of iteration is that game theorists have shown that a cooperative strategy can develop and survive in an iterated Prisoner's Dilemma under certain circumstances. In the standard, one-time Prisoner's Dilemma Game, the naturally tendency of the players acting in their own self-interest is to defect, with the result that both end up with the lowering payoff of P.

A variety of solutions to the dilemma and the likelihood of mutual defection have been suggested, such as the making of threats and commitments or changing the players' payoffs. Of particular interest are recent studies arising out of computer tournaments pitting competing strategies against each other in a Prisoner's Dilemma Game.[45]

This work has shown that mutual cooperation can develop and become a stable state of affairs if the game is repeated and if the players attach a certain level of significance to future payoffs.

Participants in cooperative R&D ventures can find themselves in a Prisoner's Dilemma with regard to personnel recruiting. Many cooperative R&D ventures plan to obtain research personnel from the member companies. The hope is that the companies will nominate top scientists and researchers from their ranks for cooperative R&D venture assignment. This use of company people rotating through the cooperative venture is often seen as a critical element of the technology transfer process.

Not surprisingly, companies often do not nominate or suggest their best people but instead offer second-tier talent. Although each company may be well aware of the importance of accumulating top-notch researchers for the successful venture, each company hopes that the top talent will be sent by the other shareholders.

Figure 2.3
The Prisoner's Dilemma (Recruiting Top People from Shareholders)

Company 1

	A Send Top People	B Send 2nd Rate People
Send Top People (x)	R, r	S, t
Send 2nd Rate People (y)	T, s	P, p

Company 2

Required conditions $\left\{ \begin{array}{l} (1) \quad T > R > P > S \\ (2) \quad R > (T+S)/2 \end{array} \right.$

To help simplify the analysis, imagine a cooperative R&D venture with two participating companies. Assume that the two companies, 1 and 2, are trying to decide what quality of researcher to send to the cooperative R&D venture. To further simplify the example, further assume that each company is faced with only two decisions. This staffing situation can be described using the Prisoner's Dilemma model. For Company 1, Decision A is the decision to send its top research talent. Decision B is the decision to send less-qualified personnel. Likewise, for Company 2, Decision x and Decision y are the decisions to send top talent or not, respectively. The payoffs for these Decision pairs are (r,R), the reward in terms of R&D that could be produced if both Company 1 and 2 send top talent. The payoffs for single defection (either the decision pair B/x or A/y) are expressed as (s,T) and (S,t). And finally there is the punishment payoff (p,P) if both companies send second-rate talent to the cooperative R&D venture.

Given this description of the situation, does it satisfy the requirements of first condition above, namely, $T > R > P > S$? Although assigning exact numbers to each of these terms would be a highly subjective task, such an exercise is not necessary. It is only necessary that the relationships in the first required condition hold. Therefore, for the assignment of personnel, can one make the case that the required relationships are present?

First, is $T > R$? T is the payoff to a company if they send second-tier talent and the other company sends top talent. R is the payoff if both companies send top talent. The case for asserting that $T > R$ can be derived from the data. Top talent in the areas of interest was (and is) an extremely valuable commodity to the companies. If a company can tap into the top research talent of its competitors while protecting its own top talent from competitors, there is a high likelihood of competitive advantage being derived. In other words, the company may perceive a benefit from being a free rider on the R&D talents of its competitors.[46]

Next, is $R > P$? Can we say that the payoff for both companies sending top talent (r,R) is greater than the punishment (p,P) for both sending second-rate talent? The ability of a collaborative R&D venture to produce the desired technology and knowledge is especially dependent on the nature of the talent conducting the research. Often, the R&D contemplated is just not feasible for less than world-class researchers.

Finally, is $P > S$? Can we say that the payoff for both companies sending second-tier talent (p, P) is greater than the sucker's payoff (s or S) that would accrue to the company that sends top-talent when its competitor does not? This is the most difficult condition to meet but also appears true for the following reasons: If Company 1 sends its top talent (Decision A), then we can presume that its internal R&D efforts will be negatively affected. If Company 2 decides to keep its top talent and send second-rate personnel (Decision y), Company 2 will reap the benefits of Company 1's researcher without making a significant contribution. Therefore, Company 2 will get the exclusive benefit of its top researchers as well as the shared benefits of Company 1's top researchers.

The second required condition is a bit more difficult to analyze because it requires us to determine the average of non-quantitative payoffs. The requirements of equation (2) can be satisfied under the following conditions: if the R&D output is sensitive to the critical mass of researchers accumulated to work on the problem and related areas, and if each company can afford a few top-notch researchers, but none can afford to accumulate the critical mass of talent that is necessary for truly major breakthroughs. This is essentially the situation described in Figure 2.4 below.

Figure 2.4
R&D Output vs. Input

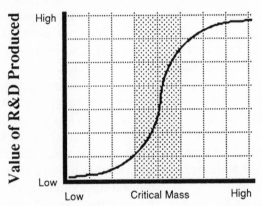

Number of Top Tier Researchers

Many believe the proposition that a collegial body of top-flight researchers lends itself to the cross-fertilization of ideas. If this is the case, then one can say that the total benefits to companies in assembling this critical mass of researchers $(r + R)$ is greater than the benefit that could be derived by any company conducting research alone in less than critical mass situations and alternating between sharing it and not sharing it with competitors $[(t + T + s + S)/2]$.

If the personnel problem facing cooperative R&D venture management in the early stages of the organization's growth can be seen as a form of the Prisoner's Dilemma, then one important way to circumvent the deterioration into a suboptimal non-cooperative situation is to introduce communication. Since the absence of communication is one of the conditions defining the Prisoner's Dilemma, then the increased use of communication can be a tool to break the dilemma and encourage cooperation.

By establishing a network of communications, management can communicate the consequences of non-cooperation and provide a mechanism for the exchange of promises and threats. This situation emphasizes the importance of establishing and maintaining an effective communication system by the collective venture management.

MANAGEMENT THEORY

Clearly those studies that specifically claim to examine the management of joint ventures are an important part of the body of relevant literature. For the past twenty years the collection of studies and analyses that focus on the management of interfirm cooperation has steadily grown. One of the early studies by Aiken and Hage examined collaboration by health care organizations and concluded that cooperation was a function of organizational complexity.[47]

Many of the studies directed at the management of joint ventures seek to establish the determinants of cooperation through quantitative analysis of an available database. For example, Boyle, using Federal Trade Commission data on the formation of joint subsidiaries that was first collected in 1965, concluded that two-thirds of the joint ventures he observed were in manufacturing activities and that the size of the parent firm was an important determinant of joint venture participation.[48] Hlavacek, Dovey, and Biondo developed this further and argued, as one might expect, that relative size of parent firms was significant in determining joint venture behavior.[49] The three authors, studying the use of cooperation to introduce new products, found that in all of the twenty-three collaborative ventures they examined each had a "small" and "large" partner (relative to each other).[50] This finding regarding the significance of parent firm size can also be found in the research of Pfeffer and Nowak.[51]

Other researchers have focused on other characteristics of sponsoring parent companies. For example, Edström found that financial strength of the parent companies could be used to predict collaborative venture behavior, at least with regard to Swedish manufacturing companies.[52]

Aside from seeking the determinants of joint venture activity based on characteristics of the parent firms, the management literature also contains efforts aimed at assessing the reasons firms might engage in cooperation. A number of authors have claimed to have found evidence that companies use interfirm cooperation to create and enhance market power. One such author is Fusfeld who based his conclusion on an examination of the iron and steel industry. In the discussion of his research Fusfeld argued that the firms he studied used cooperative ventures to create market power by means of complex supply channel linkages.[53] Similar conclusions have been suggested by Pfeffer and Nowack[54] and Mead[55] who argued that horizontal linkages between parent firms augmented market power. These authors should be contrasted to Berg and Friedman, who in their analysis of a wide variety cooperative ventures came to the conclusion that "JVs tend to knowledge-acquiring and risk-reducing activities, rather than market-power generators."[56]

Much of the management literature devoted to cooperative ventures focuses on cooperation between domestic corporations and foreign partners. This is not surprising when one considers that, as one author put it, "[m]ost U.S. joint ventures were previously regarded as a means to enter foreign markets."[57] In the early 1970s two pioneering studies of joint ventures emerged that helped lay a solid foundation on which subsequent work would build. One was the oft-cited publication of the research conducted by Stopford and Wells regarding the management of multinational enterprises[58] and the other was Franko's equally well referenced analysis of collaborative ventures undertaken by multinational corporations.[59]

Stopford and Wells examined the formation and survival of cooperative ventures involving domestic multinational corporations and foreign partners through the use of questionnaires and formalized interviews. They found that pursuit of certain strategies, such as those emphasizing production rationalization, marketing of differentiated products, new product development, or raw material control, led multinational firms to prefer the unambiguous control associated with wholly-owned subsidiaries, rather than collaborative action.[60]

Franko specifically limited his study to an examination of "joint ventures between multinational firms and host country corporations, individuals or family groups."[61] The aim of his research was to explore the stability of collaboration, and he was able to conclude that the durability of cooperation was dependent upon the level of maturity of the U.S. parent. In particular, Franko found that for the foreign joint ventures in his study, the "tolerance" for joint venture arrangements lessened as the U.S. parent corporation organized into an area or area-functional structure.[62]

The analysis of joint ventures involving domestic multinational firms and foreign partners still forms a major part of the management literature devoted to cooperative action. Hladik in her recent analysis of joint ventures limited her study to U.S.-foreign business partnerships agreements.[63] The doctoral research of Gomes-Casseres, with its implications regarding when firms might find collaborative action beneficial, specifically focused on multinational ownership strategies.[64]

One of the persistent themes that emerges from the literature is that cooperative ventures are complex and difficult to manage and exhibit a relatively high failure rate.[65] As Harrigan has reported, "it has been estimated that over half of the joint ventures ended recently were ill-conceived at birth because the objectives of the joint venture were unclear, because their parents' capabilities were poorly matched, or because they aspired to achieve more than was possible in the industries where they competed."[66]

The evidence to support such a conclusion is not as strong as might be desired. Some authors[67] merely cite Franko's work on the durability of foreign joint ventures and others rely on executive anecdotes and interviews.[68] Despite this perception of a high probability of joint venture failure some researchers have uncovered evidence that, in general, firms have had highly satisfactory experiences with interfirm cooperation. For example, Young and Bradford, after analyzing the responses of 106 companies that were members of the Financial Executives Research Foundation involved in 410 joint ventures, report that 73 percent of the companies had joint venture experience rated as satisfactory or better.[69]

The reluctance of executives to embrace cooperative activity because of the managerial complexities involved may not necessarily be reflected in the success or failure rate. For one thing, it is difficult to judge joint venture "success" from afar, since, as one pair of authors put it, joint ventures have "built-in, self-destruct characteristics."[70] Dissolution of a joint venture may not represent failure but rather the end of a normal and productive life. In one research effort that involved twenty-five selected case studies the data indicated that firms continued to follow the joint venture route because it is often the only way to hold or secure a solid share of some particular market or because it offered a very profitable way to gain a competitive market share.[71]

The general management literature also offers some insights into why companies might be motivated to try interfirm cooperation.

Herzfeld listed four reasons for seeking partners: limitation of investment, limitation of risk, overcoming nationalistic prejudice, and merging skills and strengths.[72] Other studies have been more general in the observation, noting only "defensive" and "positive" reasons for collaboration.[73] On the other hand, Roulac's four motivations for entering a joint venture reflect his financial viewpoint.[74] Berg and Friedman in their series of 1978 articles, while not specifically enumerating the reasons for interfirm cooperation, do note that their data indicate that joint ventures "serve as an external substitute for internal knowledge acquisition."[75] Later, when joined by Duncan, the trio offered three primary incentives for joint venture participation in general terms: risk avoidance, knowledge acquisition, and market-power creation.[76]

In a recent study of thirty-eight cooperative ventures conducted by Yankelovich, Skelly, and White for Coopers & Lybrand, the researchers documented an increased acceptance of interfirm collaboration as the "concept of the corporation as a self-sufficient entity" comes "under question."[77] The study notes that corporations "are abandoning their ideological stances of the 1970s" as a result of what the authors feel is a new and pragmatic outlook on the part of many firms in response to market pressures.[78] The four reasons for interorganizational cooperation most often cited by the forty-four executives interviewed were: complementary strengths (80 percent), shared resources (48 percent), joining a winning team (43 percent), and sharing risk (39 percent).[79]

DEFINITIONS OF JOINT VENTURES

Before one can begin to absorb the prior research and assessments of joint ventures one must try to determine just what is meant by the label joint venture. As noted above, the literature contains many studies of joint ventures, but one cannot say without hesitation that all have examined the same phenomenon. Failure to embrace a common definition makes subsequent comparisons difficult, if not impossible, and renders conclusions not universally applicable. As a consequence, a review of the prior management literature regarding such cooperative activities must examine just how widely or narrowly various authors and researchers have cast their nets.

As alluded to in the introductory chapter, cooperation between organizations can take on a broad range of forms, from the short-term spot contract to the establishment of independent equity ventures of extremely long duration. In studying such collaborative action it is important to note just what types of cooperation will be included in the analysis and what types excluded. In some studies the scope of purview is not explicitly stated but must be inferred from an examination of the database used. In others the boundaries are set forth with greater detail.

This need for definitional specificity is complicated by the fact that the wide variety of forms for cooperation makes succinct and noncontroversial classification a difficult task. As one paper on the subject aptly stated, "[e]very joint venture is a special arrangement in which the participants fashion an almost infinite variety of arrangements."[80] This great diversity means that classification can be done along a wide range of characteristics. Some authors use "separateness" of the cooperative activity as an important criterion.[81] Others examine the duration of cooperation to determine inclusion or exclusion.[82] Cooperative ventures with government partners are often excluded but are specifically included in others.[83] The following examples help illustrate this classification confusion and point out the difficulties that can be encountered when one tries to compare the findings of one research study with the others.

Berg and Friedman are best known for their pioneering studies of domestic joint ventures.[84] Their definition of what constitutes a joint venture is one of the broadest, partially because they were trying to amass as large a database as possible in order to overcome what they considered to be "a paucity of data" which limited large-scale quantitative analyses of the type they had in mind.[85] Berg and Friedman's database of joint ventures encompassed a wide variety of activities, including all those in Thompson's 1970 study of the chemical industry, as well as the joint ventures monitored by the Federal Trade Commission (FTC).[86]

The breadth of the data did facilitate the type of analysis sought by Berg and Friedman and permitted the authors to draw conclusions regarding various differing subtypes of cooperation. In fact the authors explicitly recognized "the heterogeneity of joint venture activity" noting that such inherent differences discouraged large-scale quantitative analyses.[87]

Just as Berg and Friedman purposefully included a wide range of collaborative action in their study, others have limited the scope of their research so as not to confuse their observations by a cacophony of data deriving from extreme heterogeneity. For example, Harrigan, in her recent work on joint ventures, only included those ventures that had active businesses as parents, thereby excluding cooperative ventures with government involvement or with passive investors (such as many real estate partnerships).[88] In addition, Harrigan excluded collaborative action that did not take the form of a separate entity created by the parents as a vehicle for cooperation.[89]

Figure 2.5
Announced U.S. Joint Ventures (1964–1975)

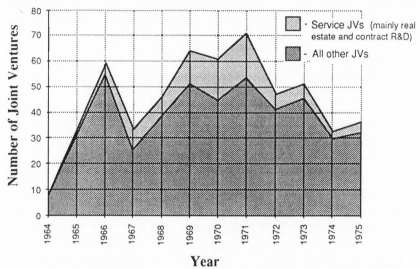

Year

Data Source: Database collected in connection with Jerome L. Duncan, "The Causes and Effects of Domestic Joint Venture Activity," unpublished doctoral dissertation, University of Florida (1980), as reported in Harrigan, *Strategies for Joint Ventures* (Lexington Book, 1985), pp. 8–9.

Roulac, in his article on structuring joint ventures, adopted a much wider definition. Although he never explicitly defines the term joint venture, he does state that "[a] joint venture may be thought of as a resource-aggregating and risk-allocating mechanism that brings together explicit talents to pursue common objectives."[90] In contrast to Harrigan, Roulac does not dismiss passive financial partnerships as readily. This is not surprising, in that Roulac is the president of a financial consulting firm and teaches financial courses at the Stanford Business School. In fact, Roulac seems to focus on financial risk-sharing cooperation.

The heterogeneity of joint ventures also can be seen in the cyclical popularity of certain types of collaboration when compared to oth-

ers.[91] For example, in the late 1960s to early 1970s there was a surge
in popularity of real estate and contract R&D joint ventures.[92] (see
Figure 2.5). Also during the 1960s and 1970s, joint ventures involving
domestic companies were more closely associated with entry into
foreign markets.[93] As a consequence of this foreign market entry
objective, many prior studies of joint ventures focused on cooperation
between domestic enterprises and foreign participants.[94] Whether or
not such foreign joint ventures constitute a unique subset of joint
venture activity is open to serious consideration.[95] Perhaps the for-
eignness of the cooperators is not an important characteristic on which
to classify the cooperative activity. For example, Richard Young and
Standish Bradford, in their examination of joint ventures, used the
following definition:

> [A joint venture is an] enterprise, corporation or partnership,
> formed by two or more companies, individuals, or organizations,
> at least one of which is an operating entity which wishes to
> broaden its activities, for the purpose of conducting a new, profit-
> motivated business of permanent duration. In general, the own-
> ership is shared by the participants with more or less equal equity
> distribution and without absolute dominance by one party.[96]

Such a definition would exclude a number of foreign joint ventures
included in the research studies of others not merely because they
involve a foreign partner but because there is clear dominance by the
domestic multinational partner. According to the authors such an
undertaking is not a joint venture but rather a simple minority investment by private shareholders. For example, many of the twenty-five
cases examined in Business International's Management Monograph
No. 54 would not pass muster as a joint venture under Young and
Bradford's definition.[97] Likewise, the joint venture operated by W. R.
Grace and Pinturas Colombianas in Colombia between 1945 and 1955
would be excluded.[98] Young and Bradford sought to exclude such joint
ventures on purpose. They did not feel that such undertakings were
true examples of interfirm cooperation, but rather were investment
vehicles for private shareholders. In such ventures, Young and Bradford argue, business policy, product and process decisions, and administration are mainly controlled or dominated by the large,
multinational parent corporation.[99]

The permanence of the cooperation is also a source of difference
regarding what should or should not be studied. Some studies specif-

ically are limited to collaboration that has a more or less permanent duration,[100] while others would include contractual joint ventures of specific and limited duration, provided that there is a "discrete management" rather than the "part-time attention of the participant's management."[101]

The importance of an explicit definition of what exactly constitutes a joint venture is less significant in this particular research project than in those covering a large number of cooperative ventures, in that in this research project, decisions regarding which cooperative activities to include and which to exclude need not be made. But recognition of the wide variety of joint venture definitions is important when one attempts to fit the data gleaned from the study of research joint ventures into the accumulated data from other studies.

The diversity of interfirm cooperation that is illustrated by this definitional variety also helps emphasize the uniqueness of collaborative research ventures. As one can see, researchers and authors have found a number of characteristics on which to distinguish and classify cooperative action. By examining just a select few of those suggested, such as partner situation or characteristics, managerial separateness, degree of partner passivity, or organizational permanence, one can readily appreciate that cooperative research activity is often distinctive.

CONCLUDING OBSERVATIONS

Examination of the prior literature regarding interfirm cooperation in the fields of economics, organizational theory, game theory, and general management reveals a wide diversity of research methodologies and issues. Each field exhibits a distinct viewpoint concerning interorganizational collaboration. The economic literature tends to consider the whole organization as the main unit of inquiry. At that level of analysis the primary issue becomes one of why cooperation might be profitable to the organization. Organizational theory approaches cooperation from another angle and seeks to understand how individuals or coalitions can coalesce in concerted action. Based on mathematics and logic, game theory scrutinizes cooperation from yet another vantage point. And finally, the general management literature focuses on the formation and administration of cooperative action.

In trying to understand the contributions of each of the four areas of literature discussed in this chapter, one is reminded of the old proverb of the blind men and the elephant, in which each blind man examines a different part of the beast and extrapolates from his examined part to the whole. Each blind man's observation is accurate but seems to contradict the others. Similarly, in drawing insights applicable to interfirm cooperation from the various disciplines examined, it is best to take a broad, inclusive viewpoint that seeks to integrate the separate contributions of each.

3

Competition and Cooperation

This chapter examines how the courts and the political system have attempted to deal with interfirm cooperation through the promulgation and application of the antitrust laws. Although it is common to refer to our "competitive economic system," the court cases and legal literature have long sought to address the cooperative aspects, both good and bad, that are an important part of the system.

For many, competition and cooperation are seen as polar opposites. Under this view, as one increases, the other has a corresponding decrease. This is not necessarily the case. Cooperative activity can enhance competition as well as diminish it. The following example helps illustrate this point (see Figure 3.1). A group of individuals decides to have a football game.[102] At this aggregate level the game is a cooperative undertaking. Everyone participating must agree and adhere to a certain set of rules and regulations such as what are the boundaries of the playing field, what constitutes offsides, and so on. In more abstract terms the individual participants first need to exchange promises and make commitments and then set up mechanisms to enforce them. The players must first cooperate in order to establish how they will compete.

At the next level the game can be characterized as two organizations in competition, with the two teams engaged in a zero-sum conflict of moving a ball up and down a field. The next level is cooperative again, as each team tries to coordinate the activities of the twelve individual team members for the common purpose of yardage gain. And finally, at the individual level, one once again finds competition as the players struggle against each other for star status or merely to maintain a position on the team.

Figure 3.1
Cooperation and Competition in a Football Game

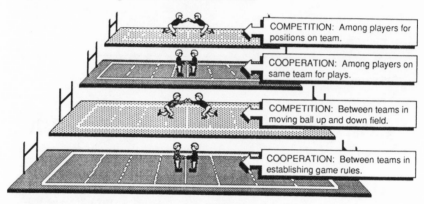

COMPETITION: Among players for positions on team.

COOPERATION: Among players on same team for plays.

COMPETITION: Between teams in moving ball up and down field.

COOPERATION: Between teams in establishing game rules.

IN PRAISE OF COMPETITION: THE CONCEPTUAL CORNERSTONE OF THE ECONOMY

Over the past decade there has been much study of competition as an important consideration in shaping business organizations and in determining corporate strategy.[103] Competition: The term appears ceaselessly throughout business management literature and is given prominent treatment in such related and complementary fields as economics, political science, sociology, mathematics, and psychology. Hardly a day goes by without some politician or business figure publicly praising the virtues of competition or our competitive economic system. Competitive forces, barriers to competition and competitor analysis are all familiar concepts to the modern business executive. With such widespread use one would think that confusion regarding the term's meaning would not be a significant problem. Each champion of competition probably has something slightly different in mind when he or she gives tribute to the workings of the invisible hand.

The word competition literally means to seek together. It is derived from the Latin *cum*, meaning with or together, linked to *peto*, to seek. The modern dictionary definition emphasizes the element of rivalry by stating that competition is a struggle with another or others for an object, prize, or situation "desired in common." Implicit in the modern definition is the notion that the the struggle is a zero-sum one, that only one of the competitors can capture the prize desired in common. Interestingly, cooperation, a term often used to mean the opposite of competition, also involves the element of a goal desired in common. Only with cooperation it is assumed that the situation is non-zero-sum.

The precise meaning of competition when used with reference to our economic system is difficult to determine. A competitive economy, though sought by many, is something that is hard to specifically identify. In the United States for the past ninety-five years there has existed a unique forum in which the uncounted energies of armies of politicians, lawyers, and business persons have been spent grappling with a practical concept of the competitive economy. Domestic antitrust legislation and enforcement is this forum.[104]

The Supreme Court once referred to the antitrust laws as "the Magna Carta of free enterprise," stating that "[t]hey are as important to the preservation of economic freedom and our free enterprise system as the Bill of Rights is to the protection of our fundamental personal freedoms."[105] Underlying the three main statutory elements of that body of law collectively known as antitrust is the notion of competition. Adam Smith in his *Wealth of Nations* cast the concept in its most memorable form: society is best served by private enterprise guided by the invisible hand of competition.[106]

The abhorrence of private restraint on competitive forces has long been a theme in American politics as expressed in the law. Discontent with the restrictive mercantile policies of King George III and Parliament had an important influence on those who would help set the mold for the economic system of the emerging republic. Concern regarding the proper nature of the economic system was not confined to academic debate and intellectual musings. Feelings about economic justice ran strong and deep. In Boston the crown-granted monopoly to the British East India Company on tea led to the venting of these emotions through now-famous violent action.

During the industrial boom that occurred in the latter half of the nineteenth century, once again the banner of unrestrained competition was unfurled, this time to do battle against the newly emerging industrial nobility. Following the Civil War, the animus of western farmers was roused in an agrarian revolt against the emerging economic order they felt was inimical to their interests. In 1889 President Benjamin Harrison called for "prohibiting and even penal legislation" against the "dangerous conspiracies against the public good."[107] A year later the Sherman Act of 1890 was enacted in an effort the curb the power of the feared combinations and trusts.[108]

The Progressive spirit that swept through this country prior to World War I also embraced the concept of fair and unfettered competition as the proper path to a just prosperity. Both Teddy Roosevelt in his New Nationalism and Woodrow Wilson in his New Freedom called for legal curbs on a perceived erosion of competition by big business during the election campaign of 1912. Victorious Wilson made good on his promise two years later with the passage of the Clayton and Federal Trade Commission acts to restore and preserve what was viewed as a deteriorating competitive economic system.[109]

Even today the byword of competition runs deep in political rhetoric and action. Over the past decade deregulation of ground transportation, energy, telecommunications, and air travel has taken place in pursuit of this elusive "invisible hand." Former President Ronald Reagan spoke of applying the tonic of competition by commercializing space and education.

WORKABLE COMPETITION: COOPERATION IN A COMPETITIVE ECONOMY

On closer examination, the conceptually ideal competitive economy that the antitrust laws, our economic Bill of Rights, seeks to preserve, protect, and promote is something of a hybrid, a mongrel rather than a thoroughbred. It must be clear, even to political orators who espouse a competitive ideology and constantly punctuate their speeches with competitive market imagery, that our economic system is far from some pure model of unfettered, atomistic competition guided by the benign and impersonal invisible hand. Oligopolies are common in some of the most successful and efficient sectors of the economy. The visible hand of government, through direct regulation and indirect guidance of the tax laws, procurement practices and entitlement distribution, abounds. And, despite constant kowtowing in praise of competition, private companies find cooperative action a necessary element of the modern industrial economy.

Although the Supreme Court made the oft-cited pronouncement that "the public interest is best protected from the the evils of monopoly and price control by the maintenance of competition,"[110] there are numerous situations where the public interest has been deemed to be equally or even better served by cooperation.[111] Competitors may meet and work with each other in trade associations to develop information for common use, or to cooperatively lobby the government. Competitors, under some circumstances, may even be permitted to set collective standards of conduct and establish cooperative enforcement mechanisms to discover and correct deviations.[112]

From industry to industry the list of cooperative activities which are believed to have a positive effect on competition and those which are believed to have a negative effect is not constant. Joint buying and joint selling arrangements are generally condemned as anticompetitive in most industries,[113] but are permissible activities in investment banking.[114] What may be classified as an unreasonable contract in the prize fighting business may not be seen as having the same competitive effect in the imported perfume industry.[115] Even industries that are similar may be judged under different standards of competition. Just compare the consequences of the limited antitrust exemption afforded professional baseball to the prevalence of antitrust litigation in professional football.

The courts have attempted to work out these inconsistencies and internal tensions through the concept of "workable" competition as opposed to perfect competition.[116] Under the concept of workable competition, certain types of cooperative activities may be encouraged, particularly if cooperation promotes "fair competitive opportunities."[117]

The judicial device used to define and illuminate this concept of workable competition is the rule of reason, whereby restraints on competition would be assessed according to their reasonableness. The need for such a rule became clear shortly after the passage of the Sherman Act. The breadth and ambiguity of the act's condemnation against all concerted action that restrains trade made circumscription on applicability necessary for companies to engage in normal trade. In the broadest sense, every contract between a buyer and a seller restrains trade in that the commercial opportunities of other buyers and sellers are thereby limited.

Immediately following the passage of the Sherman Act it was not uncommon for the courts to hold that all contracts in restraint of trade were prohibited whether reasonable or not. To this effect is *United States v. Trans-Missouri Freight Association*.[118] Despite early cases such as this, the original authors of this country's antitrust legislation apparently had in mind a notion of balance between cooperation and competition among companies. Senator Sherman, namesake of the Sherman Act, once remarked that he expected the courts to distinguish between "lawful combinations in aid of production and unlawful combinations to prevent competition and in restraint of trade."[119] In fact, it has been reported that Senator Hoar, one of the sponsors of the Sherman Act and author of the section permitting treble damages for private litigants, "advised a group of wire manufacturers that a proposed price-fixing and profit-sharing agreement designed to avoid destructive competition would probably not violate the Act."[120]

Representative Stewart of Vermont gave one of the clearest statements of opinion on this issue:

> [T]here are two great forces working in human society in this country to-day, and they have been contending for the mastery on one side or the other for the last two generations. Those two great forces are competition and combination. They are correctives of each other, and both ought to exist. Both ought to be under restraint. Either of them, if allowed to be unrestrained, is destructive of the material interests of this country.[121]

The debate over the scope of the anticompetitive prohibitions in the Sherman Act reached into the Supreme Court with Mr. Justice Harlan arguing for a literal interpretation in the *Standard Oil* case in which he wrote that there was "no distinction . . . between restraints of such commerce as were undue or unreasonable and restraints that were due or reasonable."[122] Mr. Justice Harlan's argument did not carry the day in *Standard Oil*. Instead, the majority opinion, authored by Chief Justice Edward White, unveiled a fairly rigorous form of what would ultimately become known as the rule of reason.[123]

The history of the rule of reason is an interesting one. Before his appointment as chief justice, White was an associate justice and had written a dissent in the *Trans-Missouri* case decided by the Court some fourteen years prior to *Standard Oil*.[124] In that case, a group of eighteen railroads had formed a cartel to agree upon a common rate structure. The cartel did not seek to freeze the relative market positions of the various participants, but sought to remove rates as the means of competitive rivalry. The Court struck down the arrangement as antithetical to the recently passed Sherman Act. Mr. Justice White dissented. It seems he would have allowed the cartel to stand, stating as his reason that price-fixing was necessary to avoid ruinous competition and that the rate structure selected by the cartel was reasonable. In other words, White felt that the public interest was better served in this circumstance by cooperative action than competitive warfare.

Implicitly, White seemed to recognize that the economic situation of the railroads at the time was such that some form of cooperation was necessary. Numerous competing lines had been built in the latter half of the nineteenth century, and each competing company had an enormous fixed investment in road and rolling stock. Since the variable costs of carrying freight were relatively low, there was a tendency to reduce prices during slack times to a point where they just covered variable costs. As a consequence, full costs were not recovered. Although private efforts to deal with this economic reality were struck down by the courts, public action under the Interstate Commerce Commission to accomplish the same thing was eventually sanctioned as a legitimate method to deal with the problems of railroad over-capacity.

If one accepts the notion that some degree of cooperation among potential and actual competitors is necessary in order to achieve the desired conditions of workable competition, the next step of analysis is to determine what type of cooperation is permitted. Clearly, not all forms of cooperation are compatible with workable competition, and the courts have long recognized this fact. For example, there are cooperative actions among competitors that are strictly circumscribed by antitrust policy. These particular collective activities are those covered by the *per se* evidentiary rule. With regard to *per se* activities the prosecution need only prove that the alleged activity took place. Once this is done, judgment against the defendants automatically follows. In practice this means that the courts will not entertain any evidence put forward by the defendants in defense of the activities.

A number of collective activities have been found to be *per se* illegal. The list includes price-fixing, collective boycotts, market sharing and certain restrictive practices involving patents.[125] Price-fixing cartels are probably the most commonly attacked *per se* activities.[126] In a situation involving price fixing among a group of competitors, the courts will not receive evidence regarding the "reasonableness" of the fixed price.[127] To help illustrate this point, the facts in the Socony price-fixing case make for interesting reading.

During the early 1930s pressure was put on already weak oil prices by the discovery of vast new oil fields in Texas. Numerous small, independent oil refiners and crude oil producers, experiencing severe cash difficulties, began offering refined petroleum products at deep discount prices. While the National Industrial Recovery Act (NIRA) was in force the industry was permitted to establish administrative structures to stabilize the price. When the act was declared unconstitutional in 1935, the major oil companies continued with an independent scheme to stabilize oil prices.

The mechanism used to do this was the purchase by the large oil companies of the surpluses of their smaller competitors. The fact that the government was an active and willing participant in the effort to stabilize prices before 1935 was of no consequence in the Court's eye. In a footnote in the court's majority opinion, Mr. Justice Douglas further noted that even if the cartel had no power to put into effect the price-fixing conspiracy it would make no difference in legality.[128]

Although one can say that price-fixing does not involve any borderline questions of law, the cases often involve difficult borderline questions of fact. It is precisely these boundary situations that demonstrate that legitimate, necessary cooperation and illegitimate, unwanted conspiracy can both be present and sometimes indistinguishable in modern business practice. For example, an industry association will often collect and circulate statistical information among competitors. Such statistical information may be benevolent in that the extra information can be used to strengthen competition, or malevolent in that the information may be used to coordinate and enforce price-fixing.[129]

The real problem comes from situations where there is no explicit agreement to cooperate but implicit cooperation arises because each company realizes, without agreement or prearrangement, the utility of mutual restraint. As Mr. Justice Holmes said in *Swift and Company v. United States*, "The defendants cannot be ordered to compete, but they properly can be forbidden to give directions or to make arrangements not to compete."[130]

When one moves away from cooperative activity that falls under the *per se* rule the legal waters become much murkier. These are the situations judged under the so-called rule of reason. A good example of the difficulties encountered can be found in *United States v. J. I. Case Company*.[131] J. I. Case, now a subsidiary of Tenneco, was a manufacturer of farm machinery equipment with a 7 percent share of the domestic market. The company, in an effort to strengthen its dealer network, entered into exclusive one-year supply contracts with its dealers. The government attacked the contracts as anticompetitive, arguing that they excluded other competitors of J. I. Case from access to the dealer network. The government lost the case. The court in denying the government's claims stated that "[t]he handling by a dealer of a few items of several full-line manufacturers might tend to discourage competition rather than stimulate it."[132] Thus, the court gave recognition to the fact that such cooperation need not necessarily harm competition, but may actually enhance it.

But one does not need to look to court-produced case precedence to demonstrate that cooperation among competitors is not always evil. Not long after the Sherman and Clayton acts were enacted, Congress passed the Webb-Pomerene Export Trade Act, which specifically permits otherwise illegal price-fixing and market-sharing activity if it is undertaken by "an association entered into for the sole purpose of engaging in export trade."[133] Of course, the act is not quite as permissive as it may first appear, in that the agreements (1) must not be exclusionary or harmful against domestic companies that choose not to participate, (2) must not have restrictive effects on domestic commerce, and (3) cannot include restrictive arrangements with foreign competitors.

Yet despite these limitations, the mere existence of the act gives some evidence, albeit limited, regarding the fine line between cooperation among competitors that is seen as beneficial to society and that which is not. Additional support of the proposition can be found in the Small Business Act,[134] which provides for a limited antitrust exemption to cooperative research ventures undertaken by "small business concerns," and more recently in the National Cooperative Research Act of 1984, which lessens the antitrust exposure for certain types of cooperative activities.[135]

Judicial recognition of the usefulness of cooperation among competitors can even be found during periods of intensive antitrust prosecution. In *United States v. Line Material Company* the court in dictum stated: "The development of patents by separate corporations or by cooperating units of an industry through an organized research group is a well known phenomenon. However far advanced over the lone inventor's experimentation this method of seeking improvement in the practices of the arts and sciences may be, there can be no objection, on the score of illegality, either to the mere size of such a group or the thoroughness of its research."[136]

One early case brought under the Sherman Act also illustrates this judicial recognition of the usefulness of collective activity by competitors. The case was brought by the government against the Chicago Board of Trade, charging that organization and its members with price-fixing. The collective activity under attack was an agreement among the grain traders that no member would buy or sell grain after the close of the market on one day until the beginning of the next market session except at the closing market prices. As a consequence, from 2:00 P.M. when the market closed until 9:30 A.M. the next morning when the market opened there was but a single price for grain trades among the Board of Trade members. The Supreme Court did not accept the government's argument and instead embraced the defendants' position that the restrictive collective activity was not intended to control prices but merely for the convenience of the trade. In his opinion Mr. Justice Louis Brandeis amplified this contention:

> Every agreement concerning trade, every regulation of trade restrains. To bind, restrain, is of their very essence. The true test of legality is whether the restraint imposed is such as merely regulates and perhaps thereby promotes competition or whether it is such as may suppress or even destroy competition. To determine that question the court must ordinarily consider the facts peculiar to the business to which the restraint is applied; its conditions before and after the restraint was imposed; the nature of the restraint and its effect, actual and probable.[137]

Use of the rule of reason to achieve workable competition is the courts' effort to grapple with the fact that both competition and cooperation must coexist in the economy in order for it to operate with efficiency and equity. The difficult task is to find that right balance of competition and cooperation for a given situation at a given time in a given industry. The legal concept of workable competition and the rule of reason analysis stand as judicial recognition of the fact that corporations do not and cannot operate as lone-wolf competitors in constant struggle against all other organizations but are enmeshed in an ever-changing web of competitive and cooperative activities.

JOINT VENTURES AND PUBLIC POLICY

Public policy toward cooperation among competitors in the form of joint ventures has been called "one of the darkest corners of antitrust law."[138] Part of the difficulty stems from uncertainty about just what constitutes a joint venture. As one oft-noted author has stated, a joint venture is "[m]ore than a simple contract yet less than a merger."[139] Of course, a definition such as this, which merely puts limits on the extremes, encompasses a wide variety of cooperative action. One of the most widely cited definitions in the legal literature is not much more specific in stating that a joint venture is "an association of two or more persons to carry on as co-owners an enterprise for one or a series of transactions."[140]

Aside from problems in clearly defining the term *joint venture*, ascertaining the public policy toward joint ventures is further complicated by the fact that antitrust enforcement efforts aimed at curbing the actual or perceived abuses of collective activity have been inconsistent. Complaints about inconsistent policies toward cooperation among competitors are not new. Gerhard Gesell, then an attorney for the law firm of Covington & Burling in Washington, D.C., and later appointed a federal judge, remarked in an address to the Manufacturing Chemists' Association over twenty years ago that government enforcement policy toward joint ventures was "ambivalent and constantly changing" and that "no coherent enforcement policy . . . can be discerned by the outside observer."[141]

Much of the ambiguity and incoherence can probably be traced to the previously discussed fact that cooperation among actual or potential competitors can have positive as well as negative consequences. Consider the situation facing the Supreme Court in *Citizens Publishing Co. v. United States*.[142] In that case there were two newspapers serving the same market. One of the newspapers was profitable. The other was not.

The two companies decided to form a joint venture to produce and distribute both newspapers in the hope that scale economies could be shared by both organizations. The news and editorial operations were to be conducted separately. Although one could argue that survival of both newspapers, and hence competition, depended on some form of cooperation, this particular cooperative activity was struck down by the Supreme Court as a *per se* violation of the Sherman Act, since profits would be pooled and prices fixed. It also should be noted that the companies made their position more vulnerable to attack by also including a collateral agreement not to form any new competing entities in the joint venture market.

Trying to untangle the legitimate benevolent effects of cooperation from the illegal malevolent ones has often been a problem for the courts and legislators. To cite an illustrative example, consider the case of *United States v. Topco Associates*.[143] This case arose from a situation where a number of small independent grocers organized a cooperative venture in an effort to deal with substantial competition from larger and more powerful rivals. The Supreme Court nullified the group's collective efforts to enhance their competitive performance through price-fixing and market division but did permit cooperation to con-

tinue in other areas such as joint purchasing, citing "legitimate purposes." To further complicate matters, the Supreme Court in deciding
an earlier joint venture case made it clear that a claimed legitimate
purpose for cooperation would not insulate suspect collective activity
from attack.[144]

Aside from concerns regarding the diminution of actual or potential
competition among the parents of a cooperative venture, there is also
some indication that the courts will consider limitations on the future
independence of the joint venture in assessing the legality of cooperative activity. For example, in *Consolidated Gas v. Pennsylvania W &
P Co.*, often referred to as the *Penn Water* case, an effort by two electric
utility companies to operate a joint subsidiary to produce electric
power for their exclusive use was declared unlawful.[145] The decision
focused on restrictions on the future independence of the joint subsidiary due to exclusivity sections of the cooperative agreement.

Nowhere has the uncertainty surrounding the judicial and legislative efforts at separating the perceived positive effects of cooperation
from the feared negative ones been more apparent than in the field of
joint ventures to undertake research and development.

COOPERATIVE RESEARCH AND DEVELOPMENT AND
PUBLIC POLICY

Antitrust policy seeks to benefit society by preserving and enhancing competition in the belief that increased competition results in
more or better goods and services at lower prices. A critical element
in the competitive framework is innovation, since it is the creative and
searching mind that is the driving force in the desired competitive
struggle. Since research and investment that leads to innovation can
be seen as both the cause and the result of competition, antitrust policy
endeavors to encourage competition in the marketplace to promote
innovation, and to encourage innovation in an effort to promote
competition.[146] The research activities leading to innovation cover a
broad spectrum that can range from basic research exploring fundamental scientific principles to market and product research seeking to
embellish a specific product characteristic.

Although research and development in general is seen as an essential and positive contribution to free and open competition, joint
research and development activities can have negative effects as well.
On one hand, joint research and development may be beneficial and
necessary to take advantage of certain scale economies, to avoid

wasteful duplication, or to facilitate wider distribution of technology. On the other hand, joint research and development conceivably could substitute a large and leisurely project for a number of smaller, more energetic ones. Another danger is that joint efforts at research and development may also facilitate joint decision-making by the participants in other competitive areas or may represent an attempt to restrict research and development investment by an industry.

In weighing the balance between the positive and negative aspects of joint research and development, antitrust law enforcement officials must conduct a multidimensional evaluation. The evaluation focuses on three main effects of the cooperative action: (1) the lessening of competition between the joint research participants who are existing or potential competitors, (2) the existence of ancillary restrictions that restrain competition, and (3) limitations placed on access to participation.

Although government antitrust enforcement officials like to point out that no "pure" research and development joint venture has ever been attacked as anticompetitive,[147] the perception of potential antitrust exposure has hung over the heads of cooperative R&D participants like the sword of Damocles. Despite the apparent truth of this qualified claim, business executives and their legal advisors can hardly be faulted for their caution with regard to cooperative research and development activities. One of the reasons for this perception is the paucity of case law regarding joint ventures in general and joint R&D ventures in particular.[148]

To help explain how business timidity regarding cooperative R&D has developed, consider how the facts in the Smog Conspiracy case, one of the few cases pursued by the government against the participants in a cooperative research and development effort, might appear to interested observers.

One of the first indications of a connection between the automobile and air pollution occurred at a 1949 football game at the University of California at Berkeley. Some of the spectators at the game were scientists and researchers who had been wrestling with the causes of Southern California's smog problem that had emerged during the war-induced boom growth of the region. At the time of the game Berkeley was relatively free of the smog that was beginning to engulf its southern neighbor, Los Angeles. The smog that developed over the football stadium that sunny afternoon seemed to implicate the thousands of fans' automobiles as the source of the pollution. It occurred to some that the peculiar conditions present that afternoon in Berkeley had turned the stadium area into a microcosm of the Los Angeles basin.

Scientific evidence supporting this hypothesis soon began to emerge and evidence mounted against automobile emissions as a primary cause of smog. In response, the automobile industry began to increase its efforts in the area of air pollution research and control. In early 1953 the Automobile Manufacturers Association established a technical committee to study vehicle emissions. In 1955 the informal cooperative venture was formalized when eleven domestic vehicle manufacturers entered into a royalty-free cross-licensing agreement to encourage the industry to pool research and technological developments regarding air pollution control devices.

Nearly ten years after the automakers had established the cross-licensing agreement, Los Angeles County pollution control officials, impatient with the pace of results, asked the Department of Justice to investigate the automakers' cooperative research arrangement. According to the Los Angeles County officials, the cross-licensing agreement and the cooperation it had fostered among the automakers were not being used as a method to encourage the development of emission control devices, but rather as an instrument to suppress it.

The Justice Department, following this same tack, conducted its own investigation, which eventually led to the filing of an antitrust suit against the vehicle manufacturers and their trade association. Because the complaint charged the defendants with a conspiracy in restraint of trade, the case is popularly known as the Smog Conspiracy case.

Both the government and the industry acknowledged that the auto-buying public seemed unwilling to voluntarily pay for cleaner exhausts. As a result there was little incentive for the automakers to vigorously compete in trying to install emission control equipment. Without this market-driven incentive, the government contended, the cooperative research and development effort turned into a conspiracy to limit competition relating to emission control. It was the government's hope that by keeping each company's air pollution control efforts hidden from its competitors that uncertainty might spur individual research and development work.

Faced with an enormous potential liability that could stem from derivative treble damage suits, the automakers decided not to run the risk of a trial to contest the government's position and theories. Instead, the defendants signed a consent decree, by which they did not admit or agree to the government's charges but did agree to abide by certain prohibitions and restrictions. One of the key terms of the consent decree was an agreed-to ten-year ban on cooperative research and development regarding emission control devices.

On November 9, 1981, after nearly three years of court petitions, hearings, and rulings, the Smog Conspiracy consent decree was modified.[149] With the ban on joint R&D lifted, activities to exploit the benefits of cooperation among the automakers on air control devices were again considered. When the National Cooperative Research Act of 1984 was passed one of the first cooperative ventures to register with the Justice Department and Federal Trade Commission was one of automakers to conduct cooperative research and development regarding pollution and emission control devices.[150]

THE NATIONAL COOPERATIVE RESEARCH ACT OF 1984

Public policy toward interfirm R&D collaboration has markedly changed in the last few years. When twelve companies in the computer and semiconductor industries announced their intention in 1982 to form a cooperative venture to develop important new technologies, the response from interested outsiders was not one of unanimous encouragement.[151] One letter in particular that was sent to the chief executives of each of the member firms as well as to Senator Howard Metzenbaum came from Joseph M. Alioto, former mayor of San Francisco and prominent antitrust attorney. This letter touched off a heated public debate on the benefits and dangers of interfirm cooperation.

In his three-page letter Alioto warned the executives that:

[I]n my opinion, your contemplated conduct is an unequivocal combination in violation of the antitrust laws of the United States. The effect that your agreement will have upon competition and innovations in the otherwise dynamic and exponentially expanding electronics industry is obvious — not to mention the destructive impact on the establishment of new submarket industries and jobs ... the mere fact that your companies utilized some non-apparent lines of communication is itself startling and would, with any other Antitrust Division, be more than enough to conduct a grand jury investigation to ascertain what these avenues are, how long they have existed, and what matters were discussed.[152]

Mr. Alioto ended his letter with this thinly disguised threat: "If your company nonetheless chooses to proceed with the combination, then at least you do so with full knowledge of the potential consequences."[153]

The national importance of the debate regarding the extent to which U.S. corporations should be encouraged to participate in forms of inter-firm collaboration quickly spread to the halls of Congress. A number of bills specifically designed to address the problems posed by the formation of the Microelectronics and Computer Technology Corporation (MCC) were introduced to clarify the status of cooperative R&D.[154] This congressional consideration of the merits and perils of interfirm collaboration marked an important shift in public policy toward the role of cooperation in the competitive economy.

Congressman Doug Walgren, chairman of the Subcommittee on Science, Research, and Technology, made the following opening remarks at a congressional hearing held in mid-1983:

Recognizing that foreign trade and our ability to compete effectively in the world marketplace is becoming of ever-increasing importance to our economic well-being, it is time to focus our attention on our situation and develop an effective U.S. response. In the hearings I mentioned earlier, we heard views expressed that we in the U.S. are wasting valuable and scarce resources by companies working independently in the same field of interest to make scientific discoveries or technological developments on their own, often duplicating each other's work. . . . The bills to be discussed today represent an attempt to eliminate the disincentive in terms of antitrust risks associated with companies joining together to conduct lawful and procompetitive research and development activities.[155]

As the pressures of competing in the international marketplace increased on domestic companies, the attractiveness of interfirm cooperation also increased. The past success of interfirm collaboration undertaken by Japanese companies was not overlooked. As Congressman Ed Zschau, who represented Silicon Valley in northern California, put it:

Although our past achievements in technology have been inspiring, we can't afford to relax. The rate of technological change worldwide is accelerating. . . . The further and faster we push the limits of our knowledge and our technology, the costlier and riskier those R&D efforts become. . . . Over the next decade, America's dominance in the computer industry will be challenged from abroad. The challenge will come from Japan. In 1981, after three years of extensive planning, the Japanese government announced a *national project* designed to make Japan number one in the computer industry by the late 1990s. . . . The Japanese research program, involving a consortium of companies coordinated by the Japanese government, could ultimately cost a billion dollars over ten years. A concerted team effort will be needed for the U.S. computer industry to meet this competitive challenge. However, a project to develop a fifth-generation computer is simply too large and too daring for an individual company (with the possible exception of IBM) to justify pursuing alone. Clearly, R&D joint ventures will be needed.[156]

Hearings on the various proposals took place throughout 1983 and into 1984. By the spring of 1984 Congress had received volumes of testimony urging, for the most part, some government action aimed at clarifying the antitrust exposure a firm might face if it decided to engage in cooperative research and development activities. By this time the most popular elements of the earlier proposed bills had been consolidated into a single House and Senate version[157] which eventually was enacted as the National Cooperative Research Act of 1984. President Reagan signed the new bill into law on October 11, 1984.

EEC AND JAPANESE POLICY TOWARD COOPERATIVE VENTURES

Lest one get the impression that legal restriction regarding cooperation among competitors is a peculiar phenomenon that is unique to the United States, a brief note of the policy toward joint ventures in Japan and the European Common Market is in order.

European Economic Community Policy

Politicians and policymakers in the United States are not alone in their praise and adulation of competition. One of the European Economic Community's principal stated objectives was "the establishment of a system insuring that competition shall not be distorted in the Common Market" [Treaty of Rome Article 3]. As the Commission of the EEC expressed it soon after the Common Market was formed:

> [C]ompetition is not only an important tool in the building of the Common Market during the transition period but will have an essential role to play in the control of the economic process on the European markets established with its aid. . . . [A] constructive competition policy is one of the most important and most effective instruments available to the Community for realizing the aims of the Treaty.[158]

The Treaty of Rome contains two main sections to implement this policy of "constructive competition," Articles 85 and 86. Article 85, generally referred to as the anti-cartel provision, prohibits agreements, decisions, and concerted practices "which have as their object or effect the prevention, restriction or distortion of competition within the common market."[159] Certain activities are specifically mentioned as incompatible with common market policy such as price-fixing, market-sharing, and production-limiting agreements. Article 86 is aimed at prohibiting the abuse of a dominant position and roughly corresponds to Section 2 of the Sherman Act.[160]

Despite the strong language of these two sections regarding prohibited anticompetitive practices, the proper balance between competition and cooperation is subject to debate. As one commentator noted over a quarter of a century ago, "the basic concepts of Articles 85 and 86 are not so clear as to exclude very important differences of opinion about their interpretation. As differences of opinion on cartel policy in the Member States are for historical reasons very great, we shall probably arrive only gradually and on the basis of specific cases at a clarification of these concepts. . . . "[161]

Van Themaat's prediction has held true as the European Economic Commission has applied and interpreted EEC competition and cooperation policy. There is general agreement that the commission has been more receptive in the past to evidence of benefits arising from cooperative action than have enforcement agencies and courts in the United States.[162]

Regardless of past differences, U.S. and European Economic Community enforcement policies seem to be converging on analysis that emphasizes efficiencies. Evaluation of the positive as well as negative effects of cooperation among competitors has long been an essential element of EEC competition policy,[163] but there are indications that domestic antitrust enforcement is beginning to follow suit.

As an example of the increasing importance of balancing positive and negative consequences of cooperation in United States enforcement policy, consider the example of the Federal Trade Commission's decision regarding the General Motors/Toyota joint venture to manufacture automobiles in California. The commission, in its majority opinion, stated:

> The Commission has provisionally determined that the proposed Fremont venture—as outlined in the Memorandum of Understanding and as restricted by the consent agreement—creates a substantial likelihood of producing significant procompetitive benefits to the American public. The Commission has concluded that these procompetitive benefits to the American consumer would outweigh any anticompetitive risks, provided that the scope of the venture is restricted. Accordingly, the Commission has provisionally accepted a consent agreement that provides the appropriate safeguards.[164]

Japanese Policy

Although Japan is often noted for its favorable policy toward cooperative activities, the country does have an official policy against anticompetitive agreements. Modeled on the antitrust laws of the United States and exported to Japan in the postwar occupation, the Antimonopoly Law, administered by the Japanese Fair Trade Commission (JFTC), seeks to curb unreasonable restraints of trade and unfair business practices. As such, the act can reach cooperative ventures that pose anticompetitive difficulties. The Antimonopoly Law was enacted in 1947 under the encouragement of the Allied occupation forces.[165]

Not surprisingly, the act relies heavily on the notions of "Anglo-Saxon individualism" that lie at the heart of Western antitrust concepts, a tradition that one observer notes "was totally alien to the cooperative business philosophy of Japan" that prevailed in the prewar years.[166] In fact, the Antimonopoly Law that was thrust upon the shattered Japanese economy was in some ways even more stringent than the U.S. counterpart. For example, the original law contained many *per se* standards, and under its provisions enforcement officials could force a company to divest part of its business where there were substantial disparities in bargaining power, without regard to abuse of that power.[167] To enforce the Antimonopoly Law, the Japanese Fair Trade Commission (JFTC) was established, modeled after the Federal Trade Commission in the United States.

It was not long after Japan recovered its independence that the Antimonopoly Law underwent a major revision that replaced many of the widely disliked *per se* standards with a balancing test similar to the rule of reason used in the United States.[168] Even with a less rigorous antitrust law the JFTC did not have a particularly easy time imposing a U.S.-style competition policy on Japanese society.[169]

Hostility toward the imported competition policy was not limited to Japanese businessmen, but also was evident in politicians and government bureaucrats. From 1952 to 1969 the role of the JFTC in the economy was limited. In fact, much the efforts of the JFTC during this period were spent struggling against a return to the prewar cartelized economic system. The older *zaibatsu* corporations such as Mitsubishi were permitted to remerge.[170] The Japanese Diet also passed numerous statutory exemptions to the Antimonopoly Law permitting otherwise prohibited activities in a variety of industries.[171]

The dominance of the Ministry of International Trade and Industry (MITI) over the JFTC in its influence on the Japanese economy was clear during the first thirty years of the JFTC.[172] During the 1970s the pendulum began to swing away from MITI domination of the economic machinery, and competition policy administered by the JFTC began to strengthen. In 1977, after three years of debate, the Diet passed an amendment to the Antimonopoly Law that invigorated antitrust enforcement. Not long afterwards a dramatic decision rendered by the Tokyo High Court in 1980 in the petroleum cartel case dramatized the evolution away from the unquestioning pro-cartel system to a more competitive one.[173]

Like their counterparts in the European Economic Community and the United States, Japanese legislators, business leaders, and government bureaucrats have been seeking that proper balance between interfirm cooperation and interfirm competition. Undoubtedly, the quest in all three economic systems continues to evolve, and the evidence indicates an evolution toward a common middle ground.

CONCLUSION

Interfirm cooperation plays an important role, both positive and negative, in our competitive economic system. In recognition of the double-edged nature of collaborative activities, the legal system has devoted considerable time and energy to efforts aimed at defining the limits of permissible and impermissible action. Although the area of interfirm cooperation is still fraught with legal uncertainty, there is increasing pressure upon firms to embrace collective ventures as instruments of strategic action. Judges, legislators, policy makers, and corporate participants must continue to improve their understanding of interfirm cooperation in order to separate the desirable from the destructive.

4

The Management Challenge
of Cooperative R&D

As discussed in the previous chapter, interfirm cooperation has always been an integral part of the competitive economy. The legal literature, as well as the literature in the fields of general management, organizational theory, and economics discloses a wide variety in the types of collaboration used by corporations in pursuit of strategic objectives.

In the past, public policy toward interorganizational cooperation has been viewed by many as a hindrance,[174] but in the 1980s there was a decided shift in outlook.[175] The increased use of cooperation among firms, or strategic partnering, as some consultants label it,[176] has focused management attention on interorganization collaboration.[177] With the public policy barriers to cooperation lowering it is not surprising to discover that new forms of collective action have begun to appear. In particular, research collaboration among companies has been heralded as a potent response to the challenges of increasing competition in the global marketplace.[178]

As strategic alliances to conduct research activities become increasingly attractive as a competitive strategy, executives must ask themselves how the management of such joint ventures differs from the management of single-entity organizations or prior joint ventures, since their ultimate success or failure will depend less on what the antitrust laws permit or prohibit than on how the organizations evolve and are managed.

Although there is a wide range of cooperative action available to the modern manager, the remainder of this book focuses on one important segment of that continuum: equity R&D cooperative ventures involving multiple and active participants that are relatively equal and competitive. The following questions will be explored: How does the management of this type of strategic partnership differ from the management of other organizations? And, if there are differences that are of significance to the cooperative venture executive, is there a management model that can be developed to assist executives in establishing and managing these cooperative ventures?

In that no one could hope to completely answer these questions, the inquiry must be broken down into smaller parts that can be executed separately, with the expectation that these smaller pieces of analysis and insight can be eventually woven together into a fabric of greater understanding. To this end three specific areas will be examined.

The first question of interest is, why would companies want to cooperate in the first place? The reasons that propel individual competing companies to cooperate in a collective research effort differ according to the ability or necessity to share costs and benefits. Prior research suggests that there are a number of possible relevant motivational categories. If there are important differences between the management tasks of single-participant research organizations and the management tasks of cooperative undertakings, then it is useful to sort out these differences and discover how cooperative venture managers seek to resolve the difficulties facing them. If one can identify specific, separate motivational categories for pursuing strategic alliances, then distinguishing organizational systems and structures, and managerial techniques might also exist and be discoverable.

The existence of multiple participants in collaborative research ventures makes the management of them measurably unique in contrast to the management of single-participant enterprises. The need to accommodate multiple participants is traceable throughout the collective organization. This increased need for management characterized by negotiation and accommodation affects (1) the strategy-making process, (2) the organizational structure, (3) the communication and control systems, and (4) the resource allocation processes.

In addition, the most important motivations of the participants will prevail upon the management functions, with the general manager making trade-offs and compromises among the various structures and systems. Likewise, conflict or uncertainty regarding the relative importance of multiple motivations is to be expected in the management of the cooperative undertakings.

It is the task of the cooperative venture general manager to devise organizational structures and systems that are responsive to the motivations that are of interest to each individual participant in order to maintain continued cooperation. This task is complicated by the fact that each participant faces its own unique combination of motivational categories and that conflict can arise in trying to make the trade-offs among the various categories.

The next question to examine is, after the companies decide to cooperate how do they decide on the specific form of cooperation? It is a long journey from the decision to cooperate to the establishment of a viable cooperative research venture, and it is along this often difficult path that many joint ventures flounder. It is here that the management of the collective effort can add significant value. The general manager of the collective R&D activity must take the reasons motivating the companies to collaborate, as well as the form in which they originally agreed to cooperate, and mold them into a working organization that produces results that are satisfactory to the participants.

The business policy literature has long stressed the importance of organizational purpose in the management of an enterprise. Chester Barnard, in his seminal work, *The Functions of the Executive*,[179] was one of first in a long string of writers and researchers to identify corporate purpose as an essential part of organizational success.[180] Barnard's theory of organization is rooted in his definition of formal organization as "a system of consciously coordinated activities or forces of two or more persons."[181] In Barnard's scheme there are three critical elements for an organization to come into being: (1) communication, (2) willingness of individuals to serve or cooperate, and (3) common purpose.[182] Related to these three elements are Barnard's essential executive functions: (1) providing and maintaining a system of communication, (2) securing essential efforts, and, most importantly, (3) formulation and definition of purpose.[183]

If the formulation and definition of organizational purpose is indeed a critical managerial concern and necessary for organizational success, then the examination of just how an organizational purpose is formed and defined for a cooperative research venture can provide important insights into the organization's prospects for success and can highlight sources of collaborative difficulty. Independent organizations decide to pool resources in the form of a cooperative research

Figure 4.1
Management Tasks

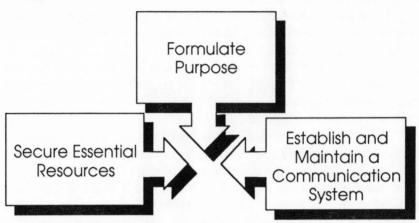

venture with some purpose in mind. In the best of circumstances the motivational goals of the independent participants will be the same, or at least compatible. Where the purposes of the cooperators are not the same or are incompatible, cooperation can suffer, complicating the management task.

The methods selected by joint venture executives with regard to (1) maintenance of a communication system, (2) securing essential effort, and (3) formulating purpose must correspond to the motivation of the participants to cooperate and the relative importance to the various types of motivation to the individual participants. This unique combination of motivations is traceable to structure and strategy elements in successful ventures.

The final question is, after cooperation is seen as desirable by the individual participants and a specific form of collaboration is chosen, what role can management play in establishing and maintaining cooperation among the participants? Maintaining an acceptable distribution of costs and benefits among the participants is one of the fundamental tasks facing the general manager of a cooperative venture.

In assessing the attractiveness of a cooperative enterprise the individual participant is basically concerned about two linkages with the collective venture. One is the individual participant's required contribution to the collective venture and the other is the flow of benefits from the collective venture to the individual participant. The decision to participate in a cooperative venture will be determined by the prospective participant's assessment of the relative value of these two linkages. The situation described is shown in Figure 4.2 below where C represents the required contribution to the collective enterprise and B stands for the benefits derived from cooperation. The required contribution and benefits include both tangible and intangible resources and assets. An individual participant has the incentive to cooperate if the contributions from the individual participant are less than the benefits received ($C < B$). It is the function of the joint venture executive to establish and manage a cooperative structure that yields benefits in excess of contributions.

Figure 4.2
Flow of Contributions and Benefits

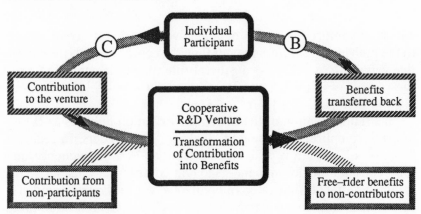

To maintain this balance, the collective venture executive can adjust the perceived value of the required contribution or the value of perceived benefits. It is expected that the success of a particular adjustment approach, whether to contribution, benefits, or both, will depend on the reason or reasons motivating the companies to collaborate. If it is shown that a particular adjustment approach is more applicable to a specific type of motivation, then guidelines regarding the establishment and maintenance of cooperative ventures of various types can be formulated to assist the collective enterprise executive.

Even if there is sufficient incentive to cooperate, there may be available other avenues to achieve like benefits at less cost. This is shown in Figure 4.3. If the benefit to be derived from pursuing an individual venture (B_1) and the benefit to be derived from collective action (B_2) are essentially equal outcomes, the preferred method of attainment will be by means of an individual venture if the contribution to the individual venture is less than the contribution to the

Figure 4.3
Flow of Contributions and Benefits for Individual Participant

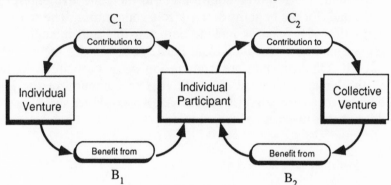

collective venture ($C_1 < C_2$), or collective venture if the contribution to the individual venture is greater than the contribution to the collective venture ($C_1 > C_2$). As a general rule the participant will prefer the greater of ($B_1 - C_1$) or ($B_2 - C_2$) [or for n possible methods of achievement ($B_n - C_n$)].

This representation of the benefit/contribution linkages as closed loops is complicated by benefit "leakage" to outsiders. In reality a "leak-proof" system is difficult to attain and as a consequence one must consider the flow of benefits to non-contributing outsiders. This free-rider effect is illustrated in Figure 4.4, which shows two individuals contributing to a collective venture (C_1 and C_2) but three flows of benefits (B_1, B_2, and B_3).

In such situations the collective venture will still be viable even with a flow of benefits to a non-contributor (B_3), if the cooperative venture can be structured so that the combined contributions of individual participants is less than the benefits flow to the participants ($C_1 + C_2 < B_1 + B_2$) *and* the benefits flowing to the free rider (B_3) do not impose extra costs (increasing C_1 or C_2) or cause a decrease in the benefits to the contributing participants (B_2 or B_3) to such an extent that the inequality is reversed.

Referring to the linkages thus illustrated one can highlight some of the required tasks of the collective venture general manager. First, the general manager of the cooperative enterprise must address the issue of the respective participants' contribution to the collective. What should each participant bring to the party? In order to answer this question the general manager must consider the participants' perceptions of the expected benefits. For example, suppose that in Figure 4.4 the perceived benefits, less contribution to the cooperative effort, is

Figure 4.4
Flows of Contributions and Benefits to and from Collective Venture

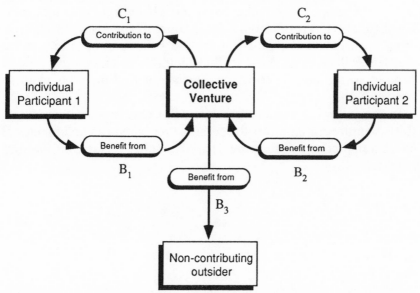

much greater for Individual Participant 1 than Individual Participant 2, or in other words $(B_1-C_1) > (B_2-C_2)$. And suppose that for Individual Participant 2 the costs of participation actually exceed the perceived benefits $(B_2-C_2 < 0)$. Because Individual Participant 2 has no incentive to cooperate, cooperation will only be possible if some of the benefits flowing to Individual Participant 1 (B_1) are somehow transferred to Individual Participant 2 (B_2), so that $C_2 < B_2$. Of course, there is a limit to how much of the benefits flowing to Individual Participant 1 (B_1) can be shifted to the benefits flowing to Individual Participant 2 (B_2), in that the contribution from Individual Participant 1 must remain such that the contribution required remains less than the benefits received $(C_1 < B_1)$. It is the task of the general manager of the collective venture to structure and operate the cooperative effort in a manner to maintain this delicate balance.

With the introduction of the free-rider problem the role of the manager of a collective venture is further complicated. Referring again to Figure 4.3, the general manager of the collective enterprise must structure and operate the cooperative effort to minimize any benefits to non-contributing outsiders (B_3) that lessen the benefits to the contributing participants $(B_1$ and $B_2)$. To the extent that benefits to a non-contributor (B_3) represent a residual benefit that cannot be enjoyed by the participants (i.e. it is a benefit of a different nature than those flowing to the participants) then the collective venture general manager need not be as concerned with its creation and capture by non-contributors. On the other hand, if the benefits to non-contributing outsiders (B_3) result from a diminution of benefits to the contributing participants (B_1 or B_2) then the collective venture general manager will be compelled to find methods to hinder the flow of benefits to the non-contributing outsider or find methods to force contribution.

In the following two chapters we will examine four cooperative R&D ventures in an effort to see how their sponsors and managers have attempted to maintain the desired benefits-versus-contributions balance.

5

The Story of MCC

Companies responded to increasing competitive pressures in the 1980s and forged new forms of collective activity to help solve problems of strategic importance. Nowhere was this more apparent than in the area of cooperative research and development. The Microelectronics and Computer Technology Corporation, or MCC, a consortium of competing United States computer and component manufacturers headquartered in Austin, Texas, is a prime example of this new breed of collaboration. MCC is a part of a worldwide effort that will help bring into being what is commonly referred to as the fifth-generation of computers, machines that will "think" or operate more like humans than their predecessors. The importance of the technology being developed by MCC is well recognized and the task facing MCC researchers is formidable. But just as formidable is the task facing MCC management who had to develop and who must continue to develop new systems and structures to deal with the unprecedented problems facing a collaborative effort of this nature.

In this chapter the formation and subsequent management of MCC will be examined. In later chapters the insights and lessons of the MCC experience will be supplemented by and contrasted with the experience of other cooperative research ventures such as Sematech and CIIT. Because of its status as a vanguard venture, and due to the openness of MCC's founders and managers, particularly Admiral Bobby Ray Inman, the experience of MCC as it struggled through its first five years serves as an unusually helpful case study for those who follow.[184]

MCC differed in some very important aspects from most previous joint research venture activity. First of all, MCC was structured so that it had multiple and essentially equal partners. This was in contrast to the common joint venture activity involving a U.S. company in which an unequal (in terms of decision-making if not equity) and generally passive (in terms of corporate strategy making) foreign partner was present. All the MCC participants were large domestic corporations, and many were competitors or enjoyed some sort of prior or potential marketplace relationship. Each was a independent strategy-pursuing entity in its own right.

The focus of MCC's activity, namely the development of technology, also makes the study of MCC unique and of special interest.[185] Unlike earlier successful joint research ventures such as CIIT that can remain more independent of the participating parents, MCC is an important element of the participants' current businesses. And, since the success of MCC and its ultimate benefit to the participants will depend on how well the technology created is transferred to the shareholders, the management and strategies of MCC and its parent companies are more closely intertwined than would be the case in other cooperative ventures. The parents of MCC must remain active participants for the technology transfer process to work. The fact that the output of a cooperative research venture is essentially a non-corporeal product, namely knowledge and technology, makes the transfer of the joint venture product to the participants all the more complicated.

As a unique solution to an increasingly important set of problems, MCC serves as a model for future cooperative research ventures. Founded just prior to the passage of the National Cooperative Research Act of 1984, MCC and its first CEO, president, and board chairman, Admiral Bobby Ray Inman, played an instrumental role in the congressional effort to clarify national policy toward interfirm collaborate research and in gaining passage of the NCRA.[186] Since MCC's founding, more companies have come to view cooperative activity, at least in the research area, with less trepidation.[187] Since the passage of the NCRA in October of 1984, a wide range of companies have filed notice with the FTC and Department of Justice of their intent to form cooperative ventures. These new cooperative ventures and those that follow will inevitably look to the experience of the pioneer, MCC, in order to manage their efforts.[188]

SECURING RESOURCES AND DEFINING PURPOSE

Underlying the analysis of MCC's management is the story of an evolving organization. It is the story of an idea being transformed into an institution. It is a story of experiments, some successful, others less so, and the acquisition of managerial talent and experience to meet the demands of a unique and difficult situation. Whatever lessons MCC may be able to provide for those seeking to extract benefits from similar strategic alliances must be drawn from this "living history."

The saga of MCC begins with a concern that gave birth to a concept championed by William Norris, the founder and former chairman of Control Data Corporation. The subsequent evolution of MCC can be divided into four phases. Phase One was characterized by conceptualization and definition. During this period the idea of a cooperative venture was transformed from a vague notion to a concrete plan of action. Phase Two encompassed the first two major implementation tasks, selection of a CEO for the new organization and selection of a location. Phase Three involved the development of administrative structures and procedures. During this phase the growing ranks of MCC executives worked out the organizational structures and systems that would be necessary to engage in high-quality research, produce superior results, and transfer the results of the research back to the contributors. Phase Four, the phase in which MCC is now operating, is characterized by the operation of the research programs to develop the technology and knowledge, and the actual transfer of this intellectual property to the shareholder companies.

PHASE ONE: CONCEPTUALIZATION AND DEFINITION

The Call for Action

As organizations grow and mature it is often to the accompaniment of legends and stories about past events. This organizational folklore or mythology can be very revealing of underlying values and corporate ethos. Although MCC is still a very young organization, certain legendary stories circulate among those who work for it, even among the relative newcomers. One such story relates to the birth of MCC. This genesis story is set in Orlando, Florida, during February of 1982. William Norris, who was the chairman of Control Data at the time, had called together the heads of a number of other companies in the computer industry to discuss the possibility of cooperative activity.

Figure 5.1
MCC – The First Five Years

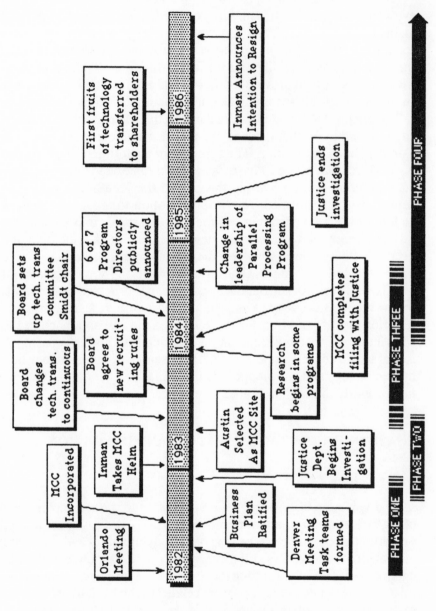

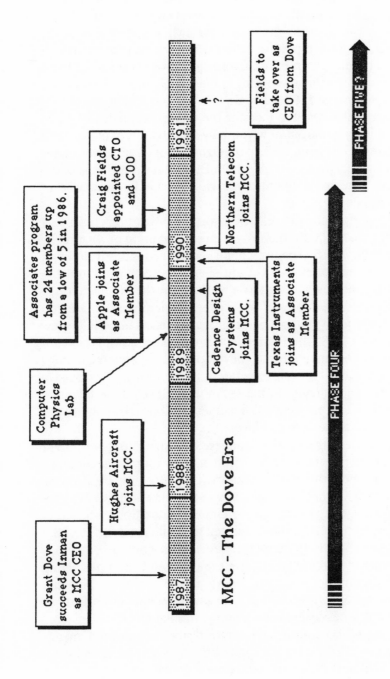

MCC – The Dove Era

| 1987 | 1988 | 1989 | 1990 | 1991 |

Grant Dove succeeds Inman as MCC CEO

Hughes Aircraft joins MCC.

Computer Physics Lab

Associates program has 24 members up from a low of 5 in 1986.

Apple joins as Associate Member

Craig Fields appointed CTO and COO

Cadence Design Systems joins MCC.

Texas Instruments joins as Associate Member

Northern Telecom joins MCC.

?

Fields to take over as CEO from Dove

PHASE FOUR

PHASE FIVE?

As the story goes, a group of these top executives were sitting around a table exchanging generally negative opinions on the idea of cooperation. After listening to the discussion for awhile, Gordon Bell, the well-known and highly respected technological wizard then representing Digital Equipment Corporation, rose up from his seat and let loose with a single sentence that, according to the legend, tipped the balance in favor of cooperative action. Dr. Bell, in a combination of concern and dismay, gazed across the faces of the assembled executives and told them, "Five years from now you may all be out looking for jobs because you insist on having these petty fights among yourselves rather than look at the real problem." After Dr. Bell returned to his seat, the story continues, the discussion resumed with a decidedly more positive attitude toward cooperation.

Interestingly, no one who tells the story now was present in that room in Orlando. No doubt the story is an exaggeration of what really happened, the facts having been embellished over countless retellings. But, the story does capture a certain shared perception about the origins of MCC, at least among those working for the organization.

Tracing the historical roots of MCC even deeper than the Orlando meeting in 1982, one would not be exaggerating to say that MCC grew out of the vision of William Norris. Norris had watched with concern the Japanese cooperative effort to develop the necessary technology to manufacture very large scale integrated circuits (VLSI).[189] Japanese manufacturers, capitalizing on the technology developed under the auspices of the VLSI project, had become a serious challenge to the dominance of the American producers.

It was in this setting that the Japanese industry and government announced an even more ambitious project to develop the technology to build the fifth-generation of computers. This effort, the Institute for New Generation Computer Technology and known as ICOT, produced a wide range of reaction in the United States. Some scoffed at the technological premise, others doubted the ability and desire of the competitor participants to cooperate, even with government prodding. At the other extreme there were the Chicken Littles predicting nothing but doom and gloom for the domestic computer industry. Between the extremes were those who saw the Japanese efforts as serious, but not necessarily overwhelming, threats.

William Norris was one such person who saw the potential magnitude of the Japanese threat to the competitiveness of the U.S. industry. What happened next is in large part a measure of the unique nature of his leadership ability in the industry. Not content to sit by and merely worry and wail about the problem, Norris set out to take corrective action. Not surprisingly, the solution advocated by Norris followed a number of cooperative venture predecessors undertaken by Control Data over the years.

Norris contacted the top executives of computer and computer component manufacturers to determine whether or not sufficient interest could be generated to begin discussions regarding cooperative action. It was decided that a meeting be held in early 1982 to provide a forum for further deliberations. This initial meeting in February of 1982 in Orlando, Florida, to discuss possible collaboration had been preceded by a Norris trip to Japan about a year earlier. In the intervening time Norris began to flesh out a plan to deal with the future problems he envisioned for the U.S. computer industry. The core of the Norris proposal was a cooperative venture called MCE.[190] Although the concept was greeted with some skepticism at first, it did stimulate discussion.

The prevailing industry climate at the time was one of deep concern regarding very severe problems — severe problems from a recession and severe problems caused by overseas competition, most notably Japan. The remarkable aspect of the solution envisioned by Norris to the problem he saw was that it called for cooperative action among competitors. This call for cooperation is less unusual when the path taken by Control Data Corporation (CDC) under Norris's leadership is examined. As a smaller competitor in a marketplace increasingly dominated by the giant IBM, CDC had been a pioneer in seeking partners for certain projects. In the early 1970s CDC and NCR were able to form a successful joint venture to develop magnetic peripheral devices. Later in that decade CDC joined with Honeywell and other computer companies in projects concerning magnetic recording media. As Norris put it, "We understand and know how to benefit from technological cooperation."

The Japanese Threat

The basic rallying cry that spurred the original participants of MCC into action was "preserve the U.S. leadership in microelectronics." The domestic microelectronics industry had grown dramatically in the postwar years and lay at the heart of the American economic future. The industry was remarkably successful, and its technology led the world.

Despite the industry's past performance and strength at the time, Norris and other leaders in the industry had become increasingly concerned about the nature of competition in the 1980s and into the 1990s. In particular, the threat posed by Japanese companies was seen, in the words of Phil Arnison of Control Data, as a "clear and present danger" to the U.S. microelectronics market.[191] The threat created by Japanese competition was compounded by four difficult conditions that were prevailing in the microelectronics industry.

First, financial resources were increasingly scarce and costly. Second, the industry was finding that the talents of people to conduct the R&D were nearly as scarce and costly as the financial resources. Third, competitive conditions had changed so that companies did not have the luxury of the leisurely five- to eight-year product development and introduction cycle that was common in the 1970s. And fourth, the proliferation of new technologies that every microelectronics manufacturer needed to master in order to remain a viable competitor had dramatically increased. As a consequence, companies had to obtain a degree of competence or even excellence in numerous technological areas, each competing for scarce money, time, talent, and executive attention. As one company official noted, "the typical high tech company doesn't have enough of these resources to generate a critical mass" necessary to be competitive in the marketplace.

The Japanese microelectronics industry faced many of the same difficulties, but the differences in their response were an element in their increasing competitiveness. First of all, because of the differences in financial practices, the scarcity and cost of funds was less of a problem to the Japanese industry. High debt leveraging led to less need for high profit margins and thus more emphasis on sales rather than bottom line profits. Larger relative capital and R&D investment on the part of the Japanese microelectronics manufacturers, especially during depressed periods in the marketplace, was just one indication to the U.S. industry that the threat of Japanese competition was no phantom. In addition, the mutually supportive nature of business and government in Japan was seen as another potential competitive advantage, especially in light of the Japanese government's public commitment to turn Japan into an information society. The U.S. industry already had evidence of just how effective this government/business cooperation could be in the form of the VLSI Cooperative Research Association, an "emergency cartel" formed under Public Law 84.

In an effort to follow the success of the VLSI project the Japanese government had announced administrative and financial support ($440 million) of not only the fifth-generation program, but two other cooperative programs as well. One was the supercomputer project, to which the Japanese government had pledged $115 million, to be added to an equal sum of money put up by industry. The other was the New Function Next Generation Devices effort funded with at least $125 million of direct government aid that was to develop super lattice structures and three-dimensional packaging necessary to support the future computers.

As was stated by the narrator in a video produced by the original MCC participants to help persuade other industry members regarding the seriousness of the situation:

> The Japanese challenge is a combination of government pro-
> moted industry cooperation, non-reciprocal trading policies and
> partitioned product lines. And, all of this is financed by a highly
> favorable low cost capital stream. That's clearly a structured
> competitive advantage. . . . The U.S. companies are playing
> against a stacked deck.[192]

It was recognized that the response to this challenge would have to fit the differing circumstances, values and environment associated with the U.S. industry. The unique structure of Japanese industry and the special relationship between the private and public sectors that encouraged the mobilization of the Japanese nation to support Japanese national goals was not likely to be duplicated in the United States. Although MCC was to be an important element in the U.S. response, even from the beginning it was not seen as the single solution to a complex problem.

The Orlando Meeting

At the Orlando meeting there was general agreement on the need to improve technology and there was recent precedent for coopera-
tion. Many of the companies present had already agreed to participate in the Semiconductor Research Corporation (SRC), which was, in essence, an effort to upgrade the technology at the university level. But, even with a general consensus on the merits of cooperation there was no clear consensus on the specifics of how that cooperation might be structured or even of what the particular subject matter of the

research should be. As stated by one observer, the general conclusion was that, "Yes, we need to upgrade our technology. We can't afford to do it ourselves. We can share the cost by participating in it jointly somehow, but what specific technologies are we going to pursue?"

As with any cooperative undertaking among competitors, the cloud of antitrust prosecution loomed. This antitrust concern was so strong that the first statement Norris made to the assembled executives at Orlando after welcoming them was a warning: "We should all remind ourselves that whenever competitors meet for any purpose, certain topics may not be discussed."[193] In interesting contrast to MITI's participation in Japan's fifth-generation computer cooperative activity, the U.S. government agency that was informed prior to the meeting and was given a summary of the proceedings afterwards was the Federal Trade Commission, the antitrust watchdog. In fact, the antitrust concern was so significant that the Orlando meeting was a gathering of chief executives and not their chief technical personnel but rather their attorneys.

At the meeting Norris did not seek commitment to a cooperative project per se but instead sought the commitment of the intellectual and business resources necessary to undertake the planning and operational definition of a cooperative venture. At the time, sixteen companies expressed enough interest in the concept (AMD, Burroughs, CDC, DEC, Harris, Honeywell, Mostek, Motorola, National Semiconductor, NCR, RCA, Signetics, Sperry, United Technologies [parent company of Mostek], Westinghouse, and Xerox) to engage in further discussions.

Norris's Reasons for Cooperation

There were three main reasons for cooperative activity cited by Norris at the Orlando meeting: pooling resources, avoiding duplication, and the shortage of scientific and engineering talent. The first argument in favor of cooperation implied that the investment required to participate in fifth-generation computer research and development was so great that it would strain the resources of individual companies.

The second argument forwarded by Norris in support of cooperative action was focused on the benefits of eliminating duplication of research and development. To Norris, neither the individual companies nor society as a whole benefited from a process that required one company to rediscover basic knowledge previously learned by another. It was Norris's contention that "the use of basic knowledge by one party should *never* preclude its use by another."[194] Sufficient competition, Norris argued, could occur in the different applications of the base technology. This notion of base technology cooperation followed by application competition lies at the heart of MCC.

The third advantage in cooperation, according to Norris, would be in sharing the limited scientific and engineering talent pool. The unstated implication of this argument was that the demand for those with particular skills and experience greatly exceeded the available supply. By cooperating, the companies demanding the talent could, presumably, avoid costly bidding wars or, perhaps worse, the inability to acquire the requisite talent at any price.

One possible explanation of Norris's concern was a belief that there were important scale effects to fifth-generation computer research and development. Companies conducting R&D at subscale levels would be at a competitive disadvantage when compared to their large rivals who could support scale-level efforts. The second possible interpretation does not require a belief in significant scale economies in the relevant R&D. Instead, the pooling of resources could be seen as a significant risk-reduction mechanism.

There were those who argued then, and now, that the goals of the fifth-generation computer efforts are especially risky from a technological point of view. The necessary discoveries may be a very long way off or perhaps uneconomical or physically impossible. Despite such risks, the potential promise of the fifth-generation computers is so great that most companies saw the need to make some commitment in that direction. Cooperation was one way of lowering the investment and at least guarantee that there would be no major surprises from the competing partners.

One could also argue, perhaps with a little less persuasion, that for a few of the later-joining companies cooperation was seen as a way to reduce costs or risks associated with strategic movement or entry. For example, Eastman Kodak's decision to join MCC could be seen as part of an overall shift in the company's strategic direction, or at least a change in the company's traditional method of doing business. Kodak had long been the premier example of a fully integrated "take control of all important aspects" company. The company manufactured its own paper for photographic supplies and at one time even managed its own forests to assure the quality of the raw material.

Deciding on a Research Agenda[195]

Following the Orlando meeting, the next steps were mainly left up to a steering committee that basically consisted of the deputies of the attendees of the Orlando meeting. The first major issue they faced was: "Which technology programs should be pursued?" Although agreement in general was possible on the notion that it was desirable to cooperate, agreement on explicit projects was more difficult. It was the task of the steering committee to get down to specific projects in which the individual companies would be willing to invest $2 million to $5 million and some valuable personnel over a three-year period.

To approach that problem a two-person team visited all the potential shareholders to try to determine areas of common interest. This team talked to the technical people in each of the fourteen or fifteen participating companies. These two people who were visiting the companies tried to understand what the technical challenges were as each individual company saw them and tried to see if they could find areas where there was a commonalty of interest.

The two people assigned to this task team were both employees of Control Data at the time. One was Phil Arnison, who acted as the general coordinator to the project and the other was Robert H. Price, who had a technical background. One of the confusing coincidences regarding the formation of MCC was that two Bob Prices were actively involved, both from Control Data. One was sometimes referred to as "the technical Bob Price" by those involved to distinguish him from the other Bob Price who was then president of Control Data. It was this task team of Arnison and Price that was able to pick a signal out of the noise, identifying those projects with some commonalty of interest.

It was fairly evident to all involved that not every company was going to be interested in every program. The companies were just too diverse for that. What was of importance to a mainframe computer company was not necessarily of importance to a general electronics company or a semiconductor manufacturer. Therefore, the task was to identify projects that would have enough commonalty of interest that there would be a broad base of support.

A consensus emerged fairly early on that MCC would conduct research "cafeteria style." This meant that individual programs would be identified and then the companies could sign up for the programs in which they were interested. According to Bob Rutishauser, then of Control Data and later a vice president of MCC, "If you had insisted that everybody join all the programs, it probably would have been difficult to get MCC off the ground because almost everyone would have said, 'Why do I want to invest in that program that is not of interest to me?' "

Although the decision to go "cafeteria style" made the formation of MCC less difficult, this particular decision would later cause complications for MCC in the creation and transfer of benefits. According to Inman this was the one major change he would have made in how MCC was structured. In his opinion it would be much better if all the members had to join all the programs. This one change would have eliminated the problems of knowledge leakage among the programs and would have simplified funding.

Once the decision had been made to offer a selection of research programs, the next question was, "What goes in the cafeteria?" Originally over twenty R&D projects were nominated as possible candidates for joint effort by the prospective members. As a result of the investigation and analysis conducted by Arnison and Price of Control Data there emerged a half dozen specific program candidates for MCC to pursue.

With the number of programs winnowed down from over twenty to fewer than a half dozen the information was presented to the steering committee. The steering committee agreed to the areas of interest, decided that the next task was spell out in greater detail just what could be done in each of those areas.

To this end there were five task teams selected, made up of one individual from each of the companies that thought it might be interested in that particular program. The leadership of the task teams was spread among the various companies: packaging was headed by someone from Harris; CAD/CAM by Robert H. Price, the "technical Bob Price" of Control Data; the advanced computer architecture was headed by a fellow from Digital Equipment; and the leader of the software team came from NCR.

It was the responsibility of the task teams to meet and define the research program. They kept massaging the objectives, the resources, and the schedules until an acceptable research plan was produced. The task teams worked diligently throughout the spring of 1982. By late spring the preliminary task team reports were becoming available, and the budding cooperative venture had passed from agreement on generalities to definition of specifics.

Originally there were five task teams formally chartered by the steering committee, but one, a factory automation team, did not

survive this stage. The task team for that program came to the conclusion that factory automation, although a promising project, would
require prior work by some of the other projects before it could
proceed. As a result it was shelved as a potential future project. Even
without the factory automation program there was a general feeling
that getting four programs off the ground simultaneously was going to
be enough of a challenge in the first year or so. Other worthwhile
projects would have to wait.

At least every other month during this period, and sometimes more
often, the steering committee met. The informal chairman of this ad
hoc group was "management Bob Price," the president of Control
Data. The commitment of Control Data to the concept pervaded the
early organization. CDC provided a staff of three people to do the
analytical and organizational work. They were, in essence, the staff to
the steering committee, and they were the people handling the day-
to-day affairs of the nascent MCC. It was their task to orchestrate all
the various activities.

In contrast to the administrative work associated with the early
start-up, the presence of Control Data was less apparent on the task
teams, which were composed of people from all over the country.
These task teams were pretty much located wherever the head of that
particular team was located rather being centralized in Minneapolis
at Control Data.

During the conceptualization and definition stage prior to incorporation, the structure of the effort was very informal. Most of the
prospective members had given no firm commitments to the concept,
other than CDC and a couple of other companies that had, fairly early
in the game, given some indication that MCC was something they
thought they would have to do. But, by and large, the companies were
in the position of saying, "This sounds interesting. Let's see what
happens. Depending on how the thing finally shapes up, we will make
a go or no-go decision."

The fact that the ideas, people, and funding did finally coalesce into
an organization of substance is attributed to a combination of three
factors by those involved. First, everybody was very much aware of the
increasing competitiveness in the marketplace. The Japanese had just
stunned the semiconductor manufacturers by taking nearly 70 percent
of the 64K chip market. The mainframe manufacturers were seeing
announcements of supercomputers from Japan and were also getting
a lot of pressure from Japanese low-end systems. It was a strong
external force that deeply affected the strategic thinking of the U.S.

companies. According to one participant the feeling was a little bit like the quote of Ben Franklin, "We may all hang together but we will surely all hang separately."

The second factor was the fact that the people who were representing the various companies during MCC's formation were very creative individuals who wanted to do something of significance. High-caliber people were assigned by the companies to the project. In other words, these were not middle management people that were merely delegated to the project. These were very senior people who almost invariably exercised significant power in their organizations. Typically the number two, three or four person in an organization was the one who was attending. They, in turn, were well prepared by their own staffs. Such high-level, high quality participation greased the road to cooperation.

The third factor was that there was some strong staff support provided by CDC to analyze the issues and prepare proposals and documents. Not inconsequentially, CDC also provided the legal expertise to help cut through the Gordian knot of antitrust facts and fears. The quality of the staff work was such that the core issues were smoked out and alternatives presented, around which meaningful and constructive discussion could take place.

The momentum grew as the participants narrowed the issues. Ideas were beginning to take shape. Discussions had reached such a state by the spring of 1982 that the steering committee decided that the preparation of a business plan was in order. The basic research programs had been identified and there was some semblance of agreement on the steering committee as to how the various management concepts could be put into action. It was felt that a formal document, setting forth the ideas to date, would be a useful catalyst to action. The steering committee wanted to have in hand a prospectus-like document that they could take to potential members and say, "Here is what we are going to do and here is what it costs to participate. Now, do you want to join or not?"

The task of preparing the actual business plan document was given to a group of four people. This group literally closeted themselves for a week at the Thunderbird Motel in Minneapolis. As vividly described by one of the four, flip charts covered the walls of the motel room turned think tank. Every conceivable issue of organization and staffing, of timing and expense levels was thrashed about. Eventually, after a week of intense work the four emerged with a business plan.

PHASE TWO: CEO AND SITE SELECTION

The Search for a CEO

Once the business plan was available and companies were able to indicate their willingness to join the cooperative venture, the next task was to select someone to run it. The business plan very clearly stated that a strong line organization was desired. It was clearly not the intention of the participants that MCC turn into a management-by-committee operation.

To this end, the business plan called for a strong CEO and strong program managers.[196] The shareholders could advise, but the decisions were to be made by the line organization. It was to be "sink or swim" for the organization on that basis. The companies specifically rejected the idea that the shareholders would have to approve detailed R&D plans. They would provide input, but it was felt that any requirement of unanimity among eight or more companies would stifle the organization.

The strategy was explicit: strong CEO, strong program directors, strong line organization, and rapid decision-making. To guard against potential abuse, some checks and balances to the power and authority of the program directors were provided by the Technical Advisory Board and to the power and authority of the CEO by the board of directors.

The steering committee set up a subcommittee to head up the search for a CEO. Once again it was chaired by "management Bob Price" of Control Data.[197] This subcommittee did most of the work in identifying and interviewing candidates. At the end of the process they had a handful of candidates who were considered quite good. It was decided that these top candidates should visit all the companies involved. In some cases the candidate was flown around to the companies. In other cases the candidates were able to meet with a group of companies in one location. Retired Admiral Bobby Ray Inman, the leading candidate at the time, came to the December meeting of the board of directors to get a better understanding of newly born MCC. At that time he had an opportunity to meet individually with most of the company representatives.

There were some CEO candidates considered from the member companies, but for a number of reasons the leading candidates were all from outside the companies. It has been suggested by one participant involved in the process that maybe some of the people knew the internal candidates too well. Another observation on the selection process focused more on the positive attributes of outsider Inman rather than on potential negative information known about insiders. As one person put it, "Inman was such an outstanding candidate that I think once people got to see him everybody looked six inches shorter by comparison."

At first blush the selection of Inman might seem puzzling. He had no private sector business experience, having served as chief of Naval Intelligence, head of the NSA, and then deputy director of the CIA until his retirement. Furthermore, although noted for his keen intellect and razor-sharp mind, he was not an expert in the fifth-generation computer technology. But, the choice of Inman had other important merits.

Many of the executives who had prior experience with joint ventures felt that one of the single most important elements in a successful joint venture was integrity. Without integrity, they argued, the partners would be constantly concerned that the costs and benefits were not being shared equally and that someone was benefiting at their expense. These nagging suspicions, it was believed, would eventually erode away the support required to make the cooperative activity work. Therefore, the person who would manage the cooperative organization, the argument went, had to be somebody of unquestionable integrity.

Inman's reputation for unshakeable integrity was well known.[198] In Washington he was known as being "squeaky clean." A person like that at the helm of MCC would make the shareholders feel more comfortable, because at least they would know that the decisions were being made as objectively as possible. Inman signed on in January of 1983, not only as CEO but also as chairman of the board of directors.

There is an amusing story that is told among the MCC staff concerning Inman's early days as head of MCC, a story that has become firmly fixed in the culture and mythology of the organization. Soon after Inman joined, MCC opened a temporary office in Arlington, Virginia, near where Inman was living at the time. Most of the administrative duties were still being handled by Control Data out of Minneapolis. In fact, MCC did not even have a phone listing in Arlington, but nevertheless, the phone was very busy. It was just Inman and one secretary working for him.

As one might suspect, Inman's selection as head of MCC had set off a round of rumors that MCC had CIA connections. These rumors persisted despite the fact that MCC had existed before Inman ever became associated with it. An amusing set of circumstances regarding the Arlington operation during the early part of 1983 did little to quell those rumors.

Sperry had donated the Arlington office space for MCC's use. The space was on the twelfth floor of an all but deserted building. When a visitor stepped off the elevator at the twelfth floor he or she would look around to see nothing but empty space. It was completely deserted. There was just a little sign saying "MCC" and pointing up a stairway. The visitor would wind up the spiral staircase only to find another five thousand square feet of empty office space. Off in the back of this vast open space, the story goes, would be Inman and his secretary — the perfect spy novel setting.

The Site Selection Process

One of the first major tasks facing Inman and the participants in MCC was to determine the organization's location. The site selection decision was especially important in the case of MCC because of a number of other decisions that were made concerning the structure and operation of MCC. The decision to operate MCC as a "freestanding" research and development organization rather than as a contracting agency was particularly relevant to the site selection process.

Had MCC's founders patterned the organization along the lines of the Semiconductor Research Cooperative (SRC, later the Semiconductor Research Corporation), the location decision would have been vastly simplified. SRC served mainly as a contract clearinghouse. Members contributed funds for research projects that were to be conducted under contract at various locations around the country. The founders of MCC, on the other hand, contemplated a centralized R&D effort, with most of the work being done at a central location by MCC-supervised personnel. This structural decision complicated the site selection process.

First of all, as a cooperative venture, the location had to be one that did not seem to confer any particular advantage to any individual participant. For example, if MCC were to locate in Minneapolis there would have been concern that the organization would or could be "captured" by Control Data, which had its headquarters in that city.[199] On the other hand, since technology transfer was one of the important goals of MCC, geographic proximity that would facilitate ready access to MCC would be a significant factor. With the participants spread across the country, finding a "neutral" location with easy access to all members was no mean feat.

The decision to conduct research at MCC's own facilities also meant that the site selected would have to be one that would be enticing to the personnel MCC would need to attract. To accomplish its goals MCC would need to assemble a world-class team of scientists and engineers. In that there was only a finite pool of exceptional talent, MCC would find itself in competition with other organizations (and possibly MCC member companies) in trying to sign up personnel. A desirable location could not but help in the talent marketplace.

The site selection process had started before the executive search process was completed, but it wasn't until after Inman had agreed to head up the newly formed MCC that the location decision-making machinery began to work in earnest. Inman walked into the middle of the process. The site selection committee originally consisted of one executive from RCA,[200] three from Control Data and one from Sperry. Inman joined this group with his acceptance of the CEO position in January. Initially, a dozen sites were slated for investigation.

As the nature of MCC become publicly known and its potential benefits more widely understood, the site selection process expanded into a nationwide search that eventually included fifty-seven cities in twenty-seven states.[201] In order to systematically classify the wide array of suitors, the search committee focused on four areas of basic concern to MCC: (1) university technical leadership, (2) quality of life, (3) technical/industry infrastructure, and (4) cost of operation.[202] Cities that passed the initial filtering process were scheduled for visit by fact-finding groups. A fact finding group consisting of George Black, Ray Kerr and Del Asmussen arrived in Austin, Texas, in late April of 1983.

Each of the four basic areas of concern was further elaborated in a written document that was sent to those promoting the various sites. For example, regarding university technical leadership, the written list broke down the area into five components: (1) number of graduate students in "double E" (electrical engineering) and computer science, (2) identity of double E and computer science faculty, (3) commitment of university and government in target locations to advance the double E and computer science departments to a degree of excellence on a par with Stanford/Berkeley, Carnegie Mellon, and MIT, (4) faculty additions to the two departments in the last three years, and (5) the joint projects between the two university departments and industry.

During the early spring of 1983 three meetings were held (one on the East Coast, one on the west and one in Chicago) during which each of the interested cities was given twenty minutes to present its case to the site selection committee. At the Chicago meeting in mid-March three Texas cities were represented: Austin, Dallas and San Antonio. Although the cities were in competition with each other, they were loosely tied together as part of the Texas delegation headed by Governor Mark White and the chancellors of the University of Texas and Texas A&M.

On April 12, 1983, it was announced that the original list of fifty-seven cities that had shown an interest in MCC had been narrowed to four: Atlanta, San Diego, Research Triangle, and Austin. One city that failed to make the final cut played an important role in the final selection of Austin. The city was San Antonio, some ninety miles south of Austin. According to MCC executives, the presentation made on behalf of that city by its charismatic mayor, Henry Cisneros, was extremely well received. They even suggested that had the University of Texas been located in San Antonio that city might have been selected as a finalist city.[203] With San Antonio out of the competition the skill and resources of the entire Texas delegation refocused on promoting Austin.

The four finalist cities were each given an opportunity to present their case before Inman and the site selection committee. High-ranking delegations from each city gave powerful arguments in favor of their particular city. Each city offered a package of inducements to MCC. The package put together by the group representing Austin was referred to as the Texas Incentive.[204] It was a thorough and broad reaching package that spelled out key commitments that would be made by various elements of the community. One key element of the package was the commitment of the University of Texas and Texas A&M, which offered to strengthen their engineering and computer science curricula as well as lease MCC facilities on nominal terms until a permanent facility could be constructed.

In the end, it was decided that Austin best met the criteria established for MCC's location. On May 18, 1983, the site selection decision was publicly announced. To give an indication of the thoroughness of preparation in the Texas Incentive program, MCC was able to open temporary offices in Austin within five days of the site announcement.

PHASE THREE: ADMINISTRATIVE STRUCTURES AND PROCEDURES

Selecting a Structure for Cooperation

Once the decision is made to pursue interfirm cooperation, the first major hurdle facing the participants is to fashion an organizational structure to help establish and facilitate the desired collective action. As mentioned earlier, cooperation can take on a wide range of forms from short-term contracts to long-term equity ventures. This abundance of choice regarding structure makes each collective venture, as one author noted, slightly different as the participants attempt to piece together a framework responsive to their particular needs and desires.[205] The same is true for MCC, and its organizational structure reflects the unique character of the collaborative undertaking.

Corporate Form

MCC is organized as a for-profit, equity joint venture with its own centralized research facility. The sponsoring companies join MCC as shareholders, with each member company having a seat on the board of directors. At the time the founders were considering just how MCC should be structurally constituted there were a variety of other organizational options that could have been followed.

First, MCC could have been established as a cooperative equity venture formed under 501(c)(3) of the Internal Revenue Code. Numerous examples of 501(c)(3) joint ventures exist to facilitate intra-industry cooperation. For example, the International Copper Research Association (INCRA), formed in 1960, and International Lead Zinc Research Organization (ILZRO), formed in 1958, are both set up as 501(c)(3) organizations. A strategic alliance established under 501(c)(3) is a nonprofit venture and must abide by the constraints and limitations placed on such corporations.

It was not the restrictions of the IRS Code that made the founders of MCC reluctant to establish MCC as a 501(c)(3) corporation. As William Norris, originator of the MCC concept, put it:

> I don't know how to manage a nonprofit organization, and I don't think many other people do it well. . . . So many of the nonprofits I know start out with enthusiasm and dedication, but when the original group or founder who imparted this [enthusiasm and dedication] leaves then survival of the organization becomes the

objective. . . . Also, I think that a nonprofit entity that would be as significant as the one we are talking about here would get a lot of political attention, possibly adverse. . . . One further reason that is very strong with me is that I believe in the profit system and therefore operate that way.[206]

Another possible organizational form was that of a Research and Development Limited Partnership (RDLP). This particular form was being promoted at the time by another visionary, D. Bruce Merrifield, then assistant secretary of commerce for productivity, technology, and innovation, U.S. Department of Commerce.[207] It was Merrifield's expressed hope that MCC would use the RDLP form of organization.[208] In Merrifield's opinion, by forming as an RDLP, MCC would have an easier job of raising funds and might have a greater degree of independence from its backers. In hindsight, despite possible benefits regarding contributions by participants, this type of structure would have complicated the technology transfer process.

Other options included a structure more like that adopted by the Semiconductor Research Corporation to conduct advanced R&D in the semiconductor field. Although also organized as an equity joint venture, SRC's original concept did not have the organization conducting its own research. Instead, SRC would determine the specifications for desired research projects and then farm out the research under contract to various university and industry laboratories. SRC was to act as a clearing house and control center for the network of research projects. It was felt by the MCC founders that such a structure would be less expensive and potentially more attractive to member companies but more difficult to manage. Additionally, a system of research contracts spread out across the country would not be able to capitalize on research synergies and cross-fertilization of ideas as well as a centralized research operation.

Of course there was the Japanese model of cooperative R&D, as painfully demonstrated to U. S. companies in the form of the VLSI project and later the fifth-generation computer program (ICOT), the Japanese programs that precipitated MCC as a response.[209] Both programs cast the government in an active, organizing role. Such a organizational approach was not feasible for two reasons. First, there was not a government agency to assume this function. Second, and perhaps most importantly, the MCC member companies were strongly opposed to government participation. As a result, "public sector entities," as well as foreign corporations, were precluded from MCC membership and equity participation.[210]

MCC Member Companies

Instability in any cooperative venture such as MCC can arise because of differences among the partners between the perceived benefits to be derived from cooperation and the costs incurred in cooperating. Among the various participants, these differences can come from a variety of structural causes, such as size of the participants, number of locations or sites within the corporations to use the technology, and the particular industry of the participating company.

Presently, MCC has twenty-one member companies.[211] Originally, the participating companies could be roughly grouped into three categories, although a number of member companies did not fall neatly into a single category. A fourth and a fifth category emerged as MCC grew.

The first group were the mainframe computer manufacturers, a group mainly composed of older companies (for this young industry) that were once known as "the Bunch."[212] With the addition of Digital, this is the group that has competed against the dominance of IBM for years in the past. Consolidation and strategic redirection have shifted the focus of some of this group, but most continue to have substantial interests in computer hardware manufacture. This group of companies was a major force behind starting MCC, particularly Control Data. Lately, the dominance of this group of shareholders has receeded, perhaps reflecting the marketplace difficulties facing these companies. Sperry, a founding member of MCC, merged with Burroughs in 1986 and the resulting company was named Unisys. In November of 1986, Unisys sold the Sperry aerospace business to another MCC member company, Honeywell.[213] Unisys left MCC at the end of 1987. In early 1989, Digital, while remaining an active participant in MCC, withdrew from the advanced computer architecture and software technology programs.[214]

The second group, and also instrumental in getting MCC under way, was made up of firms involved in semiconductor manufacturing. Included in this group were AMD, Motorola, National Semiconductor, and before its demise, Mostek. It should be noted that in addition to the companies mentioned, a number of other MCC member companies have semiconductor operations to support their products. The difference is that the semiconductor group does not have a large captive market for its semiconductor production. Being situated in a

Figure 5.2
Company Participation in MCC (Dates Companies Joined)

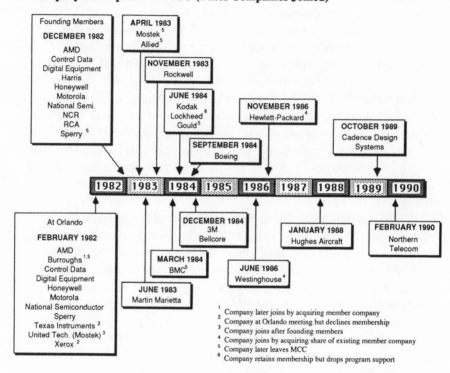

Founding Members	APRIL 1983
DECEMBER 1982	Mostek[5]
	Allied[5]
AMD	
Control Data	
Digital Equipment	**NOVEMBER 1983**
Harris	Rockwell
Honeywell	
Motorola	**JUNE 1984**
National Semi.	Kodak
NCR	Lockheed[6]
RCA	Gould[5]
Sperry[5]	

NOVEMBER 1986
Hewlett-Packard[4]

OCTOBER 1989
Cadence Design Systems

SEPTEMBER 1984
Boeing

1982 1983 1984 1985 1986 1987 1988 1989 1990

At Orlando

FEBRUARY 1982

AMD
Burroughs[1,5]
Control Data
Digital Equipment
Honeywell
Motorola
National Semiconductor
Sperry
Texas Instruments[2]
United Tech. (Mostek)[3]
Xerox[2]

DECEMBER 1984
3M
Bellcore

JANUARY 1988
Hughes Aircraft

FEBRUARY 1990
Northern Telecom

MARCH 1984
BMC[5]

JUNE 1986
Westinghouse[4]

JUNE 1983
Martin Marietta

[1] Company later joins by acquiring member company
[2] Company at Orlando meeting but declines membership
[3] Company joins after founding members
[4] Company joins by acquiring share of existing member company
[5] Company later leaves MCC
[6] Company retains membership but drops program support

Price of One Share of MCC Stock*

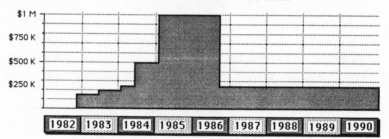

$1 M
$750 K
$500 K
$250 K

1982 1983 1984 1985 1986 1987 1988 1989 1990

* Share price is set by MCC board of directors and reflects not only value of MCC participation but more importantly the desire of MCC members to accept new companies as members.

fast moving marketplace, subjected to intense Japanese competition, the companies in this group have to be both extremely entrepreneurial and cost conscious.

The next major group consisted of the large aerospace manufacturers. In this group are Boeing, Rockwell, Martin-Marietta, General Motors' Hughes Aircraft division, and Lockheed,[215] each of which derives a substantial portion of its revenues from the aerospace market.

A fourth group which appeared later is composed of the conglomerates. These companies may have large computer, aerospace, or semiconductor operations, but need to be characterized as conglomerate because of the diversity and magnitude of their other corporate endeavors. In this group were companies such as General Electric, which acquired MCC founding member RCA, 3M, Westinghouse, and Allied Signal.[216]

A fifth group that has more recently emerged consists of telecommunications organizations. Northern Telecom and BellCore (Bell Communications Research Inc.) are the companies in this group. BellCore is itself a research consortium, since it is the collective research arm of the seven regional Bell operating companies that survived after the breakup of AT&T following antitrust litigation. Northern Telecom, MCC's most recent member, is the sixth largest captive supplier of microchips in North America and one of the world's leading telecommunications firms with 1989 revenues of over $6 billion.

There are also a number of companies that do not neatly fit into any one of these four categories. One company that seems to fall through the cracks of the five categories is Eastman Kodak. Strategically positioned as an imaging and chemical company, Kodak does have substantial interests in the aerospace market where its remote imaging and sensing technologies are used in spy and observation satellites, Inman pointed out. In addition, the company has recognized that the line between chemical and electronic imaging is quickly beginning to blur and that new technologies may be required in their traditional markets.

More recently, the addition of Cadence Design Systems, Inc. in October of 1989, marked the the first electronic design automation (EDA) member to join MCC. The company's decision to participate in MCC's Computer Aided Design (CAD) Program and the CAD Framework Laboratory was particularly significant in that Cadence brought something to the party with its proprietary framework technology that will be co-mingled with the results of MCC's efforts.

The diverse industries, as well as different company sizes, can translate into major differences in strategic outlook. Differing strategic goals can be the source of potential tension within MCC. As can be seen in Figure 5.3 there are significant differences in the sizes of the companies, measured by sales. These differences show some correspondence to the industry grouping: conglomerate companies being the largest, aerospace being next, then the computer companies, and finally the semiconductor companies being the smallest.

As a result of these differences in size and industry orientation one should expect the benefits to be derived from cooperation to differ from group to group and company to company. And since the costs of cooperation facing a participant are the same as for other companies in the same programs, one would expect the value to be derived from cooperation to vary due to these structural variables. Recognition of these structural differences can be of importance to the management of a strategic alliance, in that cooperative instability can result if these difference become too great.

Another destabilizing factor can come from the different market foci of the various companies. One illustration of this can be seen with regard to the national defense market. If one looks at the total amount of defense contracts (over $152 billion) awarded in 1985 during the Reagan defense buildup, MCC member companies received approximately 24 percent of total (see Figure 5.4). Aside from the fact that this alone is an impressive percentage, the data are even more interesting because the contracts awarded to the individual MCC member companies run the gamut from little or none to substantial.

If one examines Figure 5.5 one notices that when these defense contract awards are plotted against the total R&D expenditures for the same company, the companies fall into groupings that roughly correlate with the industry categories suggested earlier.

Not surprisingly, the aerospace companies had a high contract award registration, but at the same time the companies had relatively lower total R&D expenditures than the conglomerates, and are on a par with the computer companies. The conglomerates spent a larger absolute amount on R&D, mostly reflecting their larger size, and showed a wide variation with regard to defense contract awards. The computer companies' R&D expenditures tended to be on a par with the aerospace companies, but their defense contracts tended to be substantially less. The one computer manufacturer that was not listed

Figure 5.3
Relative Size of MCC Member Companies in 1985 (by 1985 Annual Sales Revenues)

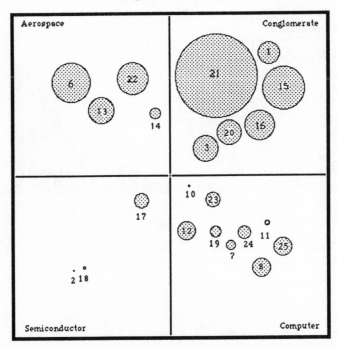

Approximate Scale: ▬▭▭ in circle diameter equals $10 Billion in sales.

| MCC Member Companies Not Listed on Grid | 0 | 5 | 4 |

Data Sources: Business Week, Corporate Scoreboard, May 19, 1986, pp. 139–164. BellCore is shown by its $900 million operating budget in that it is a captive research organization. *Business Week*, Son of Bell Labs, Dec. 2, 1986, p. 106. BMC sales ($78.45 Million for 1985) from the company's 1985 10-K report. Company reference numbers are listed in Appendix 4.

because it had few or no defense contract awards went against this trend and showed a high level of absolute R&D expenditures.

The semiconductor group is not listed in Figure 5.5 because all but one of the companies did not have defense contracts amounting to more than $148 million, approximately $1/10$ of 1 percent of the total defense contract awards. Companies with defense contracts in excess

Figure 5.4
MCC Member Company Participation in Defense Contract Awards (1985)

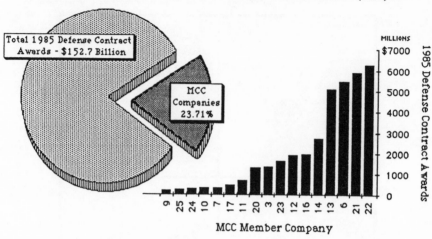

Data Source: *Aviation Week & Space Technology Report*, May 12, 1986, p. 71.
Company reference numbers are listed in Appendix 4.

Figure 5.5
Distribution of R&D Expenditures and Defense Contract Awards in 1985

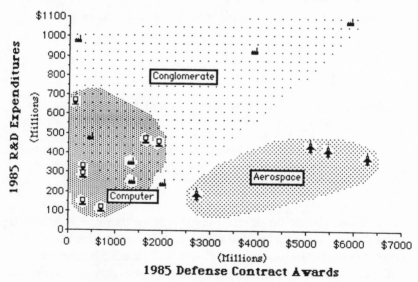

Data Sources: Defense contract information from *Aviation Week & Space Technology Report*, May 12, 1986, p. 71. R&D information from *Business Week*, R&D Scoreboard, June 23, 1986, pp. 139–156.

of this figure represent the top 100 firms in terms of defense contracts received.

It is also interesting to note the dates when the various companies in these industry groups joined MCC. (See Figure 5.2) The semiconductor and computer companies were the ones that orignally helped set up MCC. The major aerospace companies and conglomerates joined later. And finally, the telecommunications companies signed up. The aerospace companies, none of which were at the February 1982 Orlando meeting, all joined, with the exception of Hughes Aircraft, within a nine month period beginning in mid-1983. It is likely that the selection of Admiral Inman to head MCC was a significant factor in this group's joining MCC, in that Inman was well known and trusted by these major defense contractors.

Figure 5.6
1989 R&D and Profit Distribution for MCC Companies

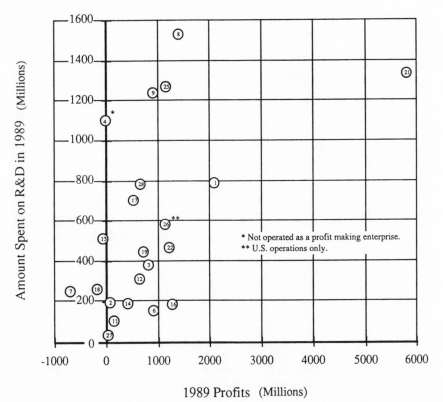

Data Source: Business Week, R&D Scoreboard, June 15, 1990, pp. 197–223.
Company reference numbers are listed in Appendix 4.

Figure 5.6 shows the distribution of R&D and profits for the MCC member companies in 1989. It is interesting to note that there is greater variability in the amount spent on R&D (the y-axis) than in the member companies' profits (the x-axis). For example, companies such as Eastman Kodak, Digital, and Hewlett-Packard have profits that are comparable to the bulk of MCC's membership but have R&D expenditures that are two to five times as great.

In support of the proposition that company differences can lead to cooperative instability, consider the situation of one particular MCC member company that exhibited a substantial difference when compared to its partners. The company was BMC Industries. In the first place, the company was on the extreme small end of the MCC member company size continuum. This alone might not be of major significance, but when small size is coupled with some other factors the unusual situation facing this company regarding cooperation in MCC comes into greater focus.

Figure 5.7
Percentage of Company R&D Funds Going to MCC

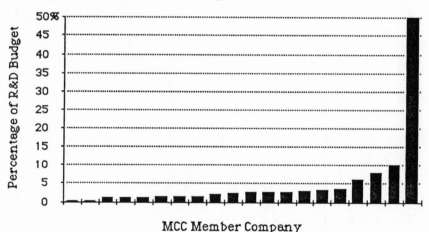

Data Source: Survey of MCC Shareholder Companies conducted by the author. Responses to Section II, Question 12.

The company joined MCC as part of a major strategic push to move the company from its traditional base businesses into high-tech marketplaces that would be served by the type of technology being developed by MCC. A substantial portion of the company's total R&D budget went to supporting MCC. As can be seen from Figure 5.7, for most MCC member companies the investment in MCC represents less than 5 percent of the companies' total R&D budget. For this particular company the MCC investment accounted for one-half of the company's R&D expenditures. When one considers that the benefits to be derived from the MCC investment are medium- to long-term, the risk inherent in this situation becomes apparent. In 1986 the company abandoned its high-tech electronics strategy and withdrew from MCC. It is interesting to note that the company for which the MCC investment represents the second highest percentage (10 percent) also expressed concern about continued cooperation in MCC.

The geographic diversity of the MCC companies further complicates the task of maintaining the value of cooperation. As shown in Figure 5.8, the executive headquarters of MCC member companies at the time of Inman's departure are congregated around three locations: California; St. Paul, Minnesota; and New York, with a string of member companies in the states surrounding New York and stretching west toward Minneapolis. The two coastal concentrations reflect the predominance of electronics companies centered around those two locations. The large number of Minneapolis companies more likely reflects the personal charisma and leadership of MCC founder William Norris, whose company, Control Data, is located in St. Paul.

This geographic dispersion of the shareholders has increased the importance to MCC management of establishing and maintaining an effective communication system.[217]

Internal Structure

The principal governing body of MCC is the board of directors, which includes a member from each of the nineteen shareholder companies. It had always been the intent of the founders that MCC be headed in its formative years not by a committee of the member companies, but by a strong CEO. The selection of retired Admiral Bobby Ray Inman to fill this role required an additional change to accommodate one of his conditions of employment. Inman was also designated chairman of the board. The board of directors would establish policy, oversee admission of new members, and provide advice and guidance for MCC top management, but Inman and his staff would be in charge.

The internal structure envisioned by the founders of MCC appears in Figure 5.9 and is somewhat different from the structure which was subsequently adopted when MCC was formally established (shown in

Figure 5.8
Geographic Distribution of MCC Member Companies during the early years.*
(Location of Headquarters)

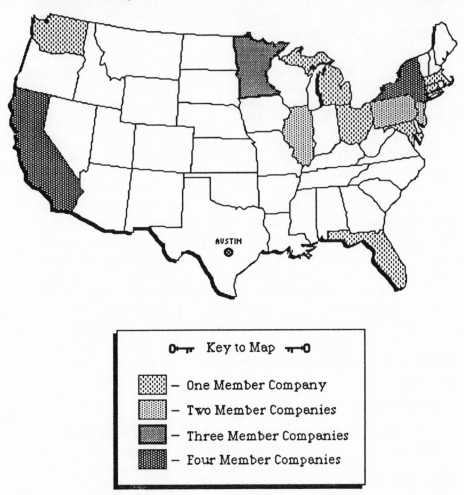

*   Map includes original MCC member companies as well as successor companies. (Mostek and BMC are not listed. Westinghouse and Hewlett-Packard are listed.)

Figure 5.10). In the original concept, there was to be a Research and Development Advisory Committee (RDAC) and a manager of the Research and Development Division (RDD). The RDAC was superseded by the Technical Advisory Board (TAB).

Figure 5.9
Original Concept for MCC Organizational Structure

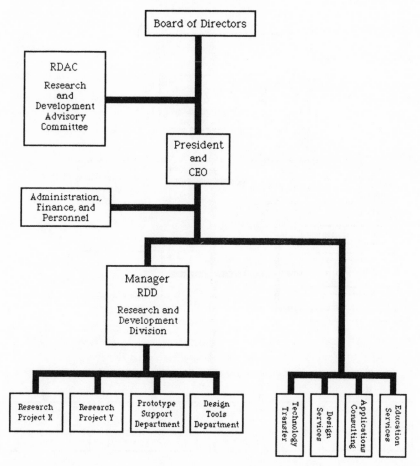

Like the board of directors, the TAB was to be composed of members from the shareholder companies, but TAB members were generally to be more technically oriented. The board members were expected to be more managerial in their outlook. Currently, the usual TAB member is a senior research executive from the shareholder company. The function of the TAB was to identify promising research and development projects and oversee the establishment of a research schedule and program specifications.

As time went on, the RDD designation disappeared when it was decided that the program director positions would be strengthened and be given substantial independence. In place of the manager of RDD, technical guidance and coordination for the programs would be

Figure 5.10
MCC Organizational Structure at Time of Incorporation

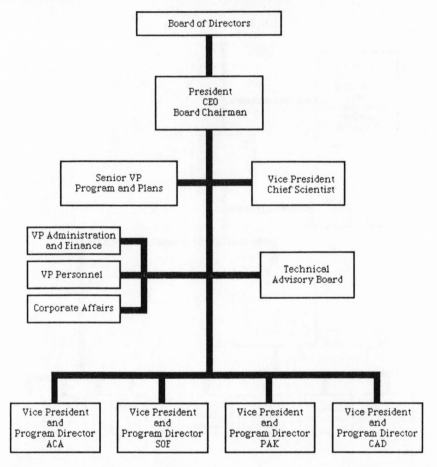

provided by the vice president-chief scientist and the managerial function would be taken over by the senior vice president-program and plans.

The CEO, the senior VP-program and plans, and the VP-chief scientist eventually became an executive management committee. It is this informal committee that oversees all of the MCC operations. The CEO, Inman, focused externally on the shareholders and important external organizations. Smidt, Senior VP-program and plans, focused internally on the management of the programs. And, the VP-chief scientist, Pinkston, oversaw the technical progress of the research programs as well as monitored technical developments of interest outside of MCC.

This organizational structure further evolved in the late 1980s to the elimination of the positions of the Senior VP-program and plans and VP-chief scientist, and the subsequent creation of Chief Technical Officer (CTO) and Chief Operating Officer (COO) positions. The evolution and flexibility in titles and positions at MCC reflects a management philosophy that instead of trying to make the person fulfill a predetermined, specific function, the function is often tailored to the skills and expertise of the individual. In 1990, Craig Fields was appointed to both the CTO and COO positions.

MCC member companies pay for only those programs they have joined. (See Figure 5.11 for a listing of the member companies and the programs in which they participate.) Although this decision made joining MCC more attractive to a number of participants, it complicated the day-to-day operations. This decision meant that the information and technology produced by one program could not be easily shared with another without some mechanism to compensate those companies that paid for developing the information and technology. These proprietary information difficulties were a direct result of the decision to permit MCC member companies to select which research programs to join.

As the organization evolved, the structure changed to reflect new situations and conditions. First, the role of the TAB diminished as program reviews were completed and the research projects became operational. In addition, the TAB ran into difficulties on the issue of protecting proprietary information, in that the TAB was composed of members from all member companies and detailed discussions of the various research programs could compromise the proprietary rights of companies paying for one program by disclosing the technology to companies not participating in that particular program.

The need for technical advice more closely related to a particular program became apparent. As a result, Program Technical Advisory Committees (PTAC) were set up. By establishing four PTACs, one for each program, many of the problems associated with the protection of proprietary information were also eliminated. (See Figure 5.13 for the current organizational structure.)

Personnel Policy

Early on it was recognized by Inman and the small group of advisors and colleagues he had assembled to help set up an administrative structure for MCC that the success or failure of the organization would

Figure 5.11
MCC Member Companies and Program Participation

	ORIGINAL MEMBER COMPANY/SUCCESSOR	ACT*	PAK	SOF	CAD	CPL†
•	3M Company		Program Participation			Company participation information not released
F •	Advanced Micro Devices		Program Participation		Program Participation	
A	Allied Signal Corporation		Program Participation Terminated			
•	Bell Communications Research	Program Participation		Program Participation		
	BMC Corporation		Program Participation Transferred to New Member			
•	Boeing Corporation		Program Participation			
•	Cadence Design Systems				Program Participation	
F •	Control Data Corporation	Program Participation	Program Participation	Program Participation	Program Participation	
F •	Digital Equipment Corporation	Program Participation Terminated	Program Participation	Program Participation Terminated		
•	Eastman Kodak Corporation	Program Participation	Program Participation			
•	General Motors-Hughes Aircraft				Program Participation	
	Gould, Inc.				Program Participation Terminated	
F •	Harris Corporation	Program Participation	Program Participation	Program Participation	Program Participation	
•	Hewlett-Packard		Program Participation			
F •	Honeywell, Inc.	Program Participation			Program Participation	
•	Lockheed Missiles and Space Co.			Program Participation Terminated	Program Participation Terminated	
•	Martin Marietta				Program Participation	
	Mostek Corporation/CTU				Program Participation Transferred to New Member	
F •	Motorola, Inc.				Program Participation	
F •	National Semiconductor Corporation				Program Participation	
F •	NCR Corporation	Program Participation		Program Participation	Program Participation	
•	Northern Telecom		Program Participation			
F •	RCA/General Electric Corporation			Program Participation	Program Participation	
•	Rockwell International Corporation			Program Participation		
F	Sperry/Burroughs/Unisys	Program Participation Terminated	Program Participation Terminated	Program Participation Terminated	Program Participation Terminated	
A	United Technologies		Program Participation Terminated			
•	Westinghouse				Program Participation	

† - New program started May 1989
* - Program restructured into ten areas, August 1989
(dark shading) - Program Participation
(medium shading) - Program Participation Transferred to New Member
(dotted) - Program Participation Terminated
F - Founding Member Company
• - Current Member Company
A - Company now associate member

depend on the quality of the personnel they would be able to attract. Without first-class brainpower no amount of shareholder funding would insure attainment of MCC's ambitious goals.

Figure 5.12
MCC Organizational Structure at Time of Inman's Departure

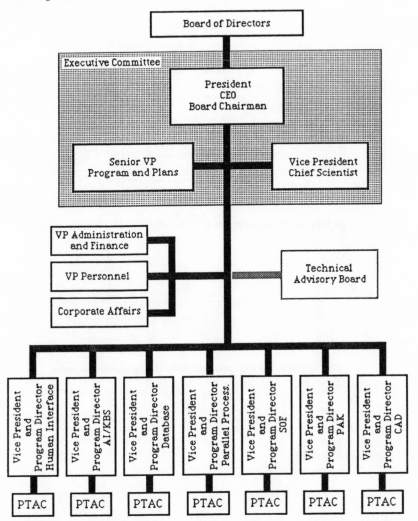

From the beginning it was envisioned that MCC would have three categories of employees: a direct hire, an assigned employee, and a liaison employee.[218] A direct hire would be someone recruited by MCC just like any other company. Barring unforeseen circumstances, that person would stay with the organization as long as he or she competently completed the tasks associated with his or her job. The assigned employee would come from a shareholder company with the understanding that that person would eventually go back to that shareholder company. The assigned employee would be assigned for

Figure 5.13
MCC's Organizational Structure (1990)

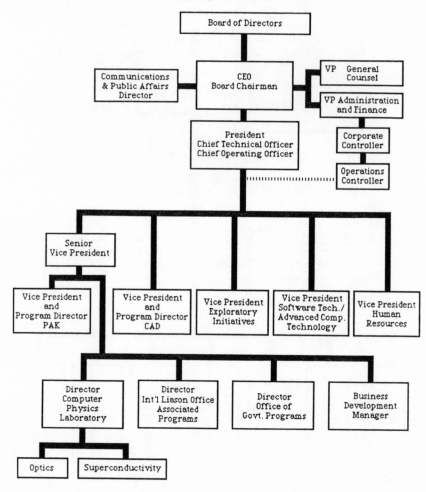

Figure 5.14
Three Types of MCC Employees

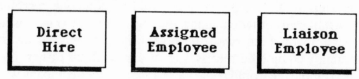

an unspecified period of time which could last as long as a few years. The assigned employee, like the direct hire, would be an integral part of the research effort.

The third type of employee, the liaison employee, would be designated as such from among the assigned employees. The liaison employee would be expected to spend about 25 percent of his or her time working on issues of how to transfer the technology back to the shareholder, communicating with the shareholder company, and generally working with MCC to ensure adequate representation of the shareholder's best interests. For the remaining 75 percent of his or her time, the liaison employee would be part of the research team.

According to George Black, vice president for human resources, the nature of the commitment of the shareholding companies to MCC during the organization's first year covered a fairly wide spectrum. At one extreme, some companies, such as Control Data, would have been willing to staff the whole organization. At the other end of the spectrum were shareholder companies that would just as soon send money. The nature of a company's commitment to MCC manifested itself in the number of candidates offered by that shareholder and by the quality of the assigned people.

It was George Black's opinion that shareholder commitment to MCC varied directly with the level of involvement with MCC. Shareholder companies that had representatives who were actively involved on an almost daily basis were more likely to understand what was required of them to make MCC work and were better able to understand and assist in the development of MCC. The company representatives who sent substitutes to the meetings, or worse, did not send anyone, would probably over some period of time, according to Black, come to the conclusion that MCC had not been a very good investment. In a way, Black added, they will be right, simply because they have not found a way to exploit the investment and take advantage of what is available.

George Black and the top MCC management originally tried to identify a clearly defined pool of candidates to staff the hundreds of research slots that would be available at MCC. In that effort they were only modestly successful. As a consequence, they decided the best way to staff the organization was from the top down. The exact size, shape, and substance of the organization would be left to the program directors, once they were identified, attracted, and employed.

With this approach in mind, the first task, and one of the most important, facing the MCC management was to identify those people who were most likely to be qualified as program directors so that recruiting efforts could begin. During the creation of MCC it was originally thought on the part of the shareholders that all of the program director positions should be filled exclusively from candidates from the shareholder companies. Very quickly the wisdom of that belief was being examined by the MCC management in place at the time: Inman, Black, Rutishauser, and Smidt.

Candidates from the shareholder companies were nominated and interviewed. The process lasted approximately three to four months and did not uncover enough people of sufficient quality to staff all the program director positions.[219] As this became recognized, a modest parallel effort was under way that began looking outside the shareholders for suitable candidates. As George Black put it, "We had people we thought might be suitable and we were trying to keep them warm at the same time we were interviewing candidates from the shareholders."

As the source of potential program director candidates expanded beyond the shareholder companies, a group of seven people from the board of directors was selected to act as the personnel selection committee. This committee met in Minneapolis for a full day's brainstorming session to try and identify the best possible candidates, without any consideration given to whether or not the person would be available or even interested in joining MCC. From this session a list of potential candidates emerged, and on that basis the recruiting process commenced in earnest.

A number of people were contacted. Those who were unable or unwilling to consider working at MCC generally were eager to suggest others who might be. As a result, a network of contacts developed and a pool of qualified candidates emerged. Just how inclusive this pool was became apparent to Black when, a few months later, he was looking through some literature concerning an artificial intelligence conference and he realized that he knew three-quarters of the people attending. Prior to joining MCC, Black did not know a single one. According to Black, only fifty people in the United States were truly suitable to be considered as director for one of the research programs.

One of the surprises experienced by the top management of MCC was that the board of directors or the technology advisory board, while prepared and willing to play some role in identifying potential candidates, were among the first to tell MCC management that the exponential growth in the relevant scientific disciplines was such that they had not been able to keep pace with the talent. As George Black told it, ten years before, the people who were senior executives in the shareholder companies knew everybody in the business. Now they did not even pretend to. In many instances they did not even know where the best work was being done. Black felt there was a number of reasons for this change. One he cited in particular was that corporate responsibilities had grown as the industry and the individual companies had, and as a consequence the senior executives no longer had the time to keep in touch with what was going on in the technical world.

Black was given the responsibility for identifying suitable program director candidates and finding ways to contact them. He would work through shareholder representatives, creating a network of contacts within the shareholders companies, in an attempt to identify someone associated with MCC and who had an established relationship with the identified candidate. If such a person was found, that person would make the initial contact.

In those situations where no such existing contact point could be discovered, Black would simply pick up the telephone and say, "I am from MCC and here is what we are all about. In my search, the name that is consistently brought to my attention is yours, and I thought I would come around and talk." Black attributed the success of many of these "cold calls" to the fact that people were generally flattered to hear that they had acquired a national reputation among their peers.

Of course, the talent search was not without its disappointments. Inman, in looking back with humor on some of the unsuccessful recruiting efforts, cited "Black's Law," which states that everyone you want cannot relocate because he or she has a daughter who is a junior in high school.

Along a more serious vein, it was recognized that some of the recruiting disappointments had resulted from how the process was managed. As Black straightforwardly put it, "One of the early mistakes we made was involving too many people in the interview process. We attempted to recruit people before we had established a facility here [in Austin] so we made the mistake of asking the candidates to go from place to place to interview shareholder representatives." Sometimes the candidate had to endure a dozen or more interviews in various locations across the country. Another practical reason for delaying the recruiting process until the site selection had been completed was that it was generally difficult to get people to take a position in an unknown location.

Even more destructive than the sheer number of interviews was a lack of continuity and cohesiveness that developed. MCC lost a couple of promising candidates early on when the candidates would get mixed signals from the various shareholders regarding the research objectives or methodology for the program he or she was being asked to run.

In the search for a director for the software program, one particularly promising candidate was lost. According to Black, this candidate survived the entire ordeal, but after each round of interviews he was slightly less enthusiastic, until the candidate eventually lost interest in joining MCC. At that point Black was able to convince Inman that recruiting efforts for the program directors would have to stop until MCC had its own facilities in Austin. After that, all interviewing took place at MCC's headquarters in Austin. Shareholder representatives were still invited to interview candidates, but they had to come to Austin to do so. According to Black, this change in process eliminated a majority of the people who had originally wanted to be in on the interviewing process. The shareholder representatives who did take the time and effort to come to Austin for the interviews were of significant assistance because they were generally well informed concerning the programs and brought well-honed interviewing skills.

The difficulties experienced in locating and recruiting key personnel caused some delays in the expected initiation of actual research. During this period some shareholders began to express concern, but the perseverance eventually paid off and MCC was able to publicly announce six of its seven program directors by mid-1984.

MCC TECHNOLOGY PROGRAMS

The MCC steering committee, which was established after the February 19, 1982, Orlando, Florida, meeting, formed task teams to look into a number of possible technology programs. As a result of this effort, four major technology program areas were identified as particularly promising candidates for MCC's efforts. Later, one of the four was further divided into four sub-programs, making a total of seven technology programs. In 1989 a fifth program was added. The original four programs suggested by the task teams and subsequently endorsed by the ad hoc steering committee were software productivity, CAD/CAM (computer aided design and computer aided manufacturing), Alpha/Omega (an advanced computer technology program), and microelectronics packaging. The Alpha/Omega program was the one that was subsequently divided into four, and later ten subparts.

As the focus of the technology programs sharpened, a number of the original program names were changed to bring into clearer focus the true nature of the technology program. For example, CAD/CAM program became the VLSI/CAD program, the packaging program was renamed the Semiconductor Packaging and Interconnect Program, and the Alpha/Omega program become the Advanced Computer Architecture Program and later renamed the Advanced Computer Technology Program. The Computer Physics Laboratory Program was added in 1989 to conduct research into superconductivity and optics as they related to electronics.

Under the bylaws of MCC, the board of directors has the power from time to time to initiate other research and development programs that are defined to be within the scope of MCC's general business purposes. Although the start of a new research program was considered in 1985, the board decided to postpone the decision until a better assessment of MCC's current progress could be made. Each of the research programs at MCC is governed by a research and development agreement that is a contract entered into between MCC and a participating shareholder, defining the scope and goals of the particular technology program as well as the rights and obligations of MCC and the participating shareholder.

Each shareholder is required to join at least one technology program for an initial period of three years. Before a technology program begins, any shareholder can join, so long as the board determines that the participation does not threaten the continued viability or operations of MCC or the technology program in question. Upon joining, each participant agrees to assume a percentage of that program's costs. A restructuring of the Advanced Computer Technology Program in August 1990 brought a change in this policy. Under the new guidelines designed to attract more participants, companies could join any one of ten specific phases rather than the whole program. This policy modification resulted in Texas Instruments and Apple Computer joining elements of the program as Associate members.

In situations where a shareholder wants to join an existing technology program the procedure is a bit more complicated. First, the board of directors has to determine an amount to charge the new participant which reflects the level of efforts already expended within that particular technology program and reflects the reduction of risk compared to that borne by the original participants.

The MCC bylaws also provide procedures for the termination of a technology program, a process that can be initiated by any one of four parties. First, a program participant can initiate termination. Second, MCC's CEO can start the process. Third, the board of directors has the power to seek a program's termination. And fourth, the TAB, or Technical Advisory Board, can request a program's termination. After such a request is made it is voted upon by the program participants. If the termination request is approved by three-quarters of the participants, the request is forwarded to the CEO, who then prepares a written report to the board of directors. This report recommends a course of action, either acceptance of the termination request or rejection. It takes a two-thirds vote of the board of directors to approve a termination request. Even if the board of directors does not approve the request after all the specified steps have been followed, any participant is permitted to withdraw from participation in that particular program.

Because of the initial decision to allow MCC members to select, cafeteria-style, among the seven programs, the nineteen shareholders of MCC are not all participants in the same programs. Some programs have a dozen or more members. Others had as few as four supporting shareholders at one time. As a consequence, one can view MCC as a consortium of seven interrelated but nevertheless semiautonomous research joint ventures, each with its own problems and promise, each with its own strategy and management style. What follows is a description of each of the research programs.

The Advanced Computer Technology Programs

In the original concept of MCC, the four programs that made up the advanced computer technology program in the early years (later to evolve into ten distinct research areas) were part of one larger program, Alpha/Omega. The reason given for the breakup into four separate programs was that it was difficult to get all potential participants to agree on what the objectives of the overall program would be. Divided into four parts it was easier to get participant agreement on program objectives. In August 1989 the ACT program was restructured into ten research areas, and participants were permitted to select which of the ten they individually wished to support.[220]

The four original programs in the Advanced Computer Technology group were: human interface technology program, artificial intelligence/knowledge base systems, the data base technology program and the parallel processing program. Although the four are closely intertwined in terms of technological synergy, each was managed as a separate independent program with its own program director.

The Human Interface Program

It is the objective of the human interface program to investigate the use of voice, graphics, and video as possible interface mediums with the computer. The idea is that to support the advanced computer architecture envisioned, advances in the way the human can interface with the computer will have to be developed. Although agreement on the general objectives was possible, the original task committee set up to map out the research goals experienced some difficulty in formulating a more precise task description.

Discontent with the original task description continued even after the program was initiated and it was up to the program director, Ray Allard, to remedy the problem. After consultation with the participants it was decided that a departure from the original task description would be desirable. As a result, the technical focus of the program's activities was changed. According to Allard there is now a fairly good acceptance of the program's focus, with one or two exceptions.

As mentioned, the original head of the human factors technology program was Ray Allard. Allard was unique in that he was the only program director who came from one of the shareholder companies. He previously had served with Control Data, where he was vice president of Pacific operations, vice president of International Services, vice president of corporate pricing and vice president of product line management. The fact that Allard was the only program director from a participant company is all the more interesting when one notes that the original notion of MCC was that most, if not all, the program directors would come from the member corporations.

Artificial Intelligence/Knowledge Base Systems Program

In this particular segment of the ACT program, the inference engine necessary in expert systems will be developed. Expert systems usually have two elements: first, a body of factual information or knowledge; and second, a method to apply and use the body of facts accumulated in the first part. This second element is referred to as the inference engine.

Essentially, what the ACT program will be looking for is a way of tying a body of knowledge to what is called a "rules or an inference engine." The combination of a rules or inference engine with a particular knowledge base system is the essence of an expert system. It is the inference engine that makes the "expert" choice based on the knowledge.

Part of the problem in developing such an inference engine is incorporating some level of common sense. If an expert system lacks common sense, then the system may be incredibly smart in its particular expertise but still make unwise decisions that would violate everyday normal common sense.

Dr. Woodie Bledsoe headed up the original program and came from the University of Texas in Austin, where he was a well-known professor of mathematics and computer science. In the past he served as the chairman of the Department of Mathematics. Dr. Bledsoe came to MCC with important connections to two of the country's most fertile computer education institutions, having taught at both Carnegie Mellon and MIT.

More recently, MCC efforts in this area have been gaining some popular publicity.[221] The on-going development of the ambitious Cyc (as in en-*cyc*-lopedia) computer program has sparked both interest and controversy as MCC staffers try to develop a computer with basic common sense.

The Parallel Processing Program

Presently, most computers generally work by means of serial processing along the lines originally worked out by the brilliant mathematician von Neumann. With serial processing, the computer deals with one bit of information after another. Despite the fact that technological advances have allowed the construction of computers that can do serial processing at extremely fast speeds, serial processing cannot handle the amount of information required in the next generation of computers. One way to increase the amount of information handling would be parallel processing.

With parallel processing, a variety of information is simultaneously processed and then woven together into a coherent whole. It is like having trains run on parallel tracks, each carrying a cargo of information. While the description of parallel processing is simple, the mechanics of developing such a system are very difficult. Using the train analogy, one of the difficulties in parallel processing is designing the switches and controls so that the speeding trains on parallel tracks come together in an orderly fashion and not one huge wreck. It is the objective of this program to work on parallel architectures, so that tools can be developed that will allow for practical parallel architectural simulation, which in turn would eventually lead to the development of the parallel architecture in the computers.

In trying to meet these objectives, the program has had difficulties. The shareholders were not pleased with the direction the program was going. Concern about the program spread to the executive management group, which at the time was made up of Palle Smidt, John Pinkston, and Inman. According to some MCC officials it was felt that the vice president in charge was being "consensused to death," that he was being too responsive to the various and sometimes conflicting viewpoints of his participating shareholders. As a consequence, the program was being bogged down by an apparent inability to take a direction and stick to it. The decision was made that the original program director would be moved to the position of principal scientist and a new program director was selected.

Data Base Program

The last element of a fifth-generation, artificial intelligence or expert computer is the data base. The data base collects and organizes vast amounts of information which then will be accessed by the inference or the rules engine. The required speed to accomplish this accessing is to be provided by the parallel processing program, and the necessary ease of use is to be provided by the technologies developed by the human factors group. Together these technologies will form the basic elements of the desired artificial intelligence machine. As part of its task, the data base program will be looking for strategies and techniques for handling mixed data. This would be data that would be text, graphic, and video, all being merged and mixed within a single data base.

The Software Technology Program

The software program is based on the idea that computers will become more and more a part of people's lives and as this happens the need for personalized computer applications will rise. It is expected that the computer user will want to have the computer do certain specific tasks. The need is not for programming but for solutions. The users do not necessarily want a computer program, instead what they really want is a solution to a particular problem. In the past, to use the computer in finding these solutions a program had to be written, but the user is generally neither interested in nor capable of writing a series of instructions for the computer.

Since most computer users have neither the time nor the skill to write a computer program to help solve their own specific problems, a computer program is purchased from someone who does. As a result, the computer program is either a relatively inexpensive general purpose one that may or may not fit the specific needs of the users or it is an expensive tailor-made one.

It is the goal of the software program to help in the development of a system where the user can interact with the computer at the level of problem definition and the computer itself will "write" a program to solve that user's problem. More specifically, the software program will create software tools through which the ultimate users will be able to personalize computer use. Basically, it is envisioned that the software program will develop a type of expert system to which the participating shareholder companies will each add their own independent knowledge base. Together these two elements will form a complete system that will enable end users to conduct interactive problem-solving sessions with the computer.

The actual "products" MCC hopes to deliver to the program participants are the software tools that the program participants may use to develop the user application processes necessary in such an expert system.

The VLSI/CAD Program

One of the main goals of ICOT, the Japanese fifth-generation program, is focused on development of certain Computer Aided Design (CAD) systems to help produce microelectronic chips with very high densities of components on them. At MCC, the VLSI (Very Large Scale Integrated circuit) /CAD program is trying to meet goals at least as aggressive as those set by the Japanese. The idea is to develop a computer aided design system that will allow users to lay out a basic design for a semiconductor chip with 10^6 or 10^7 transistors on it in less than one month, and to develop an optimized layout for such a chip in under six months.

An important part of the MCC VLSI/CAD program strategy is to involve non-MCC companies that are in the computer aided design industry, so that they can provide the necessary support hardware and software for the future. As a consequence, part of the strategy is to produce hardware description languages, data bases, system interface designs, testing lay-outs, and other technologies that will be necessary to support a CAD system. The CAD project is also designed to develop strong interactions with other centers of excellence in the area, such as those existing in certain universities. Another element of the CAD program strategy is to evaluate already available CAD tools and see how well they might fit into the MCC's program goals. The ultimate objective of these various strategic elements is to adopt or develop, and then integrate the various CAD tools into, a prototype VLSI/CAD system.

The Semiconductor Packaging and Interconnection Technology Program

Most of the semiconductor chips that lie at the heart, or rather brain, of the modern computer are connected to the rest of the machine by wire bonding. Although other interconnect technologies exist, such as tape automated bonding, solder bump, and beam leads, it is wire bonding that predominates. As technological advances lead to semi-conductor chips of increasing complexity with more and more compo-nents crammed into smaller and smaller space, the number of input-output connections on the chips increases. Advanced high-den-sity interconnections are required so that these modern superchips can communicate with the outside world.

As the density of connections grows larger and larger, difficult problems arise. For example, in the modern high-density chip the cumulative heat produced by the myriad electrical currents weaving throughout the chip and between the chip and the rest of the computer becomes a serious concern. The result is a need for sophisticated thermal management of the chip and the substrate on which the semiconductor chip is found. It is a task of the Semiconductor Pack-aging Technology Program to help solve some of these interconnec-tion difficulties.

The semiconductor packaging industry is composed of a large num-ber of extremely diverse companies. Historically, the semiconductor business has grown on a supporting infrastructure of numerous small equipment companies, big equipment companies, and material sup-pliers. Yet even with this diversity of corporate involvement, there is not a wide variety of technologies employed. Basically, there are only a few accepted technologies that have become either the formal or de facto standards, and the supporting equipment and materials compa-nies have grown up using these standards.

The reason so few technologies have been adopted by this support-ing infrastructure is not that there is a lack of technological diversity available or that a few of the best technologies have prevailed. Instead, this lack of technological diversity can be partially traced to the number and diversity of companies supporting the semiconductor industry. This giant infrastructure has made it very difficult to make substantial changes, even changes for the better, because any change requires changes in a vast number of separate, independent companies. The difficulty of ad hoc or marketplace coordination of so many independent players has meant a certain reluctance to adopt new and different methods.

According to Dr. Barry Whalen, MCC vice president and program director of the semiconductor packaging interconnect program, inducing significant technological change in the industry is like trying to turn a battleship that consists of thousands of rowboats. Therefore, adds Dr. Whalen, one of the objectives of the MCC Semiconductor Packaging Technology Program is to demonstrate to this diverse group of suppliers that a significant and critical mass of companies is going to approve, adopt, and support a certain type of new technology. This will, in turn, encourage these supplier companies who are not necessarily members of MCC to invest capital in meeting the needs of this new technology. Of course, a company like IBM can become a standard setter because the company size is sufficiently large. But smaller companies might not have a sufficient critical mass to cause the supplier industry companies to change their strategies and convert to supporting a technology which the smaller companies might desire.

Interestingly, Dr. Whalen came to MCC with prior experience in interfirm cooperation. He worked with the Semiconductor Research Corporation (SRC) on a program called Leap Frog, which was a collaborative attempt to accelerate the development of the next generation of semiconductor processing equipment.

With Leap Frog, the problem faced by the participants was the same that faced the participants in the MCC program, namely, that any one of the companies acting by itself was not large enough to significantly influence the diverse equipment manufacturers. The Leap Frog program, much like the MCC program, was designed to encourage the suppliers to invest in the development of the the next generation of equipment by accumulating a sufficiently large group of potential customer companies. Although the Leap Frog program had a very specific charter in the beginning, which was essentially to collect money from the various participants and then support research in universities, its focus broadened over time. Through the experience gained came the understanding that what the semiconductor industry really needed for the next round of international competition was the development of certain equipment, not just the development of certain research ideas. As a consequence the Leap Frog program, originally a part of the regular SRC effort, was separated and is being operated more along the lines of MCC.

THE ADMINISTRATIVE REVIEW PROCESS

Once the program directors were on board, the task fell on their shoulders to develop structures and establish procedures to carry out their assigned research objectives. One of the primary differences between MCC and a single-entity company as noted by the program directors concerns the administrative review process. At MCC the administrative review process with regard to obtaining the necessary approvals or resources was more complex than that of a standard company. Dr. Eugene Lowenthal, vice president and program director, speaking from his years of experience as an executive of Intel, made the point that in the normal company structure it was fairly clear to whom you had to sell a project. In such standard situations there was essentially an upward sell to get that comfortable level of "buy-in" or sanctioning of direction. At Intel he understood the path that he had to take. Even in a matrix organization, even though the path was more complex, he said that a project leader would understand it. It may be a dual path and there may be three or four bosses to please, but it was still a clear path.

At MCC things were more complex and vague in this regard. Every shareholder had, in Lowenthal's words, "his own ax to grind." Therefore, at MCC the program director had to be stronger than normally required and had to have the courage of convictions to say, "OK, here is what MCC is going to do." The danger was that if the program director waited and tried to get a consensus going by the initiative of the member companies, nothing would get done and the program director could wind up getting, in his words, "thrashed" by the shareholders.

The MCC program director had to have his or her own vision and the strength to resist the haphazard random inputs from the members. The program director could not afford to be overly responsive to the shareholders. As one program director put it, if the program director was too sensitive to each and every need and desire of the member companies that program director ran the danger of "being matrixed to death."

A program director at MCC with weakly defined goals would be caught in the middle of a circle of shareholders and would be pushed all around the circle. As a consequence, having more than one sponsor could be a real danger if the program director did not have this vision. On the other hand, the program directors were quick to note that multiple sponsors had positive benefits as well. Having more than one sponsor did give the program directors a certain amount of independence, in that they could play or balance the members off against one another.

At least one program director at MCC ran into difficulties trying to walk this narrow line and by mutual agreement with MCC top management decided to leave MCC to return to an organization less prone to these dilemmas. It is interesting to note that this particular program director lost his effectiveness by being too responsive to the shareholders. As a consequence, the program director "got pushed around" in the opinion of the top MCC executives. The diverse and sometimes conflicting demands of the participating companies made it impossible to move ahead with the program on schedule.

When talking about this required vision that each program director must have at MCC, Lowenthal mentioned one difference between an organization like Intel and MCC regarding continuity in motivational management. The company like Intel was started by an entrepreneur or group of individuals who had a clear idea of just what it was the company was trying to do. Lowenthal said if he as a manager ever forgot where it was the company was headed he would just go and talk to one of the founders, one of the people with the original vision.

At MCC the people who put it together were no longer directly involved. Therefore, a program director could not go to the founder, the person with the original vision, to seek guidance. The program director did not have the luxury of being able to stop Bill Norris in the hallway and ask, "What is it that we are doing here?" Despite this absence of original founders, MCC did have mechanisms to preserve and disclose the organization's purpose. As one program director described it, the founders of MCC put together a collection of materials, reinforced by certain oral and written traditions, on why MCC existed, what the purpose of MCC was. An "MCC bible" as one observer called it.

When a program director was having difficulties dealing with a shareholder experiencing pressing current problems, the program director could use these materials as reference to help resolve conflicts. By having these materials on hand, the program directors could resist the temptation to change direction in response to the shareholders' short-term crises. By going back and rereading and looking at these materials put together by the visionary founders, the program directors could withstand the slow incremental drift away from MCC's long-term goals.

Importantly, the program director could undertake this goal assessment process independently of the current inputs from the shareholders or even his own employees. As Lowenthal said, "The people that wrote down the vision may be dead, but if they did a good enough job of encoding and expressing this visionary message and made it flexible enough so that it can be used by each generation, then it will be a very useful set of materials for the current and future managers."

For MCC the visionary message was captured in a number of places: the bylaws, the research program plans, the documents that set forth what exactly the technical mission of MCC was to be, and even a set of videotapes. One program director, who felt that the videotapes were particularly important, made the comment, "It is like getting a videotape from the people who framed the Constitution. It is like having Thomas Jefferson tell you what he meant when he wrote the Declaration of Independence."

The existence of these "constitutional" materials to help guide program directors in dealing with multiple sponsors permitted Inman to be less of a direct supervisor of the program directors. Inman allowed the program directors a lot of leeway with regard to management of their particular research program. Inman's primary function, from the viewpoint of the program directors, was to create a unified front with the board of directors and the senior people of the member companies.

Dr. Woodie Bledsoe, the vice president and program director for the artificial intelligence knowledge-based systems program, said he was a little surprised initially that Inman had not assumed more direct control of the programs.[222] But he noted that Inman had a tremendous amount of charisma that could substitute for more direct methods when it came to getting people to do something in particular. Bledsoe said that Inman knew what was going on but tried to let it come together on its own without his direct intervention. Formal plans for each research program satisfied a good deal of the need for his direction. Inman's style was to find and hire people he trusted and then give those people a great deal of leeway in executing the formal plan.[223]

With the program directors in place, staffing proceeded quickly. In February of 1984 MCC had only fifty employees. By the end of 1984

MCC had over two hundred employees, 80 percent of whom were researchers. The time had come to shift from the personnel and administrative tasks associated with building the organization to producing R&D results. For two years MCC struggled with getting the results of its research out the door, with mixed results. The honeymoon was over and the sponsors were looking for tangible results from their investment.

In some ways this transition called for a new style of leadership. Perhaps sensing that his major contribution to the organization was behind him, Inman informed the MCC board of directors of his intention to pass the helm onto someone new. Bobby Ray Inman, a major force in shaping MCC and guiding it through its formative years, left the organization in December of 1986.

With the departure of Admiral Inman, MCC entered a new, potentially treacherous, era. MCC was no longer a dream, no longer a start-up organization. It was a real and on-going concern that had to move quickly from promise to performance.

To succeed Inman, the MCC shareholders turned to Grant Dove, the executive vice president of Texas Instruments. Dove, a respected engineer and manager, had 28 years of experience at TI.

Like Inman, Dove was a native Texan, but their respective management styles differed significantly. Dove had a reputation as a soft-spoken and easy-going manager, one who relied heavily on his listening skills to develop strategic alternatives from which he could make his decision. One example of the difference in the manner of leadership between the two men could be seen in how each communicated with shareholders and the public. Inman, perhaps in keeping with his CIA and NSA background, "was high-profile on the outside, while keeping the wraps tightly drawn over the inner processes."[224] Dove, on the other hand, was inclined to maintain a lower profile but exercise a greater openness about internal MCC activities. Dove's understanding of the subtle and often byzantine politics of large corporations was in sharp contrast to Inman's sometimes frank and public discussions of pressing issues that could alienate some of the MCC's more sensitive shareholder executives.

Dove saw technology transfer as one of his most important tasks. Dove knew that at the end of 1988 many of the MCC shareholders would be reevaluating their five years with MCC. Would the rewards be seen as out weighing the costs? Although by December of 1988 MCC had acquired 11 patents and had applied for 50 more (by July 1990 MCC had accumulated 47 patents) and had transferred 84 technology packages to its members, translating technology to bottom line profit was difficult. To make matters worse, the worsening economics of the maturing computer and micro-chip businesses began to take its toll. Member companies had to make hard choices between funding MCC research or their own research laboratories. For example, in early 1989 Digital announced its withdrawal from the advanced computer architecture and software technology programs citing competition with internal company research efforts.

Dove focused MCC on shorter-term projects and improving technology transfer in an effort to help MCC membership survive corporate cost cutting. The exodus of members was eventually halted, and the trend was reversed with the addition of Hughes Aircraft in 1988, Cadence Design Systems in 1989 and Northern Telecom in 1990. Dove's "mid-course correction" for MCC included the addition of a new program on superconductivity in electronics, and a major restructuring of the ACT program.

Perhaps of even greater significance was the resuscitation of the associates program. The associates for a $25,000 annual fee are kept abreast of MCC research and can participate in selected MCC research programs for additional funding. From 13 associates in 1984, the program shrank to 5 in late 1986. Substantial efforts by MCC both in terms of more attractive structuring and increased recruiting brought the number up to 17 by the fall of 1989. By the summer of 1990 the number had reached a high of 24 associate members, including such industry leaders as Apple Computer and Texas Instruments.

With membership on the rebound, and bolstered by a solid record of technological achievement, in July of 1990 Dove announced the appointment of Craig I. Fields as Chief Technical Officer and Chief Operating Officer. But Fields was more than CTO and COO. He was slated to take over from Dove as CEO in 1991. The choice of Fields marked a return to an Inman-type leader for MCC. Like Inman, Fields had extensive government experience, having worked at DARPA for sixteen years before being named as director in 1990. But, unlike Inman he was scientist. In April of 1990, Fields was unceremoniously removed as DARPA's director in a policy dispute with the Bush Administration.

Fields was seen as the type of manager who could reestablish the foresight and outlook necessary for the long-term success of MCC. As Douglas B. Lenat, the director of MCC's research efforts in artificial intelligence, put it, Fields was expected to "rekindle the technical daring and vision that Bob Inman provided."[225] Dove reemphasized this point when he noted during the announcement of Fields's appointment, that it "signals the start of a smooth transition to the next generation of leadership for MCC."[226]

Fields summed up the situation facing the cooperative venture by stating that, "MCC has proven that competitors in an industry can collaborate on high-risk applied research, providing significant competitive advantages to the participating companies."[227] But what he did not clarify was whether the difficulties and costs associated with inter-firm collaboration in a dynamic industry are outweighed by the benefits when compared to alternative approaches. Clearly, one of Fields' primary tasks will be to convince the paying shareholders that the balance falls in their favor.

6

The Chemical Industry Institute of Toxicology: A Collaborative Research Success Story

Despite all the uncertainties and difficulties facing companies wishing to engage in cooperative research ventures, there have been notable successes, even prior to the passage of the National Cooperative Research Act in 1984. The Chemical Industry Institute of Toxicology is just one such example.[228] Although its unique research objectives facilitated inter-firm cooperation, it does help illustrate those situations where collaborative efforts among marketplace competitors can yield positive results to the participants, customers, and workers.

The Chemical Industry Institute of Toxicology (CIIT) was formed in 1974 by eleven of the largest U.S. chemical companies.[229] The original eleven were quickly joined by seven others and the membership hit thirty-four companies by the summer of 1979. Although most of the founding members had been concerned with chemical toxicity questions for a number of years prior to CIIT's formation (for example, Dow Chemical's labs had been testing for toxicological effects of chemicals since 1934),[230] the dramatic disclosure in the early seventies of a link between vinyl chloride monomer (VCM) at very low concentrations and cancer brought the issue of chemical toxicology or hazard to a heated and at times acrimonious public debate. VCM was one of the first chemicals to be tested at low concentrations. Before this time, chemicals, VCM included, were tested for short periods at high concentrations to determine acute toxicity. This testing practice resulted in the setting of exposure levels thought to be safe. In the case of VCM this level was discovered to be too high. The industry's painful passage through the VCM controversy,[231] as well as similar ones surrounding benzene and Agent Orange, was such to encourage a few industry leaders to search for better methods to help find the VCMs of the future and avoid the problems of having to react and research simultaneously when questions about a chemical's biological effects were raised.

THE VINYL CHLORIDE ISSUE[232]

Vinyl chloride (VC) gas is the basic building block of polyvinyl chloride plastic (PVC), one of modern society's most ubiquitous products. Found in hundreds of thousands of products, PVC spawned a prosperous and glamorous industry in the postwar economies of Japan, the United States, and Europe. By the early seventies the PVC business had annual sales in excess of $60 billion and was directly involved in the employment of some two million workers in the United States alone. A stunning announcement by a major PVC manufacturer was to forever change the PVC business and the chemical industry as well.

In January of 1973, B. F. Goodrich announced that three of its VCM workers had died of angiosarcoma, a rare liver cancer. Soon thereafter similar reports from other polyvinyl chloride makers emerged. A total of thirteen VCM-related deaths were uncovered. An emergency exposure limit of 50 ppm was clamped on the industry in April by OSHA while the legislators, regulators, industry members, and workers tried to sort out and react to the rapidly developing story.

By May of 1974 OSHA was proposing a very strict "no detectable level" limit for VC exposure. Such a limit, according to an Arthur D. Little study commissioned by the Society of the Plastics Industries, would cause massive shutdowns, with some 1.6 million workers losing their jobs and lost sales and production in excess of $65 billion. Nonetheless, strict vinyl chloride standards were quickly implemented and just as quickly contested in the courts. The controversy spread from courtroom to factory floor. In 1974, a Uniroyal PVC plant in Painesville, Ohio, was struck by members of the United Rubber Workers over concerns about the carcinogenicity of vinyl chloride.

As the dust began to settle on the VCM controversy and the industry adapted to the exposure standard without incurring financial disaster, certain facts became clear. First, there had to be a better early warning system to detect chemicals harmful to humans and the environment, so that health dangers could be minimized and long-term resource allocations optimized. And, secondly, all concerned parties — government, industry, workers, and the general public — would be better served by a more complete understanding of a chemical's toxicity potential before human exposures and capital resource expenditures.

THE ROLE OF CIIT

The potential task facing CIIT was formidable. There are over two million chemical products registered worldwide. To this list over five hundred new chemical products are added annually. The growing sophistication of testing techniques, not to mention the expense associated with such sophistication, further compounds the testing problem. To test a chemical compound for possible harmful effects to humans requires the coordination of a number of diverse scientific fields. Perhaps the best one-sentence summary of just what toxicological testing entails is found in the 1980 Annual Report of CIIT: "Toxicology is a multidisciplinary science that seeks to discover and to predict the potential adverse effects of chemical agents on living systems."[233]

For the most part, standard laboratory animals (rats, mice, and guinea pigs) are employed as surrogates for humans to test chemical toxicity, since actual human testing is not feasible. But there are serious questions being raised within the scientific community about these "biological models." The interpretation of the "rat test" results and extrapolation to humans is a difficult and not fully understood area of science.

To make its task more manageable CIIT limited its testing program to commodity chemicals, those everyday chemicals that are the basic building blocks of the modern chemical industry. Although this reduced the possible universe of test candidates to a few thousand, thoroughly testing even this smaller number of chemicals was beyond the resources of CIIT.

CIIT's first president, Dr. Leon Goldberg, envisioned the Institute as a vehicle to promote the further integration of the separate toxicology disciplines (biochemistry, pathology, epidemiology, molecular biology, and others) into a more cohesive and coherent whole.[234] In addition, the Institute sought to develop new toxicological techniques and methods so that the typical three-year, one-half-million-dollar chemical toxicity test program could be made shorter and less expensive.[235] Pointing to the sometimes antiquated testing methods, Dr.

Goldberg noted, "Bioassays are done today as they were 100 years ago."

Clarification and refinement of these testing procedures or protocols was an important task in the minds of the sponsoring companies. They needed to know just what effects chemicals would have on humans, and since the method to achieve this understanding was based on extrapolation and interpretation of "animal tests," a more complete knowledge of those tests was necessary for their correct application outside the lab. According to Richard J. Hughes, senior vice president for Union Carbide, "It was industry's desire to set up a neutral organization, which would concern itself primarily with understanding and testing the validity of current protocols employed in toxicological testing."

At its formation CIIT had six specific goals: (1) Conduct toxicological testing of chemical products to which workers and consumers are exposed; (2) Clear the backlog of toxicological testing needs; (3) Produce the highest quality science possible, including new and better methodologies; (4) Emphasize carcinogenicity at first, with later expansion into other areas; (5) Relate animal test results to human experience; and (6) Promote education and training of toxicologists.[236]

On a more informal basis Dr. Goldberg knew that one of his most important tasks during the formative years would be to establish the role of the institute as an independent, highly productive, authoritative, and, perhaps most important, credible source of relevant information. This was no easy task given the negative public image that the chemical industry was developing as a result of the PVC and other controversies (such as Love Canal). The government and the general public had a natural mistrust of an organization founded and funded by the chemical industry. At the same time, there was by no means a consensus among the industry members on what the real problems were facing them, much less their priority and possible solutions.

This problem of getting the industry together to jointly tackle the toxicity issue was no mean feat. First of all, there were antitrust problems that would naturally arise with the major competitors in the chemical industry trying to get together and do anything of a joint nature.

Milton Wessel, an attorney and moving force in cooperative problem-solving ventures such as CIIT, put the problem this way:

As with so many other issues in this whole area of socio-scientific dispute resolution, the matter of "how" poses the most difficult question. Individual members of industry must compete and struggle to survive. Each alone can no more take on the burden of solving the problems of the world regarding risk assessment than can the individual regarding the need for additional hospital facilities in his community. There must be joint action by those who recognize and understand their own self-interests and their societal obligations. Joint action even by individuals seeking to build a modern hospital in their own community is hard enough. Joint action by giant competitors poses far more serious issues, including complex antitrust and other legal concerns.

To help wind a path through the legal uncertainties facing a collaborative research venture prior to the 1984 passage of the National Cooperative Research Act, CIIT's founders set forth four basic operating policies: (1) CIIT members must not gain competitive advantage over nonmembers by virtue of their CIIT membership; (2) CIIT activities must not result in unreasonable harm to third parties; (3) CIIT activities must not result in unreasonable lessening of competition in the chemical industry; and (4) CIIT must in all respects adhere to the highest standards of law and general morality.[237]

To alleviate some of the antitrust concerns, CIIT's founders knew that the institute would have to be run strictly as an independent entity and that the results of CIIT research (for which they would be paying) would have to be publicly disseminated. This meant that the companies sponsoring CIIT might find themselves paying for information that could be used against them by noncontributing competitors, or the government regulators. The passage of the Toxic Substances Control Act (TSCA) mandated public disclosure of discoveries made by individual companies regarding a chemical's toxic effects. In some instances this has led to premature disclosure and overreaction based on incomplete data.

Dr. Neal, CIIT's second president, pointed out that the institute's independent status can sometimes be more of a help than a hindrance when it comes to disclosures: "We (CIIT), unlike the chemical companies, have no obligation under current laws to report possible adverse health effects in animals that may arise as a result of our testing. This allows us to continue the testing until there is a suggestion of possible human health effects. In this sense we can operate like a university laboratory. They, too, don't have to report results until a study has been completed." Although not legally bound by TSCA disclosure rules, CIIT has made early release of "real" results its policy.

This means that CIIT could avoid the sensational stories so popular in a mass media world ("Lab rats die in test of common chemical. Possible cancer links suspected") and whose retraction is seldom remembered. "Our disclosure policy," Dr. Neal added, "is that we do not disclose data until we are reasonably sure there is a real effect, and we then disclose it so that everyone has equal access to it. This includes members, nonmembers, the government, and the general public alike."

THE STRUCTURE OF CIIT

"I think that this is the only way CIIT is going to be able to operate, to maintain credibility. There is just no other way it can be structured, but it makes for an interesting kind of organization to manage. So often you're walking a tightrope," says Dr. Neal.

CIIT is an independent, nonprofit organization whose membership is open to all companies that produce or use chemicals and chemical products. Starting with a nucleus of eight staff people and eleven sponsoring companies in the beginning of 1976, CIIT grew in less than six years to over one hundred professionals and twenty post-doctoral fellows, an annual budget of nearly $10 million, and thirty-five sponsoring chemical companies, representing some 85 percent of all chemical sales in the United States.

Getting the companies to jointly develop scientific information was something that ran counter to the past ways of doing business and maintaining a competitive advantage. As Jackson Browning, director of Union Carbide's health, safety, and environmental affairs, put it, "In the past, information on toxic effects was proprietary. You would keep it secret until you had found a way to neutralize the effects. Then you would announce your discovery to the world knowing that you already had a solution to the problem."

This same observation was made by Milton Wessel: "Chemical research and development have always been the lifeblood of chemical companies. Important new scientific information is highly prized and is treated with the utmost secrecy. "But," he went on to add, "at the same time, concern about potentially injurious side effects of valuable chemicals has grown at a startling pace. There is increasing need for more basic research into the mechanisms of toxicity and the very long-term effects of widely used compounds. We desperately require greater laboratory facilities and more highly qualified scientists to work in them. These are fundamental societal urgencies, well beyond the capacities of individual companies to satisfy, acting alone."

In order to carry out the information-development mission, priorities and policies have to be established. At CIIT the primary policy-making group is the board of directors. The board is composed of top officials from fourteen of CIIT's thirty-seven member companies, one university president, and Mr. Wessel as general counsel. It is the board's task to set policies for sound financial and administrative management, formulate long-term planning, recruit new members, establish good public relations, and provide for the general guidance of the institute. While many of the largest companies have board positions, the group includes some of the smallest as well.

The job of reviewing and evaluating the actual programs undertaken by the institute is handled by the Scientific Advisory Panel, whose members are all expert scientists drawn from industry, academia, and the government. In addition to its advisory and evaluative function, the Scientific Advisory Panel performs the important function of scientific liaison, thus providing a valuable link with industry and academic laboratories in the fields of toxicology and occupational and environmental health.

Panel members are appointed by the board of directors. Following the advice of the panel and suggestions made by representatives of the chemical industry, CIIT selects a list of commodity chemicals for priority testing. To be selected, a chemical's volume of production, its physical and chemical properties, its estimated human exposure, toxicological suspicion, public interest, and the chemical's significance to society are all considered. In 1980, CIIT's priority list consisted of forty chemicals, an increase of twenty-nine in four years' time.

The commodity chemicals selected for toxicological testing are determined by CIIT with the assistance of its Scientific Advisory Panel and suggestions from various representatives of the chemical industry.[238] Criteria for selection include the chemical's volume of production, its physical and chemical properties, its estimated human exposure, toxicological suspicion and opinion, public interest, and the significance of the chemical to society. Chemicals are selected without regard for their importance to any particular member company, and specialty or proprietary compounds are not tested.

THREE AREAS OF EFFORT

To provide the information on chemical toxicity sought by its sponsoring members, CIIT assigns its resources to three broad areas which are mutually supportive. First is the area of actual chemical testing. Second is research to improve the understanding of toxic action and create better testing procedures. And third is the training of toxicologists and scientists in related fields to insure a source of needed expertise in the future.

Toxicology testing is, at a minimum, a two-step process. The first step is a pilot study that generally lasts ninety days to examine the toxicity of the subject chemical at various dosage levels. From this study dosage levels are selected for the second step of the testing program, the long-term exposure study in rats or mice. This second step generally runs for twenty-four months, which is the average lifespan of the laboratory rodent. The long-term exposure studies are frequently supplemented by experiments with additional animal species to broaden the biological base of the study.

Because toxicology itself is a new and developing science, CIIT uses a fair portion of its resources to improve the predictive value of toxicology. This means research directed at developing a more complete understanding of just how a chemical works upon a test biological system, such as a lab rat, and how the test biological system relates to humans.

As Dr. Neal puts it, "Overall, there is a substantial uncertainty about the validity of results in experimental animals and what they mean relative to human beings. One of CIIT's major activities is to improve this interpretability of these animal experiments. This means basic research on the mechanisms of chemical toxicity."

This difficulty in linking the results of testing done on laboratory animals to human risk was demonstrated early in CIIT's history. After a two-year mice and rat study done on formaldehyde under CIIT's sponsorship, it was found that some of the rats had developed cancer in the nasal passages.[239] If formaldehyde were found to be carcinogenic in humans there would be major economic consequences, in that nearly 6.5 billion pounds of formaldehyde are consumed in the United States each year for manufacturing plastics, insulation, cosmetics, pharmaceuticals, and pesticides. The problem with intepreting the animal tests showing formaldehyde toxicity is that rats do not (and cannot) breathe through their mouths like humans. This biological difference means that the surface area of chemical exposure is very different for rats and humans given the same concentration of form-aldehyde in the air.

Professional training of toxicologists is CIIT's third main area of endeavor. According to Dr. Etcyl Blair, formerly of Dow Chemical and later chairman of CIIT, the training program of CIIT was of particular interest to the smaller chemical companies. "They see that the critical shortages of good toxicologists is hurting them in the long term since all it does is jack the salaries up higher and higher," he said. "They can't afford three-year, one-million-dollar studies. Not that the major companies can either." The heightened awareness and concern about chemical toxicity, coupled with the increasing importance of vast numbers of chemicals in modern society, has produced a world-wide need for professionally trained toxicologists who can design, conduct, and interpret chemical safety studies. To meet this need CIIT offers both pre- and postdoctoral training programs. In addition, the institute participates in an interuniversity program of toxicology and an annual twelve-week survey of particular problems in toxicology. The latter program involves the National Institute of Environmental Health Sciences (NIEHS), the U.S. Environmental Protection Agency (EPA) and the Burroughs Wellcome Company, as well as CIIT.

Because resources limit the institute's work to a small subset of the two million chemical products produced worldwide and the few thousand commodity chemicals, it is inevitable that some chemicals important to a particular sponsoring company will not be tested. In fact, Union Carbide, a founding member of CIIT, has not had the most important chemicals it produces tested by CIIT. According to Richard Hughes, senior vice president of Union Carbide, "This isn't as much of a problem for the company as it might appear, since the chemicals being tested by CIIT are better models that will teach us things about how major categories of chemicals affect living systems."

Dr. Leon Goldberg amplifies this sentiment. "The amount of work to be done in toxicology is staggering. The more one contemplates recent scientific and regulatory developments, the more mind-bog-gling the prospects become. CIIT's list of 40 priority compounds, important though these are, is a pitifully small proportion of the chemical agents that are out there requiring study. This means hard choices and even harder work which does not court popularity."

Risk assessment is based on data, and CIIT's primary goal is to produce these data. Richard Fleming, formerly president of GAF and the past chairman of CIIT's board of directors, expressed it this way: "While our tools and our thrust are scientific, our chief concern is that the information which is our work product should prove useful and be properly used, in both detection and control of chemical hazards." To this he adds, "As we move into the decade of the 1980s, the pressures to achieve immediate and widespread enactment of regulatory controls on toxic hazards seems to be growing exponentially, regardless of whether or not a solid understanding of the risks involved is arrived at, or at least the best possible assessment of them is made. . . . As the scope of [CIIT's] research and activity expands, we are constantly reinforced in our conviction of the absolute need for dispassionate scientific development of facts, and of procedures for producing them more quickly, economically, and reliably. It has always been easier to raise concerns than it is to soundly validate data that can answer these concerns."

Dr. Blair expressed the same sentiment in a most pertinent manner: "We all need to get a lot more information for the dollar than we did ten years ago."

CIIT is one of the success stories in collaborative research and development among otherwise competitors. By using a cooperative venture, the industry members have been spared the unnecessary expenses that would result from duplicative efforts. At the same time both customers and workers have benefitted from the joint effort. Unfortunately, CIIT can not be classified a total success. As was noted by its members on the occasion of its tenth birthday, CIIT still did not receive support from two-thirds of the chemical industry — companies benefiting from CIIT's efforts but acting as free riders.[240] Despite two years' efforts aimed at increasing the 1984 membership from thirty-three to fifty companies, CIIT was only able to add one addition corporate sponsor — Procter & Gamble.[241]

In September of 1988 CIIT inaugurated its third president, Roger O. McClellan. Efforts to expand the membership have recently increased, with five new corporate members in 1988 and four more approved for 1989.[242] Even after fifteen successful years, CIIT faces new challenges. According to Dr. McClellan, "Much future insight into chemical toxicology, will be provided by new tools in molecular and cellular biology and the ability to use some of these new tools and techniques to understand mechanisms." In addition, new techniques such as using computer-based modeling to increase the understanding of the effect of chemicals in humans need to be explored. CIIT plans to continue to pool and focus industry resources on these critical problems.

Although the unique situation facing CIIT may limit its direct applicability to other research ventures, it does reveal that cooperation among competitors can work, not only to the benefit of the participants, but also to the benefit of society as a whole.

7

High Hopes and False Starts: Sematech and U.S. Memories

Semiconductors, those tiny silicon hearts of the machines that run the information society, are increasingly labeled "made in Japan." U.S. manufacturers, once the undisputed world leaders, are scrambling to hold on to their market shares and mount a counterattack. Although U.S. semiconductor manufacturers still enjoyed 40 percent of the world computer chip marketplace in 1988, their share had fallen from 60 percent ten years earlier. Even more alarming was the rise of Japanese manufacturers who during the same period had gone from 25 percent to 45 percent of the market.[243] Important to both civilian and military markets, the semiconductor chip is a symbol of the industry of the future. Fiercely competitive and innovative, U.S. manufacturers are hardly prime candidates for commercial defeat. If these companies, America's best, brightest, and brashest, cannot survive in the rough-and-tumble global marketplace, what fate awaits autos and steel?

The semiconductor industry faces formidable challenges that make cooperative activities attractive. First is the challenge of capital. The industry's demand for capital is staggering. A first-rate chip production facility cost around $200 million in 1988. To support a plant of this size requires a sales volume approaching $1 billion per year.[244] By the early 1990s the cost is expected to rise by 50 percent to $300 million. And the costs will not stop there. According to G. Dan Hutcheson, a market research analyst for VLSI Research in California, the trend of current technological advances indicates a likelihood of $1 billion plants before the decade is over.[245]

The problem of high capital investment is complicated by relatively low returns that make attracting the vast sums of funding necessary for building state-of-the-art facilities difficult. According to Shearson, Lehman, Hutton, the average return on stockholder's equity of even the domestic industry's best performer, Motorola, was an unglamorous 10.4 percent for the 1982–1988 period. As if the high costs and low returns were not discouraging enough, the industry is plagued by cycles of abundance and shortage. These cycles can be partly traced to the long lead time required to put a new plant into operation (currently about two years) and to the lumpiness of adding capacity due to the ever-increasing size of plant capacity.

Couple with these factors the vagaries of international currency exchange rates and customer industries, also in transition and turmoil, and it becomes clear that only large companies with either captive uses or massive financial strength can afford to support the projected costs of production for commodity chips. Hovering around this core of commodity chip manufacturing are companies using small, flexible manufacturing facilities to turn out custom and specialized chips.

For an activity that hardly existed twenty years ago, semiconductor fabrication has become "the foundation of the electronics industry, which employs more Americans—2.6 million—than the steel, auto, and aerospace industries combined."[246] The significance of the industry and the seriousness of the threat is such that Charles A. Fowler, chairman of the Defense Science Board, was quoted as saying "at some time in the future [the waning U.S. leadership in semiconductors] may be looked upon in retrospect as a turning point in the history of our nation."[247] The CIA's assessment was equally apocalyptic. According to the agency in its report to the Pentagon in 1987, "The U.S. semiconductor industry is at a crucial turning point. It fundamentally cannot compete in its current form."[248] Although not all have been driven to such hyperbole, few doubt the gravity of the situation. Unfortunately, it is the solution that eludes consensus.

Industry analysts, company executives, government officials and academics[249] have come to the conclusion that interfirm collaboration is part of the solution to the malaise.[250] MCC was the pioneer in 1982.[251] As the drive of the Japanese continues others have followed. Perhaps the best-known and most controversial is Sematech.

Sematech[252] is a jointly funded, industry-government research consortium whose broad and ambitious objective is to reestablish U.S.

world leadership in semiconductor manufacturing, specifically with regard to the Japanese. The Semiconductor Industry Association (SIA)[253] created an activities task force in September 1986 to define objectives and create an organizational framework for an industry consortium. Charles E. Sporck, chief executive of National Semiconductor Corp. in 1987 was Sematech's primary architect and champion.[254] The following March a fourteen-member start-up team began operations in Santa Clara, California. A June 1987 secret meeting of executives from the major U.S. semiconductor manufacturers took place at the Hyatt Regency in Monterey, California. In August 1987 Sematech was incorporated as a Delaware nonprofit research and development corporation. Over the next few months twenty-four similar meetings took place throughout the country in Boston, Dallas, and Tampa. What brought together a group of normally intensely independent competitors? In a word, survival — survival against the unrelenting onslaught of Japanese manufacturers.

Many believed that the Japanese used government-industry cooperation, coupled with American aversion toward such partnerships, to target the semiconductor industry. According to Gilbert F. Amerlio, president of Rockwell International's Semiconductor Products Division, "Their [the Japanese] strategy was intentionally devised to overwhelm anything that private industry can do by itself."[255] But interfirm cooperation is not without controversy and critics. "The idea of the consortium is experimental. It's a relatively new concept and the jury is still out," according to Dr. Smilor of IC[2] Institute, a technology study group at the University of Texas.[256]

The structure of the industry invites cooperation and at the same time makes it difficult to achieve. The semiconductor industry is highly fragmented. At one end are the high-volume merchant producers who sell their chip output to other manufacturers for use in their equipment. A few semiconductor producers, like IBM and NCR, are vertically integrated, using the chips they fabricate in their own products. Next come the semi-custom manufacturers such as VLSI Technologies, Inc., and LSI Logic Corp. And finally, there are the design and process specialist companies such as Brooktree Corporation.[257]

The strategic objectives, not to mention corporate temperaments, of fiercely independent and aggressively competitive smaller companies differ from those of the giant U.S. commodity chip manufacturers, such as IBM, AT&T, and Texas Instruments. Some industry executives charge that interfirm collaboration is merely a crutch for the large merchant chip manufacturers. For example, T. J. Rodgers, the president of Cypress Semiconductors, a small (by semiconductor standards) but successful chip maker with $140 million in sales in 1988, complains that the large players "managed to get themselves a government subsidy."[258] Elaborating on his criticism of Sematech, Rodgers notes, "Only two companies with sales below $500 million have joined Sematech."[259] According to Rodgers the fees, which start at $1 million per year, exclude the small companies like his that are "the lifeblood of the industry."[260]

Disparate size is not the only problem. Cultural conflicts can also threaten industry consortiums. Some companies encourage and reward irreverence in their employees and other do not. One example of the problems that can arise from such cultural collisions occurred during the earlier days of Sematech. The consortium's first chief operating officer was the highly respected Paul Castrucci, a former IBM plant manager. After eight months on the job at Sematech, Castrucci resigned after reported discord with the freewheeling Robert Noyce, Sematech's original CEO and founder of Intel.[261] In his understated manner Castrucci remarked, "Consortiums are the wave of the future, but they sure are hard to manage."[262]

As was evident with MCC, different strategic objectives can further complicate a consortium's management. To cite one example, IBM manufactures over a third of its chips in Europe.[263] When IBM wanted to join the Joint European Submicron Silicon consortium (JESSI) the European members balked, citing Sematech's policy against foreign members. It is interesting to note that talks are currently under way between JESSI and Sematech to explore avenues of cooperation.[264] One possible idea under consideration is the granting of automatic membership privileges in both consortia to members in either.[265]

In pursuit of its overall goal of catching and eventually surpassing the Japanese, Sematech has outlined a three-phased approach lasting five years. Its 1990 operating plan, approved in April of 1989, called for U.S. semiconductor manufacturers to achieve parity with the Japanese by the middle of 1993. This was a slight retreat from the earlier goal of parity by the end of 1992.[266]

Sematech differs in one extremely important aspect from prior cooperative R&D efforts in the industry, such as MCC, in that the government is a significant participant. Fourteen semiconductor manufacturers comprise the industry side of the collaboration.[267] The Department of Defense is the government participant. Technically, the government is not a formal member but shares access to Sematech's technology.

As noted in chapter five, high-technology industry enthusiasm for government participation in cooperative ventures is not especially great. In the fiscal years 1988 and 1989 Congress appropriated $100 million for Sematech. A similar amount was designated for 1990, but has come under fire. The uncertainties of government funding can also be an impediment to effective industry-government cooperation. In late 1989, ideological preferences[268] and increased budget scrutiny of defense programs spawned rumors of an "intense struggle" within the Bush administration over continued government funding of Sematech.[269]

The rumors were sufficient to prompt President Bush's top science adviser, D. Allan Bromley, to explicitly deny them. Even while some administration officials were said to recommend cutbacks in Sematech funding, an "advance edition" of a government-appointed National Advisory Committee on Semiconductors' report urged additional funding for the consortium.[270]

Some of the strongest criticism of R&D consortia such as Sematech has been leveled at government participation. Technologic Partners, a technology consulting firm, conducted an informal poll of 300 chief executives and institutional investors in the advanced computer industry of their opinions regarding government-industry cooperation. Not surprisingly, there was very little support shown for government-industry combinations.[271]

Government involvement goes beyond funding and extends into the strategic planning function. The National Defense Authorization Act for fiscal years 1988 and 1989 mandated that the annual operating plans for Sematech be developed in conjunction with the Department of Defense and Sematech's Advisory Council on Federal Participation. This Council is to be composed of five senior government officials and seven business leaders. The structure of the council was purposefully weighted in favor of business to permit Sematech sufficient managerial freedom.[272]

By late 1989 the council industry appointments had yet to be made. Since April of 1988, interim governmental oversight, originally performed by the office of the Secretary of the Defense, has been provided by the Defense Advanced Research Projects Agency (DARPA) to generally favorable reviews. The reason for DARPA's favorable response from usually hostile and independent business executives can probably be traced to DARPA's impressive technological expertise and past experience in nurturing high-risk/high-technology programs and ventures. It is interesting to note that the GAO discovered that "DARPA has helped improve SEMATECH's strategic planning efforts without micromanaging SEMATECH's activities or influencing it into performing defense-related research," an opinion the GAO attributed to SEMATECH's chief administrative officer.[273]

The member companies are required to provide at least 50 percent of the consortium's operating budget. Each Sematech member contributes 1 percent of its annual semiconductor revenues.[274] The size of the member companies' financial commitment to Sematech is significant. As Grant Dove, MCC's current chairman has noted, consortiums are born of kings, but the bills are paid by barons.[275] This means that although the chief executives may initially support interfirm cooperation and may actively play a role during the early years, they eventually turn their attention to other projects. In these later, critical years, the funding decisions may be at lower levels in the member organization, even in the hands of those in charge of internal research programs that are "competing" for funds.

This issue of assured funding for the longterm is so important that one commentator listed it among the three factors necessary for interfirm cooperation: "leaders who are inspired, angry, even scared; goals that are limited and well-defined; and a dependable source of revenue."[276] To assure funding to match the long-term nature of the research, each sponsoring company formally commits to support Sematech at full funding levels for its first four years of operation. In addition, a member's exit requires two years' notice.

In general, the level of a member's contributions determines the number of employees it may assign to the consortium's research programs and who can help transfer the resulting knowledge back to the member company.[277] In addition to specifics of funding, the participation agreement that each member must sign before joining Sematech also outlines the policies for handling proprietary information and intellectual property rights.

Sematech's stated objective is "to develop advanced semiconductor-manufacturing technology on a compressed schedule and then quickly and effectively transfer this technology to its members."[278] As with MCC, or any collaborative venture that produces knowledge, the technology transfer process is critical to ultimate success. To help avoid the problem MCC originally faced in enticing top talent from the member companies to join them,[279] many of the research employees of Sematech are on two-year assignments from the member companies.

To help guarantee the highest quality talent Sematech developed the following criteria for the assigned employees: five to ten years of directly related experience, among the top 10 to 15 percent in their field, recognized within their field for the quality of their work, and capable of adapting to a consortium environment. By September 30, 1989, over 180 engineering and managerial positions at Sematech had been filled by assigned employees from the fourteen member companies.[280] As was appropriately noted in the GAO report on Sematech made to Congress, "Attracting qualified assignees from member companies is critical for achieving SEMATECH's objectives because of their role in developing advanced manufacturing technology and transferring it to member companies."[281]

The success of these personnel policies can be seen in the results. Half of Sematech's researchers are on loan from its member companies, compared to 15 percent currently on loan at MCC. Only positions in finance, law, communications, supplier relations, and human resources normally are filled by permanent employees, since their roles in technology transfer are relatively minor. While at Sematech the assigned employee is paid by the assigning member company, although the member companies are reimbursed by Sematech for these expenses. This helps reinforce the assigned employee's loyalty to the sponsoring company.

The other side of the staffing issue is employee repatriation. If Sematech is too attractive a place to work there may be difficulties in getting employees to return to the sponsoring corporation. This problem of repatriation of assigned employees has been helped by Sematech's promise not to hire any assignee as a permanent employee without the approval of the member employer.[282] As of November 1989, forty-one assignees had left Sematech: twelve completed the assignment period and returned to the member company as planned, three either were sent back or mutually agreed to return to the member company because they did not fit into Sematech's operations, and one left early to accept a position offered by his member company. Of the remaining twenty-five, nine were part of the original California start-up team and left when Sematech relocated to Texas, eight were on temporary assignment, and eight either retired or resigned from their member company.[283]

In addition to assigned employees, Sematech encourages member companies to visit its facilities. On average, five visitors per day from member companies go to Austin. Not only does this constant interchange facilitate technology transfer, it also improves Sematech's prospects for future funding and ensures that Sematech will be part of the member companies' long-term planning.

Similarly to MCC, Sematech invited states to submit proposals on siting. By late 1987 the slate of candidate sites had been reduced to twelve. Austin, Texas, was announced as the winner in January of 1988.[284] The original vision was for a 200,000 sq. ft. plant operating round the clock, staffed by 700 people fabricating silicon wafers. While not designed for commercial production, the plant was to function as a realistic demonstration facility to develop, test, and authenticate production technologies. The members would then take this jointly produced knowledge and make whatever competitive use of it as they saw fit.[285] Construction of a fabrication facility for Sematech in Austin began in February of 1988 and it was dedicated the following fall.

The first formal technology transfer occurred in November 1988 when a workshop was held and a technology package given to the member companies on the construction of the semiconductor fabrication facility. Six members have announced plans to replicate the transferred technology by upgrading existing fabrication facilities or constructing new ones, and all fourteen reportedly will use some aspects of the facilities' technology.[286]

The consortium's operating divisions were reorganized in May of 1989 so that better use of project teams, with wider experience and expertise representation, could take place.[287] Prior to that time Sematech had used a functional organizational structure that was similar to that of its member companies.

As the purpose of a consortium gets closer to the marketplace, there is a concern that the cooperative structure could interfere with the decision-making process. According to Tony Holbrook, president of Advanced Micro Devices, a participant in both MCC and Sematech, "Sematech's management by committee could be a problem. It might not be as responsive to the marketplace as a company."[288]

Sematech's focused and limited goal, to provide a model fabrication plant where members can learn fast and efficient production techniques, should give it some advantages over cooperative efforts with broader and less well-defined objectives, such as MCC. As one observer suggested, consortia with clear and limited goals, inspired leaders, and strong industry support are much more likely to succeed than a "consortium that is just an industrial policy in a new dress" such as the proposed High Definition Television (HDTV) project.[289]

U.S. Memories, Inc.

One set of baggage hindering interfirm cooperation in manufacturing is a persistent viewpoint among U.S. companies (and public officials) that R&D and manufacturing are separate functions. According to Robert Reich, one of the more vocal promoters of interfirm collaboration, "American firms draw a sharper distinction between R&D on one side and production and marketing on the other."[290] Domestic antitrust perceptions seem to follow this outlook with their encouragement of R&D cooperation and their less clear signals on manufacturing collaboration.[291] As an example of this notion that R&D function is somehow separate and distinct from the functions of manufacturing and marketing, consider Robert Noyce's observation that Sematech, a research consortium, is "precompetitive cooperation."[292]

The Japanese, on the other hand, appear to appreciate the important interrelationship between R&D activities and production engineering/design activities. As long as American participants in R&D consortia subscribe to this view of R&D as separate from manufacturing and production, they will expect product designs or technology to emerge market or factory ready from collective research efforts. Since this is unlikely to result, one can predict a high level of disappointment. The path from innovation to market is not a smooth and linear one but is iterative. Continuous and incremental input from both researchers and production engineers, not to mention marketing specialists, is critical to the development of a successful high technology product.

Of course there is a concern that cooperation in the early stages of product development may lead to anticompetitive behavior as the product comes closer to market. Perhaps a lesson here can be gleaned from the Japanese experience. While Japanese companies are adept at interfirm collaboration, they appear to have mastered the difficulties of moving from cooperating partners on research and development to fierce competitors in the marketplace.[293]

If R&D and manufacturing are importantly intertwined, and if, as mentioned in the beginning of this chapter, industry-wide collaboration to share the staggering costs of new fabrication plants is a potential solution to some of the industry's troubles, then efforts to establish industry cooperation in manufacturing would be expected. True to expectations, some members of the semiconductor industry began efforts to form a cooperative manufacturing venture in the summer of 1989. Dubbed U.S. Memories, Inc., the effort was spearheaded by seven companies: Digital Equipment Corp., Hewlett-Packard, IBM,

Intel, LSI Logic, National Semiconductor, and Advanced Micro Devices, all major chip makers, users, or both.

The plan was for the original seven participants to drum up additional members to help foot the expected $1 billion cost of the shared production facility to make DRAM (dynamic random access memory) chips. Commentators noted that "it is rare, almost un-American, for U.S. manufacturers of advanced products to band together this way."[294] As another put it, "[T]he real barrier to further action is the mistrust of other companies built on years, even decades, of competition. Quite apart from possible antitrust problems, it appears easier for Motorola to bring itself to team up with Toshiba than for two U.S. competitors to share a factory."[295]

For IBM, the world's largest producer of semiconductors, the capital costs of semiconductor manufacturing were not a driving force. Of all remaining domestic DRAM producers, IBM had the most assets to draw upon for battling the Japanese. U.S. Memories offered to solve a different problem for Big Blue. For years, IBM, a large captive user, debated over selling chips, chip-making equipment, or technology to its competitors. On one hand, selling the chips, equipment, or technology would help IBM recover its massive investment in semiconductor production. On the other hand, any competitive advantages IBM might enjoy from its captive production would be lost. With U.S. Memories IBM had a way to license its technology without "actually plunging into the market."[296]

IBM's interest in the project is reflected in the fact that the seven founders of U.S. Memories designated Sanford L. Kane as president and CEO. Kane, a former vice president and twenty-seven-year veteran of IBM, had played an active role in forming Sematech.[297] Wilfred J. Corrigan, chairman and CEO of LSI Logic, was named U.S. Memories' chairman.

Kane was soon on the road trying to solicit additional support. Compaq, Tandy, and Apple, significant chip consumers, turned the group down.[298] Apple's demurrer was particularly disheartening in that the computer maker had suffered the consequences of 1988's DRAM chip shortage when it was forced to buy chips at inflated prices on the spot market to keep its production lines moving.[299] Other chip users reportedly feared that joining the consortium might offend their Japanese suppliers.[300]

The business plan for U.S. Memories, which cost each of the seven founders $50,000 each, envisioned around twenty companies together putting up $500 to $800 million,[301] with $400 million to be raised later, most likely through a public offering. Production of four-megabit chips, based on IBM technology, would begin in 1991.

Seven months after its formation, U.S. Memories was in trouble.[302] Failure to win the support of any additional backers made the project untenable. The decision to fold the effort came at a meeting in Dallas on January 10, 1990, that included the seven founders as well as representatives from potential investors, AT&T and NCR Corporation. According to one report, Hewlett-Packard, one of the original seven founders, announced that it wished to withdraw from the project at the Dallas meeting.[303] Hewlett-Packard had become concerned that a substantial portion of their future chip purchases would have depended on U.S. Memories. As Hewlett-Packard's manager of corporate planning put it, "We'd be betting our company on a new company that hadn't even started yet."[304]

The lessons to be learned from U.S. Memories' failure will be the subject of debate for many years.[305] For some the collapse marked a retreat of U.S. chipmakers from a market they once dominated. Others, such as Gordon E. Moore, current chairman of Intel, felt that the failure was "not a very strong endorsement of getting together to solve problems."[306] W. J. (Jerry) Sanders III, the outspoken chairman of Advanced Micro Devices, was more directly critical of his compatriots when he said, "The consortia idea is too large a leap for the entrepreneurial mentality."[307]

Conversely, U.S. Memories critics, most notably T. J. Rodgers, CEO of Cypress Semiconductors, felt vindicated. Some expressed mundane concerns regarding a consortium with unproven ability to accomplish its objectives. The sheer size of the effort alone was enough to cause pause in the cautious. The consortium had planned to produce 8 percent of the world's memory chips by the mid-1990s.[308] For others the opposition was more philosophical and deep-seated. According to Rogers, "Consortia are damping our entrepreneurial environment."[309] Perhaps Charles Ferguson, an entrepreneurship scholar at MIT, had the best response to this notion of the fiercely independent entrepreneur when he said, "I'd like to see him two years after Fujitsu lines him up in its sights."[310]

8

Learning to Think Together: Lessons for Cooperative R&D Management

From the accumulated information on cooperative R&D ventures, what can be determined that may be of value to managers of these enterprises, policymakers who may wish to promote or prosecute them, and potential participants? As with any research into a relatively new and rapidly evolving subject, the data seem to generate more questions than they answer. Nevertheless, some interesting and potentially useful insights regarding the management of collaborative R&D activities are possible. This chapter is devoted to the interpretation of the information collected and a discussion of its implications.

Some of the findings indicate areas in which further data collection and analysis would be most productive. Other findings vividly demonstrate the complexities of managing R&D cooperation among equal, active, and competing partners, and the problems associated with trying to make simplified models and theories fit ambiguous and complex reality. There is no final theory or single model dictated by the data for the proper management of a strategic R&D alliances. Rather, the information tells an ongoing story of the evolution in managerial skill and experience necessary to cope with cooperative activity to achieve competitive strategic objectives.

THE COMMUNICATION SYSTEM

Unlike other cooperative ventures where the purpose might be to produce physical goods, the main objective of a research and development joint venture is the creation and dissemination of information. This fundamental difference in the nature of such collaborative efforts magnifies the importance of the communication system and strategies adopted by the organization to deal with the flows of information when compared to a joint venture dealing basically in hard goods.

There are three main information pathways that are part of a cooperative R&D venture's communication system: (1) the flow of information from the venture participants to nonparticipants, (2) the flow of information within the joint venture, and (3) the flow of information from the joint venture to the contributing participants. (See Figure 8.1 below for a diagram of the three information pathways.) Each of the three can be analyzed separately but they also can be consolidated into an overarching conceptual framework, an overall communication system and strategy.

Generally the first to evolve, although not necessarily first in importance, is the flow of information from the joint venture or its sponsors to the general public, the public relations strategy. The reason this information pathway is usually the first to appear is that it often forms a critical function in recruiting potential collaborators during the formation phase.

The second part of the overall communication system deals with the flow of information between the participants within the context of the cooperative venture. This can be extremely important in that the various participants may not all be privileged to receive the same information. A difficulty also arises in access to information and knowledge brought by the players to the collaborative activity. Since it is highly unlikely that all partners will be equal in this regard, a crucial management task will be to determine what is shared with whom and how. Claims or aspirations to proprietary information only complicate the situation further.

The third part of the communications system is perhaps both the most important and the most difficult. This is the flow of information from the cooperative R&D venture to the participating stakeholders, the most important part of which is the transfer of the developed technology.

Although each of the three main information flows can be seen as having distinct strategies, these sub-strategies are interwoven into an

Figure 8.1
Three Elements of the Communications System for a Cooperative R&D Venture

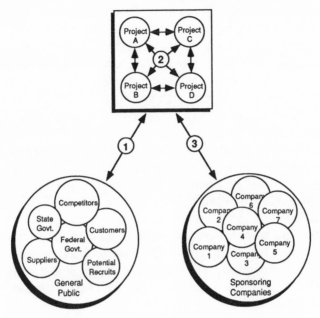

(1) Flow of information to and from the cooperative R&D venture and the general public and non-contributing constituencies.

(2) Flow of information within the cooperative R&D venture among the various programs and projects.

(3) Flow of information to and from the cooperative R&D venture and its contributing sponsors.

encompassing communications system strategy, which in turn is an integral part of the overall joint venture strategy.

1. THE FLOW OF INFORMATION FROM THE JOINT VENTURE TO NON-PARTICIPANTS AND THE GENERAL PUBLIC

Chronologically, the first element of a cooperative R&D's communication strategy that usually appears is the one concerning the flow of information from the cooperative venture to the general public. What eventually becomes a public relations strategy that in turn becomes an element of an overall communications strategy is usually not developed as a conscious strategy but grows out of a number of public relations policies adopted by the joint venture and its sponsors during the critical start-up period.

For many cooperative R&D efforts, maintaining a high degree of public visibility might be important to enhance recruitment of sponsoring companies or research scientists. In the glow of this publicity the public awareness of the particular cooperative venture is quickly raised. For others, where recruitment of a sponsor or scientific talent is less a problem or has already been achieved, more secrecy would be appropriate, if only to prevent competitive targets from rallying in response.

Although a collaborative venture may embrace an open-door policy of communication and public relations during this initial phase of operations, it should be remembered that the information that freely flows to the public may have to be of a limited nature. For cooperative R&D efforts where the purpose to is develop information and knowledge that might be of competitive importance, total operation in the sunshine is not possible. It is a fine line to walk between enough information to enhance recruitment and image, and enough secrecy to protect the proprietary results of the R&D collaboration and not tip off the competition.

How MCC Found a Balance

As an example of this dilemma, some MCC member companies expressed concern regarding the level of publicity MCC generated during the start-up period and the issue was debated at the board level. It seems that some members had hoped that MCC would be a hush-hush "skunk works" type of operation. But despite disagreement regarding how much information should flow from MCC to the general public, there was agreement on the need to keep certain information confidential. In particular, the research conducted at MCC would be kept under wraps.

This difference of opinion among participating companies is not surprising when one examines how differently the various companies handled the release of MCC-related information to the public. Some of the companies such as AMD were fairly open about their activities. Others played it much closer to the vest. In an effort to accommodate the extremes, MCC adopted a policy that left the disclosure decision on certain information to the individual shareholders. For example, MCC did not originally disclose which companies participated in which programs, nor did MCC release information about shareholder program costs.

The coverage of MCC in the press during the strategy of high visibility can be divided into a number of fairly distinct stages. The first stage covers most of 1982, and the press coverage mostly consisted of relatively short stories about MCC, about how MCC was organized. Many were no more than announcements that a new consortium was forming, and many emphasized the theme around which the cooperative entity coalesced: U.S. companies join to meet Japanese challenge in computer technology.

The Justice Department's tentative approval of MCC in December of 1982 marked the beginning of the new stage in press coverage and a number of publications ran detailed stories about MCC.[311] Again, a common theme was: MCC — America's answer to the Japanese. During this same period, from January to May of 1983, MCC was searching for a suitable location for its operations. Not surprisingly, during this period there were also a significant number of articles on the site selection. Inman's continued visibility and accessibility also meant that there was still a steady, even if not so frequent as before, stream of press coverage that focused on Inman.

After the site selection had been made, MCC experienced a third stage in its relationship with the press. As a direct fallout of the site selection process a number of articles appeared, asking, "Why Austin?" These were quickly followed by a spate of articles on Austin and its efforts to woo and win MCC specifically, and on the battle among cities for high-technology businesses in general.[312]

Press coverage seemed to hit a slump in the early summer of 1983. In response, Inman decided to make even more frequent public appearances and to grant numerous interviews during August, September, and October. As a result of this effort, press coverage picked up and articles began to appear that examined Inman's personal outlook, his view of MCC, his vision of the future.[313] The reason that press coverage was seen as important during the early fall of 1983 was that the creation and communication of an MCC image was seen as a vital element of the recruiting process that was currently under way. With little more than shareholder commitment, a strong, well-known CEO, and a skeleton administrative staff, MCC was out head-hunting for some of the top talent in the computer technology field to head the seven programs.

When the program directors were publicly revealed in a press conference on April 9, 1984, the critical importance of the public relations strategy to the personnel strategy changed. Although the high-visibility policy continued, it was not as important or intense after the program directors joined. The world-class reputation of the program directors was a boost to MCC's overall reputation and eased the need to establish and augment the organization's image through public relations activity. Additional personnel recruiting could now be based on the talent and reputation of researchers already assembled.

With the announcement of the program directors the locus of the press coverage began to shift. From late summer through early fall of 1984 there was a noticeable decline in popular press coverage and a corresponding increase in trade press attention. This change meant a change in the type of information sought from MCC. The trade press wanted more details from a business standpoint and more technical information about the programs. With regard to technology details MCC closed the door on the unrestricted free flow of information.[314] But it was not possible nor perhaps desirable for MCC to barricade the technical information pathway completely.

Many of the researchers who had joined MCC were noted authors in technical journals, and many of them fully expected to continue the practice of scientific discourse through publication. It was MCC's policy to permit publication so long as the proprietary rights of the shareholders were not jeopardized. And even if public discussion of the specific technical details regarding the programs was prohibited, researchers were permitted to give background technical information to the press.

There were three main reasons underlying MCC's strategy of keeping the technical details of the programs secret. The technical plans were still evolving and a number of people from the member companies were involved in their development. The management of MCC felt that it would be an unnecessary distraction if outside skeptics had the opportunity to criticize incomplete, evolutionary plans. Once the plans were well formed and became more publicly known, then MCC researchers would speak out in detail at scientific and technical conferences.

Although release of technical plans that were still evolving was generally restricted, MCC would sometimes test the merit of an idea in a presentation made by someone from MCC, such as a program director or a research scientist. Information about the idea was released for discussion but not in such a way that it carried the MCC stamp of approval. According to Stotesbery, this method of controlled information release was a useful method to test whether or not a particular idea had support among the scientific community, without MCC, the U.S. fifth-generation project, stepping forward and saying, "Here's what we are going to do."

The second reason for keeping the technical plans confidential had to do with the proprietary nature of the information. As the management of MCC was quick to point out, MCC was in the business of producing information at the expense and for the benefit of the shareholders. Technical information secrecy was part of MCC management's effort to make sure that proprietary material and information did not flow to those who had not paid for it.

The last part of the reason for maintaining technical secrecy was that MCC wanted to insulate to some degree the program directors and researchers from the demands of public appearances and interviews. The top priority of the research staff was research, not public relations.

Even when a communications strategy regarding the flow of information to the general public is as well planned and managed as MCC's, problems can and will arise. For MCC the first real difficulty appeared one morning in a *New York Times* article.[315] The *Times* article, which spoke of problems and shareholder disagreements, was both a mild shock and a disappointment to Inman and the management of MCC. Although MCC was already beginning to change its communications strategy to the public, the *New York Times* article gave an extra boost to the retrenchment effort. According to William D. Stotesbery, the director of government and public affairs for MCC, the net result of the *New York Times* piece was that MCC became more sensitized to the dangers of revealing everything to the press. MCC became more careful about what information it passed to the general public and how it did so.

One of the main difficulties with managing the communications between a cooperative R&D venture and the general public can be traced to the heterogeneity of the participating companies. Member companies usually handle R&D information very differently. Some companies are very open about what they are doing and others do not release that type of information. As a consequence, MCC did not even release which companies participated in which programs, nor did it release individual dollar investments of the particular shareholders.[316] Some member companies like Advanced Micro Devices (AMD) generally maintain extremely high public profiles and continued with that policy in dealing with the press about MCC. Other companies do not wish to discuss their involvement with MCC publicly and are reluctant to discuss any R&D matters with outsiders.

It is important to note that even though there may be an official policy with regard to communication the policy will constantly evolve and change. Perhaps the best advice when it comes to dealing with the fourth estate is to clearly state those things that you choose not to discuss publicly and then make it clear that you will not talk about those issues. As for subjects not so identified, it is better to deal openly. Subterfuge and deception is a poor policy and companies or organizations that try it quickly find out that it does not work well.

Maintaining an announced shield of secrecy around certain subjects, such as the results of the research efforts, also has benefits. Some secrecy can help create a "skunk works" mystique around the cooperative R&D effort that can be beneficial to the organization's image. Secrecy, and the mystique surrounding secrecy, can be of benefit with regard to personnel recruiting and building a special esprit de corps among the research staff.

2. THE FLOW OF INFORMATION WITHIN THE VENTURE

In order to make MCC more attractive to prospective members during its start-up period, participation in the technology programs was set up cafeteria style. The shareholders were free to pick and choose from among the seven programs when they joined. There was no requirement that each company had to participate in each program. Although the bylaws called for each shareholder to join at least one of the seven programs, there was a wide range in program participation among the various companies.[317] Some joined the minimum one program, others signed up for two, three, or four programs.

This early organizational decision to permit shareholder-determined participation was the cause of later organizational difficulties. Inman often remarked that the one clear lesson that was learned during the start-up phase of MCC was that the shareholders should have been required to join MCC as a whole rather than pick and choose from among the programs. As a consequence of this cafeteria-style membership, management of MCC in some ways was more akin to the management of seven joint ventures rather than a single one.

One particular difficulty this caused had to do with the transfer of information internally within MCC. Since not all shareholders were paying for the development of the same information there was a need to devise organizational structures and procedures to insure that a company which had paid for a certain set of technology or information to be developed in one program did not inadvertently benefit a nonsupporting shareholder in another program.

This might not have been such a difficult task for MCC management if it were not for the fact that there were significant research synergies among the various programs. Each program director noted that there were important benefits to be gained from the various programs working together. Information that was useful in one area could be of immense help to researchers in another area. In that one of the reasons MCC was created was to eliminate duplication of effort, there was a clear need to work out a communication system among the programs that respected the proprietary nature of the information while at the same time permitting the free exchange of ideas. The difficulty in designing and operating such a communication system arose from the conflicting nature of the two elements. Mechanisms to protect proprietary information tended to restrict communications, whereas exploitation of research synergies or cross-fertilization of ideas was maximized by a nonproprietary free flow of information.

Arrangements to accommodate both of these needs developed within MCC on an ad hoc basis. One example of such an arrangement arose between the Artificial Intelligence/Knowledge Based Systems Program under Woodie Bledsoe and the VLSI CAD program under John Haney. Shortly after the two programs were under way, the two programs were trying to put together a working relationship so that certain useful information could be exchanged between the two separate programs. The hope was that an expert system developed by the Artificial Intelligence group could be made part of a computer aided design product developed by the VLSI CAD group.

Although the beginnings of a workable communications system between these two programs was in place by the summer of 1985, not all the details of just how such a system would operate have been determined. According to Dr. Bledsoe, an interesting point in the relationship will be reached when they get to the point of having a piece of technology that is ready to be licensed to the program participants and the particular technology is part of an expert software system to do certain kinds of CAD work. Determining who owns what in such a system, noted Bledsoe, may not be a trivial task.

Reflecting on how such a problem might be resolved, Dr. Bledsoe believed that there will be some recognition that the group that puts in the most effort will own the most. This in turn will require organizational systems and procedures to help document the time and effort expended by each of the cooperating programs.

To help avoid future difficulties that might arise from the internal flow of information, the ad hoc efforts of the program directors to work out informal communication networks were formalized by a set of guidelines developed by Executive Vice President Palle Smidt. Although the guidelines did not solve all dilemmas and conflicts regarding inter-program transfers of technology, they established a useful framework for solutions to be worked out. There was a strong feeling among MCC management that MCC-developed technology would be recognized as so worthwhile that the continued functioning of MCC would be the highest priority of the shareholders and that compromise and accommodation would be encouraged.

To avoid these difficulties regarding the flow of knowledge and information within a cooperative R&D venture, it is advisable to have all sponsors as equal participants. This would make the knowledge compartmentalization efforts undertaken by MCC unnecessary.

3. THE FLOW OF INFORMATION FROM THE COOPERATIVE VENTURE TO MEMBER COMPANIES

The third element of a cooperative R&D venture's communications strategy deals with the flow of information from the venture to the participating sponsoring companies. This information pathway is at the heart of the cooperative efforts operations, for this is the pathway through which technology will be transferred to the member corporations. It is critical that this technology transfer process be well understood by management of the cooperative venture as well as sponsoring companies.

One of the most important issues is the technology transfer process: How does the technology that the cooperative R&D venture's scientists and researchers develop get transferred back to the participating companies? To give an idea of the importance of this issue consider the comments made by John Rollwagen, the president of Cray Research, Inc., a supercomputer manufacturer. Cray Research was approached to join MCC along with Texas Instruments,[318] Intel, and several other companies which later decided not to join. According to Rollwagen "[MCC] really could be a yeasty place to work, but how the technology gets transferred back to the member companies is a mystery to me. There'll be a technological exchange – it may be positive for the country, but it won't be for the individual companies. Our system is based on individuality, not a sense of community as in Japan."[319]

How MCC, the pioneer cooperative R&D venture, approached this critical issue is instructive. The original concept of technology transfer was that the member companies would donate workers to MCC, and later those same workers would take the ideas and the technology back to the shareholder companies when they returned. It was also thought that the technology would be assembled into a unit or a package called the standard technology package (STP). It was envisioned that this hypothetically complete package of the technology, together with all the necessary support, would be the "product" that MCC would transfer to the contributing companies.

Regarding technology transfer in general, the management of MCC began to focus on three primary aspects: process, use, and timing. This meant that MCC management would be looking at the process by which technology is transferred, the use to which that technology will be placed, and the timing of the transfer. Inman on many occasions noted that the creation of superior technology and even its successful transfer to the participating companies would be of little matter if the shareholder companies did not use the transferred technology competitively to earn value in excess of the costs of supporting MCC. Although the charter of MCC required the shareholders to utilize the transferred technology, getting the shareholders to act accordingly was another matter.

Although an unnecessarily fettered information pathway could hinder the technology transfer process, an unrestricted flow of information to the participating companies was also seen as a threat to MCC's overall strategy. Early or premature disclosure of valuable information could bring about inequities in the distribution of the technology. Therefore, on one hand MCC management wanted the shareholders to be well informed by a continual flow of information. On the other hand, they did not want a situation to develop where every company heard everything automatically whenever it happened. The task was to design and operate a communication system that transmitted certain information to the member companies while at the same time blocking the transmission of other data.

MCC management worked out such a complex system and will be fine tuning it for years to come as more knowledge and information is created and transferred. But even in this relatively early stage, certain elements of the system are clear. For one thing, MCC has established a rule that information cannot be taken back to any company without some form of MCC permission. In essence MCC is saying to the members that the transfer of technology and information from MCC to the shareholders will not be automatic and that it is for MCC management to control the valve.

The real question for MCC management then becomes, "When and how do you let this technology and information flow back to the companies?" Part of the answer was that the flow will not be automatic. On one hand MCC management and the member companies would like a continual flow of information. This would keep the member companies well informed and up to date on progress within the research programs. On the other hand, MCC management does not want a situation where every company would be told everything that happens at MCC. It remains a tricky issue. Mechanisms, procedures, and systems to accommodate both needs must be established.

The tension is seen as particularly difficult for the liaison employees, since they are still technically working for the member companies and it is their function to communicate. Therefore, MCC management has made special efforts to inform the liaison employee that he or she is not privileged to send everything back to their sponsoring company. If all the speculations, plans, and ideas that were being considered in a research program were to go back to the member companies there is a danger that these formative concepts could be interpreted as official MCC policy. This would be disruptive since it is expected that the companies would respond with disagreements and criticisms to what is really just contingency planning.

The management of MCC recognized that it was going to be very difficult for the researchers and scientists to sort out all the complexities of the communication process. As a consequence MCC has developed training programs to help clarify the issues to its employees. This complexity is viewed as greater than that which would normally be expected for a single-entity firm of similar size.

To cite an example, Dr. Gene Lowenthal, formerly an executive at Intel and now MCC program director, said it was very different joining MCC when compared to a company such as Intel. At Intel it was a black-and-white procedure. The nondisclosure agreements were extremely straightforward and the employee contract was simple. In contrast, when he signed on with MCC the employee contract was, in his words, a small book. Much of this complexity stems from the various loyalties present. There is the loyalty to the member company. There is the loyalty to MCC. And, there is the loyalty to the research program. The potential conflict between these loyalties is something that has to be worked out and controlled.

To help untangle and manage these issues, the communication policy has been made into an ethical and cultural issue. For example, consider the situation of the liaison employees. Basically, these people are researchers and are encouraged to view themselves as such within MCC. The image of company spy is discouraged. This shifts some of the policing burden regarding the flow of information away from rigid systems, control mechanisms, and guidelines onto the individual employee. Unfortunately, this can on occasion put the liaison employee in an awkward situation.

Sometimes the liaison employees are in a position where they feel as if they have to choose between their mother and their father. As one program director put it, "It is like mom saying don't tell this to dad and then you feel guilty because you feel that they have to be open with both." One suggested solution to this dilemma is to have each company send a letter to its liaison employees explicitly stating that it is all right in certain circumstances for the liaison "to wear the MCC hat" alone.

MCC management feels that open and informed communication with the member companies can be maintained even while restricting the flow of certain data. One method of doing this is to communicate everything but the crucial details about a project or operation. By keeping the key details or facts confidential the shareholders can be kept abreast of MCC's work without the danger of compromising proprietary rights in the technology.

In an effort to cut through this Gordian knot of complexity regarding technology transfer the board of directors formed an ad hoc committee to specifically look into the issue. At the board meeting of MCC shareholders on September 5, 1984, technology transfer was discussed. One of the difficulties that arose regarding the use of the transferred MCC technology involved the licensing fees that would be due to MCC from the shareholder company using MCC-developed technology. At the meeting the concept of a paid-up license was proposed by some of the members for consideration. What this would mean was that once a license had been bought the user could use it without limit during the time period covered. Under this type of licensing arrangement a company would pay the same fee for using the technology in one or in one million products.

This paid-up licensing concept was a departure from the original licensing system agreed to by MCC's founders. In the bylaws, licensing was to be handled on an ongoing basis.[320] Once a company received the technology it paid a continuing royalty, with an amount equal to three times the company's investment being treated as prepaid royalty. What this meant was that each participating company using the technology received from MCC would incur a royalty obligation to MCC for each use, and that each participating company would be credited with prepaid royalties equal to three times its contribution to the program developing the technology.

The concept of the paid-up license had been opposed from the start by Control Data Corporation for a number of reasons. First, the representatives of Control Data felt that it was not fair among the small and the large users. It was argued that a large user could make more use of the technology than a smaller one; therefore, the paid-up license which would cost the same to a small and large user would be more beneficial to the large company that had more opportunities to use the technology. Second, opposition was voiced because it was felt that paid-up licenses reduced the potential pay-out pool for individual contributors. And third, it was suggested that the paid-up license concept would reduce royalties to fund new programs at MCC.

The ad hoc committee apparently did not agree with the argument that royalties would be significantly reduced by going from a paid-up usage of three times the participant's investment to a fully paid-up concept. Yet despite the ad hoc committee's endorsement of a fully paid license, there was a not unanimous consent, and because the bylaws required unanimous vote at the time, the licensing proposal did not pass. The bylaws were subsequently amended and a unanimous vote would not now be required.

Inman and the management of MCC were not disinterested parties in this debate among the shareholders, although the focus of concerns was somewhat different. At the meeting Inman stressed three points with regard to the licensing fee issue. First, the minutes of the board meeting reflected Inman's strong conviction that rapid transfer of technology from MCC to the shareholders was most important and that any licensing/royalty plan must not impede this rapid dissemination. Second, he made the point that the shareholders might be reluctant to incorporate the MCC technology into products if the royalty payments could not be determined with some reasonable accuracy at the outset. His final observation was that any licensing plan adopted would need to fulfill the commitment that MCC had made to the senior technical personnel, namely, that they would receive a significant long-term payoff for any outstanding technology that they had invented.

This issue of how to structure the licensing of MCC-created technology illustrates the difficulties associated with managing a strategic alliance among diverse strategy-pursuing entities. At the heart of the technology transfer issue are the managerial problems associated with the production, measurement, movement, and protection of intellectual property. How does an organization best create, enhance, document, control and transfer a product that has little or no physical attributes? Managers are well versed in inventory and production systems for physical property. Intangible property is another matter. In an effort to deal with some of the problems of managing intellectual property new systems must be instituted that can protect that which is confidential and proprietary.

Unfortunately, a policy of strict confidentiality can be in potential conflict with the researchers' desire to publish their work in professional journals. This may be important to many of the researchers and play a significant role during the personnel recruitment process. Trying to balance these two potentially conflicting policies can be difficult. To accomplish this segregation of proprietary from nonproprietary materials, the model used for years by Bell Labs regarding publications by its researchers may be useful. Bell Labs gives the professional staff the right to publish the results of their research, but at the same time establishes systems of prepublication review and editing that endeavor to exclude the publication of certain confidential and proprietary information.

One useful step in the technology transfer process is a readiness evaluation of each sponsoring company.[321] The evaluation requires a critical examination of each participating company's preparations to receive and use the cooperatively developed technology. If nothing else, such a comparative evaluation might spur slackers into action.

It is important to note that though a "technology package" may remain as a part of the technology transfer concept for accounting purposes, in that transfer of the package might start the clock with regard to the licensing, by the time a company receives a completed technology package, the company should already have a substantial part of the technology.

The licensing situation may be further complicated by the fact that a company may begin utilizing the technology even though a complete package has not yet been transferred on the books. With a continual flow of information and knowledge, technology transfer will be hard to control and measure. Part of the problem stems from the fact that it is difficult to assess the proprietary nature of the sponsors' independent research and development. It is very likely that a participating company will mingle cooperatively derived technology with proprietary technology generated by the company. Close examination of utilization of the technology may be precluded due to the proprietary and confidential nature of any technology added by the member company.

To help manage, measure, and control the transfer of technology, a receptor organization within the member company is suggested. The receptor organization is then responsible for transferring the technology to the appropriate operating division or unit within the shareholder company. There were four possible links in this transfer chain. First, there is the cooperative R&D venture. Second, there is a technology transfer agent. Third, there is an individual or organization within the sponsoring company serving as the primary integrator. And fourth, there is a developer user group, individual, or group of individuals within the sponsor.

The technology transfer agent plays an essentially passive role in the process. This individual or group receives the information and then sends it on, fanning it out to the other groups where necessary. Basically, the technology transfer agent acts as a switchyard, making sure that the right information gets passed on to the right channel. The role of the primary integrator is to be involved in the documentation of the technology, making sure that the technology works, a more active role than the technology transfer agent. The function of the developer/user is to integrate the technology into a product.

The long range success of any cooperative R&D venture will depend on how well technology gets transferred. The extent of each sponsoring company's preparations to receive cooperatively developed technology will mark the difference between effective technology transfer and subsequent utilization, or wasted funds and effort. This in turn will affect how each member company views the cost/benefit assessment of continued cooperation.

One concern is that the vigor and vitality of the technology transfer process may diminish over time without active and creative management. This is particularly true as contact points to the sponsoring company start to weaken over time. The transfer agent or liaison employee comes to the cooperative venture with an established power base and a network of contacts in the member company. The longer the liaison employee is away from the shareholder company, the less powerful these connections become. In some ways the transfer agents and primary integrators have to sell the technology to the companies. Making the cooperative venture an integral part of the sponsoring company's planning and culture is one way to alleviate the decline in communication that could accompany the passage of time and physical separation.

It is important to remember that technology transfer is an ongoing process. The need for support prior to and during the actual transfer is well recognized, but there is a need for post-transfer support as well.

A number of methods for the post-transfer support of transferred technology are possible. One would be the construction of a pilot plant or facility near the cooperative R&D venture where the sponsoring companies would send employees to learn how to use the technology. Another method would be the establishment of a technology consulting organization within the venture, which would assist the member companies after a technology transfer on a fee basis. A third method would encourage the member companies to establish receptor organizations within their companies and/or locate on-site support offices near the cooperative R&D venture so that contact could be both frequent and convenient.

Although there is a recognized need for establishing some method to support technology transfer there is often not enough money to fully

Figure 8.2
Possible Post-Transfer Support Systems for the Transfer of Technology

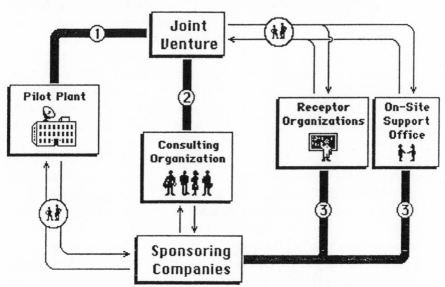

fund both the research to develop the technology and the support systems to assist in transferral and learning processes. A critical management task is to find the proper balance of emphasis between research and subsequent support given the resource constraints.

The Motivation to Cooperate

In this chapter a number of findings, suggestions and observations are covered. In seeking an answer to the question of what motivates the companies to cooperate in joint R&D activities, it was discovered that participant motivation can be viewed as having various layers, like an onion. At the broadest level, there is the common motivation to become more competitive through cooperative action. Of course, there are wide differences in what each company perceives as the competitive benefit from cooperation.

The issue to be discussed is how the motivation or motivations for cooperation are translated into organizational structure and systems. Because most coopeartive R&D ventures face multiple and diverse motivations on the part of its sponsors, the development of an organization to accommodate these participant desires is both incremental and complex. As action is taken to address participant heterogeneity on one level, consequences appeared at another. For example, a decision to structure the collaborative organization with cafeteria-style program participation such as with MCC, vastly complicated the management of information and knowledge within the organization. As a result additional structures and systems may have to be devised and implemented to deal with internal information management.

The third important area of emphasis is the critical role of management in establishing and maintaining interfirm cooperation. In developing an organization to deal with the diversity of motivation to cooperate among the participant companies, cooperative venture executives face a number of constraints. First, the cooperative venture has to be effective not only at creating the desired technology, but also in transferring that technology to the sponsoring companies. Some cooperative R&D ventures, such as Sematech, have government participation similar to that seen in Japanese interfirm collaboration. This can help with regard to organizational legitimacy and purpose. Additional factors, such as an ambiguous lifespan and diverse competitive focus among the participants further complicates the development of organizational purpose for collective R&D efforts.

As a consequence of these forces that stem from lack of sponsor homogeneity, joint R&D venture executives are often prompted to seek and maintain organizational independence. To establish and maintain interfirm cooperation, despite increased independence from the sponsors, forces the cooperative venture management to devote careful attention to three distinct but related areas: sponsor contribution, creation of benefits from the contributions, and transfer of benefits to the sponsors.

THE EVOLUTION OF ORGANIZATIONAL PURPOSE

In taking action that will increase the perceived value of cooperation, the joint venture executive can engage in activities that either affect the costs associated with collaboration or the benefits to be derived from it. One particular item that has an important impact on just how a cooperator will assess the benefits flowing from cooperation is the purpose of the collaborative venture. A cooperative enterprise may be be extremely effective in pursuing a specific purpose, but if that purpose is not consistent with or complementary to the purposes sought by the individual cooperators, then the perceived benefits, and therefore the value of cooperation, will be less when compared to collaborative action where there is a consensus of purpose.

The role of organizational purpose and how it has been stressed by a number of researchers and authors is important for the successful management of an enterprise.[322] Likewise, defining an organization's purpose has been long cited as a key executive function.[323] Building on these insights regarding single-participant enterprises, one can argue that defining purpose is significant for multifirm enterprises as well. Although in many ways analogous to the situation facing executives in single-participant organizations, the development of organizational purpose for a collaborative R&D venture, involving separate, strategy-pursuing firms, is complicated by the presence of multiple participants and the various (and often conflicting) objectives of the independent collaborators.

For example, the original purpose envisioned for MCC was that held by William Norris, then president of Control Data Corporation.[324] In Norris's mind, interfirm cooperation was viewed as part of the solution to some of the difficulties his company, and others similarly situated, faced. A cooperative venture would help solve some of the problems computer companies like his were encountering in competing with Japanese firms in the marketplace. Moreover, such difficulties were projected to worsen in the future. In this original concept of organizational purpose, the cooperative activity was to strengthen the competitive position of the domestic computer manufacturers in their battle against the foreign enterprises, not to mention domestic competitors such as IBM. Since one of the main battlegrounds in the computer marketplace centers on the manufacture of the semiconductor chips that are at the heart of the hardware and since the semiconductor manufacturers were also facing stiff foreign competition, these companies were seen as natural allies to the effort and were invited to join in the collaboration.

When one examines the companies that attended the original planning meeting for MCC at Orlando, Florida, in February of 1982, the list reflects the two main types of companies originally seen as potential beneficiaries of this type of cooperative action: the computer hardware manufacturers and the component (semiconductor) manufacturers. These are two different categories of companies that faced different, yet not necessarily incompatible, situations. In fact, the two industry groups were importantly related. The computer hardware manufacturers depended on low-cost, high-quality chips to construct their computer equipment, and most enjoyed some degree of captive semiconductor manufacturing. Yet despite the common ground both groups shared, there were important differences, not the least of which was firm size.

As was discussed in the chapter on MCC the corporate size differences of the MCC participants is quite substantial. Consequences of this size heterogeneity can be seen in the organizational structure adopted by MCC. The decision by MCC founders to embrace cafeteria-style program participation in part reflects the differing resources available to MCC members. The cafeteria-style program participation also reflects another aspect of the cooperators' heterogeneity, namely, the lack of common motivation for cooperation.

This initial diversity of shareholder companies increased as MCC matured and new members joined. As MCC expanded from the original ten members to twenty-one, and then experienced membership changes as mergers and departures took their toll, two additional industry groups became apparent among the MCC participants, aerospace and conglomerates. The companies in these two groups further exacerbated the size range among MCC member companies, with the companies in these latter two industry groups experiencing annual sales revenues greater than nearly all firms in the original two industry groups.

The inter-cooperator tensions arising from lack of cooperator homogeneity, such as those that posed difficulties for MCC management regarding defining and formulating organizational purpose, can be traced to other sources as well as those listed above. For example, the competitive pressures placed upon the participants by marketplace competition will not be the same for all. Some information will be more competitively significant to some sponsors than to others. This dilemma was faced by some of the CIIT contributors who found themselves contributing to research into chemicals produced by competitors. The relative strengths of companies in the domestic and international marketplace can range widely, as well as the value of research into specific arenas.

There are also differences among cooperative venture participants that derive from the variations in use to which the developed technology will be put. To cite an example from the MCC experience, consider the mainframe computer manufacturers and the aerospace companies. The mainframe computer manufacturers are in the business of designing and building complete hardware/software configurations that they then sell to their customers. According to MCC executives, the aerospace companies, on the other hand, have a broader "systems view" of their product, and microelectronics is but a part of this larger system. This difference in viewpoint has manifested itself in the desire of the mainframe manufacturers to receive MCC technology in more complete packages, along the lines originally envisioned regarding technology transfer.[325] In contrast, the aerospace companies that can more readily plug MCC technology into their existing products are more anxious to receive MCC-developed technology in small bits and pieces that they can work into their systems.

The Lack of Motivational Homogeneity

The first question that needs to be answered is whether companies should pursue interfirm cooperation as a means to achieve their objectives, given all the complications. From the prior literature discussed earlier in Chapter 2 a number of possible motivational categories that could be applicable are suggested.[326] For example, cooperation as a means to reduce risk has been cited by a number of researchers as an important motivation for joint ventures.[327] Based on this list derived from the prior literature and further elaborated upon by information obtained from executives of cooperative R&D ventures and their sponsoring companies, a more comprehensive list of motivational categories developed. The reasons the companies might find interfirm cooperation attractive can be grouped into eight motivational categories. The eight are shown in Figure 8.3.

Figure 8.3
Eight Motivational Categories

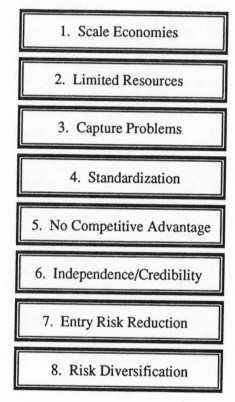

1. Scale Economies

2. Limited Resources

3. Capture Problems

4. Standardization

5. No Competitive Advantage

6. Independence/Credibility

7. Entry Risk Reduction

8. Risk Diversification

1. Cooperation as a Way to Attain Scale Economies

Achievement of scale economies is often an important element of a individual company's motivation to participate in a cooperative venture, but there is an important limitation to scale economies as a motivating force for corporations. If the projected benefits from the cooperative effort are seen as yielding significant improvements in competitiveness it is unclear that a corporation would want to share these benefits with potential competitors unless the scope of the investment was so great as to exceed the resources of the individual participant. But because individual corporate resources vary from company to company the "power" of this motivating category will differ. For example, the VLSI project in Japan, an earlier collective research and development effort in advanced semiconductor technology, changed the relative market positions of the participants.[328] As a direct consequence of the cooperative venture some companies improved their competitive position vis-a-vis other participating companies, and for some their relative competitive strength was weakened. For the companies with more limited resources the allure of cooperation to attain scale effects was greater than for companies more favorably situated.

2. Cooperation As a Method to Permit a More Efficient Use of Some Limited Resource

The second motivation category is also related to the attainment of scale economies but differs from the first in important ways. First of all, it encompasses more than those situations where there is difficulty in amassing the resources (generally financial) necessary to achieve efficient operations, but instead reflects a shortfall or limitation in access to a particular necessary resource. Secondly, the limited resource may or may not be scale sensitive. To cite an example that illustrates both points, in certain "frontier" R&D projects such as those at MCC, the resource constraint is not money needed to hire top-flight talent but rather the people themselves, in the form of trained scientists and researchers. This was the situation facing the Japanese VLSI project regarding expertise in working with crystals of exotic materials and facing the chemical industry regarding trained toxicologists when it formed the Chemical Industry Institute of Toxicology.[329] This is currently the situation facing MCC regarding experts in artificial intelligence and other highly specialized fields.

3. Cooperation to Facilitate Individual Investment in the Development of a Product That Is Not Readily Owned by Those Investing in Its Creation

Companies are naturally reluctant to make investments if the results are difficult to "capture" or "own." For example, investment that yields improvements in personnel skills rather than an actual material product are less likely to be funded, since the investing corporation has less ownership or control over the investment output, in this case, people. Because of this dilemma, it makes sense for the total class of potential beneficiaries to cooperate in conducting the effort. As an example, witness the formation of cooperative ventures like the Semiconductor Research Corporation[330] and the Council for Chemical

Research[331] which seek to develop qualified specialists in much-needed disciplines without having an individual corporation run the risk of funding its competitors' training.

Another set of examples in this category would be investments in basic, or fundamental, research. Since this type of research often results in ideas and concepts that quickly spread (and whose spread is difficult if not impossible to legally contain) cooperative efforts in this area are also attractive. One of the missions of MCC is to develop talent and technology that is difficult for the investors to completely capture.

A third set of examples in this category are those investments in which the ownership or control of the investment output has been curtailed. As an example, TOSCA requires that certain discoveries regarding toxicological effects of workplace chemicals be publicly disclosed so that rapid dissemination can take place. A cooperative venture would be useful to counteract the disincentive to invest. Such situations have spawned cooperative ventures such as the Chemical Industry Institute of Toxicology and the Health Effects Institute.[332]

Interfirm cooperation of this type should be relatively stable but might experience difficulties from "free riders" who stand to benefit from the cooperative R&D efforts without having to foot the bill. For this type of cooperative venture the recruitment net should be cast widely to include all potential beneficiaries and continued participation assured through long-term member commitments.

4. Cooperation as a Vehicle to Achieve Uniformity or Standardization

If it is clear that there is a competitive advantage in having complementary technology, there are two methods to assure this uniformity. One is to achieve a monopoly or dominant status and thereby dictate the standard to the marketplace. The other is to engage in a cooperative venture to assure compatibility or uniformity. To cite one example, in the telecommunications industry various devices must be able to communicate with each other. For many years Bell Labs and Western Electric through the power of the AT&T monopoly provided the necessary system uniformity and standardization. The uncertainty (and opportunity) regarding the role these entities can perform following the antitrust suit settlement has prompted other corporations to form cooperative ventures aimed at achieving some degree of compatibility and standardization. In the PBX field Sperry Univac-

Northern Telecom, IBM-Rohm, and Ericsson-Honeywell are all illus-trative examples.[333]

Evidence of this motivational category can be found in cooperative ventures between computer manufacturers and component suppliers. The recent talk of interfirm collaboration in the development of High Definition Television (HDTV) is another example. One alternative would be vertical integration, but the resources required and the scarcity of certain critical talent would be restrictive. Although inter-firm collaboration of this sort can be relatively stable, in a fast-moving industry efforts to set standards or establish uniform practices can be viewed by some as hindering rather than assisting progress. And there is always the destablizing possibility that the burdens and benefits of any standard selected will fall disproportionately on the contributing sponsors.

5. Cooperation to Develop or Produce a Product That Is Mandated or Required but Does Not Yield a Competitive Advantage

If investment is required because of a need to develop foundation technology or because of legal, moral, or ethical standards and the outcome of the investment itself will not produce competitive benefits in excess of costs, then there is a strong impetus to seek out other corporations under the same compulsion in an attempt to pool re-sources and share results. Examples in this category are cooperative activities relating to pollution control or employee health and safety.[334] This category can be contrasted with the third motivational category in which the investment output has value but that value cannot be readily captured. In this category are investments in which the output can be owned or controlled but does not have immediate competitive value. Companies already in a marketplace would be likely candidates for a cooperative venture that spreads the costs of an investment they each have to make but yields little or no individual competitive advantage. Likewise, there would be reluctance to permit potential entrants to share in the fruits of such a cooperative venture, since even a competitively valueless investment can still serve as a barrier to entry. Only those who have already paid the price of entry will be seen as attractive partners.

Although this motivation does not raise potential partners' fears of proprietary loss, it also makes it more difficult for the contributing sponsors to seriously promote the cooperative activity. It is a cruel fact that competitively important activities will take precedence over noncompetitive ones. In fact, the motivation may manifest itself as cooperation to minimize costs, as was argued by the government when it attacked cooperation by the automakers in the Smog Conspiracy.[335]

6. Cooperation as a Method to Maintain Independence or Credibility

In certain conflict situations, investments that seek to examine and resolve the subject matter of the controversy will often be more valuable if both sides to the controversy make a joint investment in the examination project. For example, R&D conducted by the automobile makers regarding the health effects of auto emissions is not likely to have a high level of credibility with certain environmental groups no matter how well the actual research is done. In such circumstances a cooperative venture, such as the Health Effects Institute, that includes other interested parties can be particularly attractive.[336] This category would also encompass projects that are subject to participatory demands by groups potentially affected.

In connection with MCC, independence and credibility was also cited as an important motivational force. Independence of the collective effort can facilitate cooperative R&D even though the participants remain fierce competitors regarding the products using the technology developed through cooperation. Additionally, independence and credibility is cited by MCC officials as easing the problem of attracting scarce talent, the motivation addressed in category two.

Of course, success in achieving independence from the sponsor brings problems of continued support. Corporate and R&D budgets are tight, and outside activities, particularly those exhibiting a great deal of independence from the paymaster, are likely targets for savings. This even seems to be true of the government as a cooperative R&D venture participant. Budget-cutting officials at OMB have reportedly advocated cutting the federal government's part of Sematech funding.

7. Cooperation as a Means to Reduce the Costs or Risks Associated with an Entry or Strategic Movement

Firms contemplating a business entry into a new endeavor or a strategic movement in an older one can often reduce the associated costs or risks by cooperating with others. The risk or cost reduction from cooperation occurs because of the differing circumstances of the participants. Reducing risks or costs of entry or strategic movement can be accomplished by cooperation with firms that are already favor-

ably positioned. The Kodak-Matsushita and the General Motors–
Toyota cooperative ventures are two significant examples of this type
of cooperation.[337] For example, in the GM-Toyota joint venture, GM
wants to develop small-car manufacturing expertise, a skill of Toyota,
and Toyota wants to learn about automobile manufacture in the
United States, an area of GM expertise.[338] By cooperating, each
partner can "purchase" skill or knowledge possessed by the other
partner, and since the "selling" partner has already fully paid for
acquiring the skill or knowledge in the first place, the "buying" partner
should be able to purchase at a lower cost when compared to *de novo*
or independent action. The difficulties appear when one of the partners acquires the strategically sought skill or knowledge before the
other and the incentive to continue cooperating disappears.

Because of the disparate strategic starting positions of the participants in cooperative ventures such as MCC and Sematech the importance of this motivational category varies among the sponsors. Some
companies trying to reposition themselves in a dynamic marketplace
view membership as a low-cost way to acquire important technology.
Others look to cooperation as a lower-cost route to help them achieve
a more important position in the marketplace. The difficulties experienced by U.S. Memories in trying to forge a collaborative enterprise
may in part be traced to the differing strategic positions of the participants, with some seeing themselves as more favorably situated when
compared with their potential partners and therefore standing to gain
relatively less.

8. Cooperation to Permit Risk Diversification or Risk Sharing

Often a firm wishes to diversify its risk by making a larger number
of smaller investments. By placing more, although smaller, bets, the
riskiness of investments can be averaged out, thereby eliminating
some of the downside risk in exchange for some of the upside opportunity. Mining and drilling companies often engage in cooperative
exploration to diversify the risks involved.[339] In some situations such
cooperation may be seen as insurance in which a class of "at risk"
entities are protected against cataclysmic change in circumstance. For
example, R&D among competitors may insure, with minimal individual investment, that none makes an independent breakthrough that
would put the others at competitive disadvantage. Of course, this type
of collaboration raises broader questions of social and economic
policy in that it may eliminate the marketplace reward for innovation.

Validation of Motivational Categories

In order to test the scheme of eight motivational categories listed above, executives from members of a particularly important cooperative R&D effort, MCC, were obtained. A survey questionnaire was designed to explore the motivations of the participants to cooperate. Each respondent was asked to evaluate the importance of each of the eight motivational categories that were hypothesized to be at play in cooperative ventures. A ninth question was also asked at the suggestion of the shareholder members after the pre-survey interviews. This question asked each respondent to disclose to what extent their company decided on interfirm cooperation not because they were interested in a collaborative venture, but because it was the only way to gain access to certain desired technologies.

The results of the survey on this subject are both interesting and informative. First of all, the survey confirmed the hypothesized categories as valid in that each received support from a number of the shareholder companies. Further confirmation is provided by the fact that very few "other reasons" were given by the respondents. None of the "other reasons" endorsed by the respondents had sufficient subscribers to warrant inclusion in the list of motivational categories. Interestingly, one of the "other reasons" given by a responding company in all candor was that the company joined the cooperative R&D effort partly as a public relations move.

But even if the various companies might harbor various motivations to cooperate, one might suppose that the reasons companies engage in cooperative R&D are clear-cut. The available information indicates otherwise. It seems that the companies have joined cooperative R&D activities for a wide variety of reasons. It also appears that each company experiences multiple motivations for cooperation. This "messiness" of the companies' motivation to cooperate was demonstrated in MCC survey, since two survey questionnaires were sent to each company and there were often examples of substantial disagreement among the answers. For example, the CEO of a participating company might rate scale economies effects as very important, whereas the executive from the R&D function within the same company might rate the same category much lower. This multiplicity of motivations to collaborate is a major complication in the search for cooperative R&D venture organizational purpose.

When I first began my research into the management of cooperative R&D I had suspected that the motivation to cooperate would be less diverse among the various member companies. I had thought that the primary insight to be gained from the research data would be an association of differing organizational structures and management practices in each of the programs that would correspond to a specific and common set of motivations to cooperate shared by the participants in each program. The facts have shown a situation vastly different from that hypothesized.

Figure 8.4
Reasons Why Shareholder Companies Joined MCC

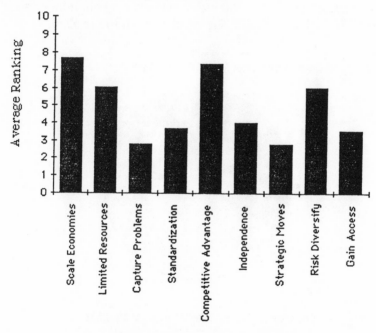

Data Source: MCC Shareholder Survey Conducted by the author. Responses
                 to Section II. Questions 1 through 9.

For example, consider the situation with regard to MCC. Figure 8.4, above, shows the reasons the various companies joined MCC when it was formed. As the chart shows, there are differences among the categories. Cooperation to achieve scale economies and cooperation to share limited resources (motivational categories one and two) were rated fairly highly. The high response to category five — cooperation to achieve something that is required but does not, in and of itself, yield significant competitive advantage—was not expected.

The precise interpretation of this finding is unclear. Perhaps it merely indicates that the real competitive advantage from the research comes as one gets closer to a marketable product, and that technology, by itself, does not offer competitive advantages until it has been assimilated into the receiving company's organization and then into products. There seems to be evidence confirming this interpretation in another section of the survey in which the respondents were asked to rank the difficulty of three tasks: (1) creating technology, (2) transferring technology, and (3) transforming the transferred technology into useful products. The latter two are overwhelmingly seen as more difficult than the first. The results are shown in Figure 8.5.

Figure 8.5
MCC Shareholder Assessment of Most Difficult Task

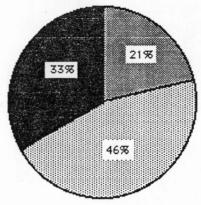

Key to Chart:

➡ Creation of useful technology by MCC.

➡ Transfer of technology from MCC to shareholder.

➡ Transformation of transferred technology by shareholder into successful product.

Data Source: MCC Shareholder Survey conducted by author. Responses to Section III. Question 4.

It should be noted that the responses in Figure 8.4 represent average responses. Although this chart shows that each motivational category held some importance to at least one shareholder company, it hides the variability in the responses. This variability within a particular category is better shown in Figure 8.6. Therefore, the task of defining and formulating an organizational purpose was complicated not only by the wide range of motivations compelling the companies to cooperate, but also by the extensive variability regarding the importance of a particular motivational category among the various shareholder companies.

It is important to note that the two most common motivational categories for joining MCC were number one (cooperation to achieve scale economies) and number five (cooperation to undertake an activity that is required but does not yield a significant competitive advantage by itself). This has significant implications for the long-term stability of MCC. Unlike cooperation to reduce the costs or risks associated with strategic moves (category seven) which becomes unstable when one of the partners achieves strategic objectives prior to the other partners, cooperation motivated by category one and category five reasons should be relatively stable. This suggests that cooperative R&D activities such as MCC can be a relatively stable form of interfirm cooperation.

For motivational category one, cooperation continues to be attractive for as long as scale economies can be achieved more economically by cooperation than by individual action. Cooperation to undertake activities that are required but are of little competitive significance continues to be attractive for as long as the activity is required. In this case the required activity is medium-term research and development. Like long-term R&D, a foundation of medium-term R&D is required for companies in fast-moving high-technology industries. Similar to the ante necessary to play in a high-stakes game, investment in research and development with time horizons greater than two or three years is required, but sufficiently distant from marketable products to have less competitive impact than shorter-term activities.

This is the type of research and development that gets a company into the game but does not necessarily make it a competitive winner. Following the card game analogy, it is the use of these "technology cards" in the play of the game that ultimately determines the payoff. Some "players" undoubtedly will make more skillful use of these technology cards and reap the benefits of their skills. Others will misplay or haphazardly discard the technology to their competitive disadvantage. Cooperation to get these technology cards in the first place, in order to be able to play the game and make use of one's

Figure 8.6
Variability in Motivation to Cooperate

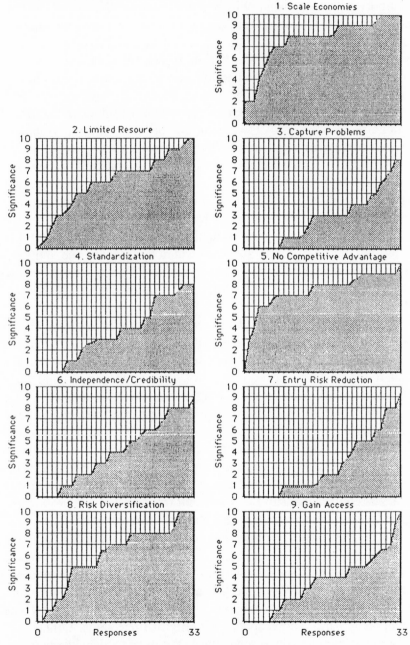

Data Source: MCC Shareholder Survey conducted by author. Responses to
Section II. Questions 1 through 10.

particular playing skills, will continue so long as it is the best method to acquire these "cards" in terms of value received.

Government Participation

The development and maintenance of a common purpose among independent cooperators in certain Japanese cooperative ventures is facilitated by active government participation.[340] In the Japanese VLSI project, the success of which led to the formation of ICOT, the fifth-generation computer project, government participation was not limited to mere strategic guidance, but also included extensive financial assistance and the operation of a research laboratory. The Defense Department plays this role in Sematech and is a significant, although perhaps not totally dependable, contributor of funding.[341] In contrast, although the Department of Defense sent "observers" to the MCC's formation meeting in Orlando in 1982, the most active United States governmental body during MCC's formative period was the Department of Justice, which was conducting an intensive antitrust examination of the venture.

In deciding on a structure for cooperative R&D, there are a number of models from which to choose. One obvious model, given that the many collaborate R&D activities have been launched in desperate defense against foreign competition, is to establish a structure along the lines of the Japanese model. One of the key players in the Japanese VLSI project and ICOT, the fifth-generation computer project, was the Japanese government. Is government participation in domestic cooperative R&D a viable option?

The Japanese model for cooperative R&D ventures such as MCC, U.S. Memories, or the Semiconductor Research Corporation, casts the government in an active role. To better assess how applicable this Japanese model of interfirm cooperation might be to the domestic strategic alliances, a section of the survey of the MCC shareholder companies devoted to a series of questions regarding government involvement in MCC is instructive.

There were four questions asked in the survey regarding this issue.[342] The first asked for the respondents' assessment of how important the technology was to the government. It was expected that the responses would indicate that the technology was of major importance, and the survey confirmed this. The second question sought to explore the shareholders' attitudes toward having the government participate in the planning process. Overall, the responses were negative. Only four respondents out of thirty-three indicated that they would be in favor of any government participation in the planning activities associated with collaborative R&D. The third question asked the shareholders' feelings toward the government as a paying member. Again the responses were overwhelmingly negative. The fourth question sought to determine how important the U.S. government was as a customer of the shareholders' products that would use technology. Again, the importance of the government as a customer was high.

The results are summarized in Figure 8.7. What the data indicate is that active government involvement in inter-firm cooperation, as is common in Japan,[343] is not likely in this country, at least not for research and development ventures such as that undertaken by MCC and involving the major U.S. companies surveyed.[344] There is a strong antigovernment sentiment, even though the technology is seen as important to the government, and even though the government is an important customer of the companies' products employing that technology.

Although this finding is probably not much of a surprise, the poignancy of the finding is reinforced when one considers the fact that many of the companies surveyed have some of the closest ties to the U.S. government of any corporations.[345] It is also interesting to note that these same companies selected a career government official to be the first CEO of MCC.[346]

One might have expected large defense contractors such as the aerospace companies to be more favorably inclined toward government involvement. The survey indicates that they were not any more positive about government participation than the other companies. One surprise in the survey was that the company most in favor of government participation, both as a potential member of cooperative R&D activities and in planning, was a highly entrepreneurial company with very little in the way of defense contracts. Perhaps this just proves the old adage that familiarity breeds contempt.

The Legitimacy of Cooperation

The absence of government participation in cooperative ventures is indicative of a lack of presumed legitimacy surrounding cooperation among competitors in the United States. This question of legitimacy is evident in the competition policy of the United States as represented in the antitrust laws. As the legal and political materials discussed in

Figure 8.7
MCC Shareholder Companies' Attitudes Toward Government Involvement in MCC

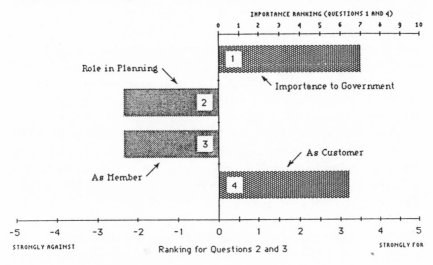

Questions Asked:

1. How important is the work being conducted by MCC to the
   United States government (or any agency thereof)?

2. Should the United States government (or any agency or
   department thereof) be allowed to participate in the planning
   process regarding future R&D programs at MCC?

3. Should the United States government be allowed to join MCC as
   a paying member?

4. How important is the United States government (or any agency
   or department thereof) as a customer of your company's
   products that will use MCC technology?

Data Source: MCC Shareholder Survey conducted by author. Responses to
             Section VII. Questions 1 through 4.

chapter 3 indicate, competition and cooperation are both integral
elements in any industry. Unfortunately, the understanding and acceptance of the legitimacy of cooperation is less than that for competition.

Domestic companies do not see themselves as part of a cooperative
network. Although enterprises may express the feeling that there is
too much competition and not enough cooperation in their industry,
the hinderances to cooperation are not merely those imposed upon
the firms by misguided politicians and lawyers. Some of the main
barriers to interfirm cooperation are internally generated. In particular, ideological resistance among executives looms large as a barrier

to effective cooperation and as such poses a problem to the cooperative venture executive in trying to forge a common organizational purpose.

One premise underlying the earlier discussion was that competition and cooperation are inextricably intertwined, and that recognition of both is necessary to fully understand business relationships and interactions. An industry is not totally competitive or totally cooperative but a combination of both, and a balance between the two or equilibrium must be maintained. Too much cooperation and cartelization can occur with sloth, high prices, and low creativity as the result. On the other hand a totally competitive market may result in firm sizes and product markets too small to enjoy scale economies or to achieve critical mass in marketing, production, and research, and may foster unproductive duplication of effort.

Finding the correct balance between the two forces is that razor's edge on which many cooperative R&D ventures must walk. One of the persistent themes that echoed throughout the preliminary meetings and discussions that took place during the conceptualization and definition phase of MCC was that the domestic microelectronics industry was marked by unnecessary and often wasteful competition, and that increased cooperation among the various actual and potential competitors could be of mutual benefit. This perceived benefit from increased cooperation was not seen as the type of benefit that a trade-restraining cartel of competitors would reap by shifting benefits from consumers to the cartel members, but instead was cooperation that was perceived to increase the competitiveness of the participants. The feeling went that if the participants could band together in the cooperative activity envisioned, then the participants would be stronger competitors against the named foreign competition of Japan and the unnamed domestic competition posed by the industry giant IBM.[347]

In an effort to better assess how the MCC shareholder companies perceived this alleged imbalance between competition and cooperation among the domestic microelectronics companies, each MCC member company was asked to evaluate the competition/cooperation balance.[348] Based on the pronouncements of the MCC founders and the discussions that took place during MCC's formation, it was expected that the MCC participants would find that the balance between competition and cooperation in the domestic microelectronics industry was not at the desired equilibrium point, but instead was skewed toward too much competition and not enough cooperation. Analysis of the responses to this question support the proposition. Figure 8.8 shows the responses of the survey participants. Although six respondents thought that the balance between competition and cooperation was correct, all the rest indicated that there was too much competition and not enough cooperation.

Figure 8.8
Respondents' Assessment of Balance between Cooperation and Competition among U.S. Companies in the Microelectronics Industry

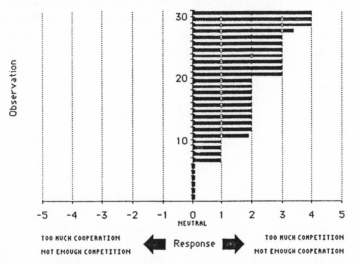

Data Source: MCC Shareholder Survey conducted by the author. Response to Section V. Question 2.

If the desired level of cooperation is not being experienced among U.S. companies in the microelectronics industry, then there must be some reasons for this failure. In order to further explore the possible reasons why the balance between competition and cooperation was perceived to be skewed against the desired level of cooperation, the shareholder participants in MCC were asked to respond to five questions.[349] The reasons that hinder U.S. companies from reaching the desired level of interfirm cooperation or from forming strategic partnerships were labeled as "barriers to cooperation."

Every respondent was asked to rank each of the five barriers to cooperation in terms of its significance on a scale of 1 to 10. The five categories were: (1) Potential antitrust liability, (2) difficulties in finding the right partner or partners, (3) difficulties in setting up a

cooperative venture, (4) difficulties in managing a cooperative venture, and (5) ideological or cultural resistance to cooperation with
actual or potential rivals. The underlying hypothesis was that all five
categories would be seen as significant barriers to cooperation. The
data confirm this general hypothesis as shown in Figure 8.9 which
shows the average response for all MCC participants.

After averaging all the individual responses, the most significant
barrier to cooperation in the eyes of the MCC participants was "difficulties in managing cooperative ventures." This finding is not unexpected. What is surprising is that the respondents, on average, ranked
potential liability under the antitrust laws as the second least significant barrier to cooperation. Only the difficulties in finding partners
was seen as less of a barrier to cooperation.

Figure 8.9
MCC Participants' Assessment of Barriers to Cooperation

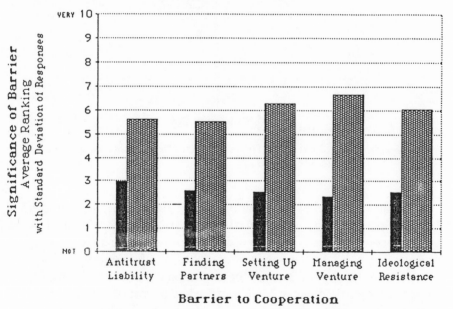

Data Source: MCC Shareholder Survey conducted by the author. Responses
to Section VI. Questions 1 through 5.

Apparently, the concern expressed by business executives and politicians regarding the antitrust laws as an important impediment to cooperative activity should be tempered by the understanding that even without the hindrance of the antitrust laws, cooperative activity in this country would be a difficult endeavor, and that the problem is not merely one of government policy but also one of managerial expertise and inclination.

Analysis of cooperative R&D ventures that have gotten off the ground lends support to the overall thrust of this book; namely, that the management of cooperative activity among competitors differs in important ways from the management of single participant organizations and that executives need to master new skills in order to successfully guide cooperative organizations. Managers of collaborative R&D seem to agree, citing difficulties in managing cooperative activity as the one of the most significant barriers to cooperation.

In addition, the identification of ideological resistance as a significant barrier to cooperation helps illustrate the contention that domestic managers are not particularly comfortable operating within the cooperative network that necessarily surrounds their individual organizations. As was pointed out in chapter three, the prevailing economic ideology in the United States emphasizes the competitive while ignoring or condemning the cooperative. The finding that ideological or cultural resistance to cooperation with competitors reinforces the point made previously that cooperative action often lacks legitimacy. This perceived lack of legitimacy in the minds of the participating executives, coupled with the absence of governmental sponsorship or encouragement, makes interfirm collaboration more challenging than in other countries (notably Japan) where this is not the case.

A Definite Lifetime for Cooperation

A limited and specified time frame can be an important element in helping to define a cooperative venture's purpose. With a definite lifespan, the goals of cooperation can be more precisely determined at the outset and incorporated into the agreement forged by the cooperators. Cooperation of ambiguous and indefinite duration may also be symptomatic, rather than causative, of a lack of purpose. If the cooperators are less than certain about the objectives to be achieved through collaboration, then it is unlikely that specific bounds on the existence of the effort will be achieved.

One cannot help but note that most of the Japanese cooperative research and development ventures regarding microelectronics and computer technology have definite terms of existence that are specified at the beginning. For example, the VLSI Project had a four-year life span and ended as scheduled in 1980. ICOT is scheduled to run ten years, the National High Speed Computer Program nine years, the National Software Program five, and so on down the list of Japanese collaborative activities.

Many of the U.S. examples of interfirm cooperation present a mixed situation with regard to the defined duration of cooperation. Although the individual research programs within a collaborative venture may have specific, finite life spans, the organizations as a whole often do not. For example, the participants in MCC agree to cooperate for a limited time with regard to each research program, but the commitment to MCC in general is open-ended. The importance of the issue of organizational longevity did not escape the attention of MCC management. At the June 4, 1986, board of directors meeting Inman noted that the issue of organizational permanence would be "a major item for discussion" at the September 3, 1986, board meeting.[350]

A Mixture of Competitive Targets

Many domestic cooperative R&D ventures are started with the stated purpose of allowing U.S. companies to better compete against the Japanese. While Japanese companies can be, and often are, significant competitors, appeals to corporate nationalism are not likely to have long-lasting results. Potential partners in cooperative R&D activities are facing many complex competitive pressures, both in the United States and abroad. Corporate boundaries span the globe. International trading relationships are difficult to avoid even if avoidance is desired. Simplistic notions of drawing up the wagons in a battle of "them versus us" are unlikely to sustain interfirm cooperation in the long run. Are U.S. companies like the ancient Greek city-states that can only be reluctantly prodded to cooperate when the Persian army is threatening? Or can domestic competitors, like their Japanese and European counterparts, embrace some forms of interfirm cooperation as necessary and useful endeavors in a functioning competitive economy? Only time will tell.

In this regard it is interesting to again look at the example of MCC. The original purpose was to increase the competitiveness of domestic companies versus Japanese manufacturers. But the responses to the survey show that the Japanese are not universally viewed by all MCC participants as the most significant competitive threat. This lack of consensus regarding target competitors contributes to difficulties in trying to establish some degree of unanimity concerning organizational purpose.

Organizational Independence

The indefinite nature of the commitment on the part of many participants, questions of legitimacy concerning cooperative action, and the difficulties faced in trying to define organizational purpose in the face of participant heterogeneity have caused the management of cooperative R&D efforts to seek methods to institutionalize and give their organizations a certain degree of permanence. This, coupled with a potential lack of homogeneity among the participants with regard to size, motivation, industry, and competitive targets, may promote the increasing independence of the collaborative R&D venture as an organization. The lack of an unambiguous, consensual purpose for cooperation among the various cooperators has prompted management, of necessity, to formulate and define an organizational purpose reflecting a certain degree of autonomy.

The factors underlying and encouraging the trend toward increased organizational independence from the parent sponsors are many and interrelated. The lack of cooperator homogeneity can precipitate certain structural and organizational choices that, in turn, further the development of organizational autonomy. For example, MCC's decision to adopt cafeteria-style participation in its research programs meant that the member companies would not be cooperating in all aspects of MCC equally. Although all shareholder firms would be equal in terms of board representation and ownership, their collaborative activities could range from a single research program to all seven.

This decision to embrace a "pick-and-choose" structure was necessitated by the lack of homogeneity among the participants. Not all prospective members were interested in, nor could they each afford, the full range of program support. With the individual cooperators each joining a slightly different cooperative venture by virtue of the differing variety of program participation, MCC's organizational unity had to be internally generated and maintained. Lest one get the impression that cooperative R&D projects such as MCC have, like some rebellious child, wrested control from their unwilling parents, it should be noted that some degree of organizational autonomy is generally anticipated and indeed sought. A vision of vigorous and independent leadership was endorsed by the various MCC founders.

The selection of the top executive for the cooperative venture is one of the most critical actions taken during the formation phase. The difficulties a collaborative effort encounters trying to satisfy a panoply of sponsors requires a strong leader with extensive negotiation and persuasion skills.

Difficulties that may be encountered in obtaining personnel from the shareholder companies to staff the cooperative R&D venture's key research positions can also lead to an increased independence. If most of the required personnel are recruited from outside the collaborators' companies their loyalties cannot be expected to flow to the sponsoring companies. In Japan, the key scientists and researchers are generally not "free agents" but have intense feelings of company loyalty. But even with this relatively secure company loyalty Japanese companies are reluctant to "loan" their best talent to a cooperative effort, particularly one that may benefit the competition. It is here that government involvement and encouragement plays a key role.

The need to recruit outside of the circle of cooperators complicates the technology transfer process and also means that there would not be strong ties of loyalty running from the collaborative R&D effort to a participating company. On the other hand, without competing bonds of allegiance to the contributing member company, a strong sense of loyalty to the cooperative venture can develop. In contrast to the top researchers in comparable Japanese cooperative ventures, the professional futures of scientists and researchers working with domestic collaboration may be associated more closely with the success of cooperative effort than with the fortunes of a particular sponsor company.

From the beginning, Admiral Inman saw cooperation among competitors in the form of an organization such as MCC as an element in the potential solution to a much larger problem than that seen by Norris or the individual participating companies. Admiral Inman, driven by a powerful desire to help maintain the strength of the United States as a world leader and knowing that an essential element of this effort was the need to sustain a strong economy that was beginning to lose ground to foreign competitors in key industries, viewed MCC as a vehicle to pursue these wider goals.

Admiral Inman's broad vision at times contrasted with the often parochial goals of the cooperators. The shareholder companies judge

MCC according to how well it satisfies their individual objectives and on occasion the resulting tension has spilled over into the public eye.[351] The concept held by Admiral Inman of MCC as part of a much larger universe was manifested in conversations regarding the Japanese challenge. While the member companies would probably have been quite content with the total disappearance of their Japanese competitors, Admiral Inman merely wanted to out-compete them, since he felt that a vigorous but not dominant Japanese microelectronics industry was in the long-run best interests of the domestic microelectronics companies and the United States in general.

Thus, the selection of Admiral Inman not only brought aboard an individual who had the stature, independence, and personal skills to negotiate with and coordinate a collection of strong-willed, independent business leaders, it also brought aboard an individual with a strong personal value system and a well-developed sense of purpose. Amidst the cacophony of individual corporate objectives and ambitions, Admiral Inman gave the organization a consistent theme, a melody line on which individual players could focus.

The selection of Admiral Inman as leader of the cooperative venture had membership effects as well. Originally formed with computer and component manufacturers, MCC's ranks were soon joined by aerospace companies, such as Martin Marietta, Rockwell International, Lockheed, and Boeing. These were all companies that were familiar with Admiral Inman and his career in the Navy and the intelligence community in Washington. The expanded membership of MCC then in turn gave rise to increased independence for MCC management for two reasons. First, the greater number of shareholders diminished the dependence of MCC on any single shareholder for continued support. And second, the inclusion of a new industry group with different competitive objectives and markets translated into an even greater reliance on MCC management to generate an organizational purpose in the absence of a clear shareholder consensus.

MCC gained an additional measure of organizational autonomy when the board of directors decided to change the bylaws in 1985 to eliminate the need for director unanimity on specified issues. The issue arose after one shareholder was able to block a change in the manner by which the shareholders would pay royalties to MCC for the technology developed.

Further evidence of MCC's increasing organizational independence can be found in subsequent pronouncements from Admiral

Inman and top MCC management that the issue of MCC's institutional permanence was of primary concern. In the eyes of MCC management, the permanence of MCC stands on two legs: (1) the ability to initiate new research programs to replace those that have accomplished their goals, and (2) the ability to secure funding that matches the term and extent of the long-term research.

The first issue was engaged in 1985 when MCC management sought approval for an additional research program. Although a final decision on the proposed program to study advanced manufacturing technologies was postponed for later consideration, MCC management has reiterated its intention to start up additional research programs beyond the seven initially approved.

The issue of secure funding is being approached on a variety of fronts. First, the number and diversity of shareholders means that MCC can easily withstand the potential difficulties posed by the elimination of any particular shareholder. For example, the demise of Mostek caused barely a ripple at MCC as a new shareholder was quickly found to stand in Mostek's stead. Likewise, the exit of BMC and the announced exit of Gould from the cooperative venture were not viewed with particular alarm. Not surprisingly, the possibility of government funding has also been considered, despite the overwhelming opposition of the shareholders to government participation.[352] In some ways the government is already an indirect source of funding for MCC, in that MCC has applied for and recently received Independent Research and Development (IR&D) approval from the Department of Defense.[353] IR&D approval means that the shareholder companies conducting defense-related work can charge some of MCC's costs against their defense contracts.

As MCC's research efforts begin to bear fruit, it is also anticipated that an additional independent stream of funding will develop from the royalty payments. The royalty payments will initially come from the shareholder companies, but after a three-year period of exclusive shareholder use, the technology may be licensed at market rates to non-shareholders as well. MCC plans to use some of this royalty stream to directly reward those researchers responsible for developing the technology. Another portion of the royalties can be used to support the program from which the technology emanated. The remaining portion of the royalties are assigned to MCC to cover general corporate costs.

Establishing and Maintaining Cooperation: Three Elements of Cooperative R&D Ventures

A cooperative research and development activity can be divided into three distinct but nonetheless interrelated elements: (1) contribution of the participants, (2) creation of benefits, and (3) transfer of benefits to contributors (see Figure 8.10). The success of a cooperative R&D venture depends on how well these three components are balanced with one another so that continued cooperation will have a positive value in the eyes of the sponsors.

Figure 8.10
Three Components of Cooperative R&D

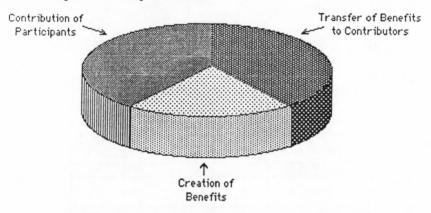

One of the fundamental tasks facing the management of a strategic R&D alliance is the maintenance of an acceptable distribution of costs and benefits among the participants. Under such a model the value of cooperation (V_c) to a participant is equal to the perceived benefits derived from cooperation (B_p), less any perceived costs incurred (C_p), or in formula form, $V_c = B_p - C_p$. If a participant believes that the perceived benefits of cooperation are less than the expected costs to cooperate ($B_p < C_p$), the value of cooperation will be negative ($B_p < C_p$, then $-V_c$) and continued cooperation will cease.

If one of the key objectives of the management of collective R&D activity is to maintain a positive value of cooperation (V_c) for each of the various participants, then it is expected that the joint venture management will engage in activities that yield the largest differential between benefits and costs and hence the largest value. To this end the cooperative venture management can work on either increasing the perceived benefits (B_p) or decreasing the perceived costs (C_p).

Figure 8.11
The Three Elements and Maintaining Value

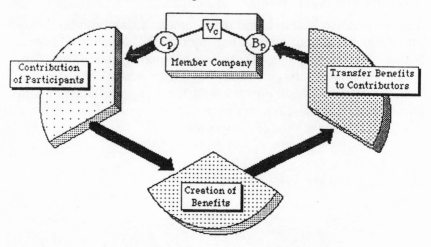

Figure 8.12
Cost/Benefit Grid

	Benefits		Costs		Value
Element One	B_1 *	-	C_1 *	=	V_1
	+		+		+
Element Two	B_2 *	-	C_2 *	=	V_2
	+		+		+
Element Three	B_3 *	-	C_3 *	=	V_3
	=		=		=
Total Venture	B_p	-	C_p	=	V_c

Managerial Action: Can affect any of the starred boxes

Managerial Objective: Maximize V_c

In that there are three separate but interrelated elements in a cooperative research and development venture, the collective venture manager can enhance the value of cooperation by increasing the efficiency in any one or combination of the elements. For example, the value of cooperation can be increased *ceteris paribus* by increasing the efficiency by which the collective activity transforms the contributions of the participants (the costs to them or C_p) into benefits (B_p). This could be accomplished through a number of ways, such as by hiring a better researcher for the same price as a less skilled one, or by providing support facilities and equipment to boost research productivity.

Since there are three separate elements, one can view the total value of cooperation (V_c) as having three components: value derived from element one (V_1), value derived from element two (V_2), and the value obtained from element three (V_3). In formula form this relationship would be expressed as $V_c = V_1 + V_2 + V_3$. Likewise, each value component can be evaluated in terms of costs and benefits associated with that particular element. For example, the value of element one (V_1) is equal to the benefits associated with element one (B_1) less the costs (C_1), or in formula form, $V_1 = B_1 - C_1$ and so on for each of the remaining two elements (see Figure 8.12 for the Cost/Benefit Grid).

Increasing the value of cooperation (V_c) by concentrating on the second element (i.e. increasing V_2) is probably the most obvious route, but managerial conduct aimed at increasing the efficiency of the other two elements can also reap handsome rewards. It is the attention paid by management to increasing the efficiency of all three elements that will spell the difference between success and failure for the organization. For example, not only must management work to attract individuals and establish a supporting organization designed to create top-notch technology (yielding a high V_2), they must also engage in activities that have increased the efficiency of the participants' contributions (V_1) and the transfer of benefits back to the contributors (V_3).

The need for management to address all three elements derives from the fact that the total value of cooperation (V_c) is of primary importance to the sponsoring company. The fact that the cooperative venture can develop significant new technology is of little value to a contributor if the efficiency of the third element (transfer of the benefits to the contributor) is low. Likewise if the collective venture executives do not pay much attention to the efficiency of element one (contribution of the participants) then the costs of cooperation will be higher than otherwise possible, and as a result the value of cooperation will be diminished.

The interrelatedness of the three elements is evident in current cooperative R&D ventures. To cite an example discussed in Chapter 6 concerning MCC, the original concept of MCC was that the shareholders would contribute personnel to MCC. These people would assist in the research and then would provide the mechanism for transferring the technology back to the shareholders when the people were eventually repatriated with the shareholder company from which they came.

Two events changed this original concept. First, the technology did not develop in neat, discrete packages that could be repatriated with a returning employee like a piece of luggage. Useful technology began to develop more or less continuously. Therefore, it had to be transferred without an accompanying researcher. The second item that caused MCC to adjust its original structural and systems design was that the shareholders were unwilling or unable to contribute the type of talent required to conduct the target research. Without this initial contribution of top-flight talent, there was no pool of researchers from the shareholder companies that could be returned with the developed technology. As MCC turned more and more to outside talent to fill its ranks, the less and less viable the original concept of technology transfer became. This example demonstrates that managerial action taken to bolster the value to be derived from one of the elements, in this case V_3, often has an impact on the cost/benefit and value of another element, in this example V_1.

This trade-off dilemma is true of a number of management choices faced by cooperative R&D venture executives. To give another example, in order to enhance element two, the creation of benefits, it was decided that MCC should be an extremely attractive place of employment. First-class facilities were designed with high levels of comfort and research support. While such an appealing work environment helps in the recruiting of top research talent and in improving their research productivity, the maintenance of such an environment has an effect on both the contribution of the participants (element one), in that such facilities are not cheap, and on the transfer of benefits to the contributors (element three), in that researchers "on loan" to MCC might be reluctant to leave such an environment and return to a less attractive work environment that may exist at their sponsoring company. In the terms of Figure 8.12, V_2 has been enhanced by the work environment decision, but at some cost to V_1 and V_3. It is the task of MCC management to make the determination that the gains in V_2 exceed the losses in V_1 and V_3 so that there is a net gain in V_c.

Another example of the same phenomenon that has been mentioned earlier is the decision by the founders of the MCC to structure the research programs on a cafeteria-style basis. Each company is allowed to pick among the four programs the ones it wishes to join. This structure was adopted so that MCC would be more attractive to potential members and would thereby increase their likelihood of joining. At the time, there was concern about attracting a critical mass of companies to launch MCC, so actions that made joining more attractive were adopted. Using the framework above, this structural decision can be seen as an effort to increase V_1, the value of element one, by permitting a larger number of members to join.

Unfortunately, this early decision had a later effect on V_2 by increasing the costs of creating the technology because of the need to segregate and protect proprietary information, as well as increasing the costs and decreasing the benefits of the technology transfer process (V_3). It is the current opinion of Inman and the top management of MCC that the gains in V_1 from the cafeteria-style structure were not greater than the subsequent loses in V_2 and V_3. As a result, MCC has tried to encourage full program participation by all member companies so that the problems associated with a pick-and-choose research effort can be diminished or eliminated.

Is Interfirm Cooperation a Formula for Competitive Success?

Judging the success or failure of any organization can be difficult. For cooperative R&D ventures such judgment is especially challenging. First of all, many of the organizations, with some notable exceptions such as CIIT, are still relatively young. Second, the creation and subsequent use of knowledge, the ultimate product of cooperative R&D activities, is difficult to track and document. In addition, by its nature R&D is both risky and long-term. How does one factor in the inherent and acceptable risk of failure, and what is the proper time span to consider? The best that can be said for many collaborative R&D efforts is that the "jury is still out."

Given the wide variety of motivations for joining a cooperative venture, the assessment of success by the participants is expected to reflect that variability, and it is unlikely that cooperation will be meeting the diverse expectations of the all participants. There are two basic reasons continued cooperation would not be attractive for a particular sponsor. The first is if the cooperative R&D venture fails to produce and deliver the technology expected by the sponsor. The second is if the strategic direction of the shareholder changes so that the technology, even if produced and delivered, would be of little competitive use to the sponsor.

Clearly, the cooperative R&D efforts that have gotten off the ground have to be judged as successful with regard to the first element of the three elements discussed above (contribution of participants). The founders and management of these ventures have been able to draw together a diverse collection of corporations into cooperative activities despite significant barriers to cooperation. Although participant contribution did not always proceed without incident[354] and continued participation is not assured, the mere fact that independent, competing companies with traditions of independence are cooperating at all is a laudable achievement. It is a credit to the skill and perseverence of the founders and management of these strategic R&D alliances that cooperation developed and was embraced by wary participants.[355]

Unfortunately, just getting the participants to cooperate is not enough to insure success. One must also look at the organization's ability to produce and deliver useful technology. It is here that the verdict is as yet unclear. There seems to be little doubt that many of these cooperative R&D efforts will be able to create useful technology. The real question is, can they successfully transfer the technology to the contributing participants?

The management of strategic R&D alliances must devote considerable attention to technology transfer and create systems and procedures to help insure the timely and efficient passing of knowledge that is competitively important to the sponsors. To some, cooperative R&D will undoubtably be a disappointment, if only because of the high expectations generated during the formation stage. In some cases these expectations are unrealistic on their face.[356] Again, using the MCC example, Inman, who was even dubbed the "computer czar" in one article,[357] noted that interfirm cooperation will not, indeed cannot, solve all of the competitive problems facing its member companies. The dollar-yen exchange rate, the relative cost of labor, company mismanagement, and ill-conceived corporate strategies are all sources of competitive difficulties that cooperative R&D activities cannot reach.

Even if interfirm R&D cooperation is not the ultimate weapon in the competitive struggle it seems clear that it is a potentially powerful one. Consider the problems facing the domestic semiconductor manufacturers. Integrated circuit manufacturing is an industry characterized by high fixed costs and extremely low marginal (variable) costs. A major component of the fixed costs facing a chip manufacturer is research and development, which worldwide has been reported at nearly 15 percent of annual industry revenues.[358] By pooling resources in R&D cooperatives, industry members can lower their fixed costs so that when pricing pressures begin to drag them toward the low marginal costs of their chips, as inevitably seems to happen, the financial risk to the individual firms is reduced and chances for survival are enhanced.

Along another dimension, the impact of cooperative R&D activities, whether a success or not, has already been felt, and cooperation among competitors will never be quite the same. The formation of the various collaborative efforts, starting with MCC, helped touch off a debate about the public policy toward interfirm cooperation that eventually led to a major revision (or some would say clarification) of the antitrust laws[359] and continues to this day with talk of extending interfirm collaboration protection to production activities.[360] Whether or not this newfound tolerance and even encouragement of interfirm collaboration will become a permanent part of public policy remains to be seen, but the change itself marks a watershed in national awareness regarding the evolution of our once-dominant domestic economy into a global economic system.

The information collected here is but a few steps down the road toward a fuller understanding of interfirm collaboration. Some successes in collaborative R&D, such as CIIT, are documented. But this may be a special case, arising from a unique set of circumstances. The ambitious goals set for other cooperative organizations such as Sematech, SRC, MCC, and other cooperative ventures have yet to be reached. It remains for future researchers to complete the story and pass judgment on these organizations' contribution to our economic competitiveness.

Appendix 1: Antitrust Laws Applicable to Cooperative R&D Ventures

The legal analysis relevant to an evaluation of cooperative ventures begins with Sections 1 and 2 of the Sherman Act, Section 7 of the Clayton Act, and most recently, Section 3 of The National Cooperative Research Act of 1984 (NCRA).[361]

SHERMAN ACT, SECTION 1

As previously mentioned, Section 1 of the Sherman Act prohibits "[e]very contract, combination in the form of trust or otherwise, or conspiracy, in restraint of trade or commerce among the several States, or with foreign nations. . . .[362]

In that Section 1 could be literally taken as a prohibition against all types of cooperation, the courts have interpreted the section to condemn only "unreasonable" restraints of trade.[363] In order to ease the burden of proof required in curbing certain of the most egregious collective activity some agreements, such as price-fixing and market division, have been deemed to be *per se* illegal. The label of *per se* illegality precludes defenses based upon the "reasonableness" of the cooperative arrangement.

SHERMAN ACT, SECTION 2

Section 2 of the Sherman Act decrees that "Every person who shall monopolize, or attempt to monopolize, or combine or conspire with any other person or persons, to monopolize . . . shall be deemed guilty of a felony. . . .[364]

Although Section 2 does not require collective action, cooperative ventures with the intent to control a market can be reached by the section.

CLAYTON ACT, SECTION 7

Section 7 of the Clayton Act is the statutory foundation regarding antitrust policy toward mergers. The Section provides that "[No] person engaged in commerce or in any activity affecting commerce shall acquire . . . the stock or . . . assets of another person engaged in commerce . . . where . . . the effect of such acquisition may be substantially to lessen competition, or tend to create a monopoly.[365]

NCRA

According to both the House Report[366] of H.R. 5041 and Senate Report[367] on S-1841, the National Cooperative Research Act of 1984 was not passed to establish new antitrust policy regarding cooperative research and development but merely to clarify existing antitrust standards. The pertinent part of the act is Section 3 that states

In any action under the antitrust laws, or under any State law similar to the antitrust laws, the conduct of any person in making or performing a contract to carry out a joint research and development venture shall not be deemed illegal *per se*; such conduct shall be judged on the basis of its reasonableness, taking into account all relevant factors affecting competition, including, but not limited to, effects on competition in properly defined, relevant research and development markets.[368]

The act also limits treble damage awards arising from cooperative R&D situations that have passed muster under the act's notification and disclosure requirements.[369] (Relief is limited to actual damages plus cost of suit including reasonable attorney fees for legal attacks on qualified cooperative research ventures.) It is important to note that while The National Cooperative Research Act of 1984 greatly relaxes the danger of antitrust prosecution to those engaging in eligible collective R&D activity, it does not grant such ventures immunity from antitrust scrutiny.

Appendix 2: Japanese and European Cooperative R&D Ventures in Microelectronics and Computer Technology

There are number of European and Japanese cooperative programs involved in microelectronics and computer technology R&D. In this Appendix four European collaborative programs and six Japanese are described.[370] The European cooperative ventures covered are: the British Alvey Directorate, the European Community's Esprit and Eureka programs, and the European Computer Research Center (ECRC) in Munich. The six Japanese programs covered are: ICOT, the High Speed Computer Program, the National Software Program, the Robotics Program, the New Generation Industry Program, and the Semiconductor Device Program.

JAPANESE PROGRAMS

One of the major forces encouraging cooperation such as Sematech, MCC, and U.S. Memories in the computer technology area has been the cooperative efforts of Japanese competitors and their successes in these efforts. The precursor to the collaborative activities that caused these responses in United States was the Japanese effort in the VLSI Project. In the mid-seventies MITI gathered five Japanese electronics manufacturers and established a program for cooperation in the area of Very Large Scale Integrated circuits. To this end the VLSI Technology Research Association was formed. Under the VLSI Project laboratories were affiliated with the member companies. They donated members to this affiliated cooperative laboratory so that staff of different companies were at different labs. The VLSI Program ended as planned in 1980. The outcome project was viewed as highly successful[371] and was instrumental in enhancing the competitive position of Japanese manufacturers with regard to integrated circuit technology.

With the memory of the VLSI experience fresh in mind, when the Japanese announced a new cooperative effort popularly known as the "fifth generation" computer effort, concern among competitors both in the United States and Europe was considerable, and there was widespread worry that the success of the VLSI Program would be repeated.

Due to extensive publicity in the United States, ICOT, Japan's fifth-generation computer program, is probably the best known of Japan's cooperative microelectronics and computer technology ventures. But ICOT is not the only cooperative effort in this area. In addition there is also the National High Speed Computer Program; the National Software Engineering Project; the Next Generation Industries Basic Technology Research and Development Program; the Optimum Measurement and Control System Project, which concerns robotics; and the New Functional Elements Projects, which is concerned with semiconductors and devices. Taken together, these six national programs have a total budget of over $1.3 billion for the eight-year period covering 1984 to 1992. Although most of the R&D is conducted at the corporate sponsor laboratories, the government also conducts research at its own facilities, the most active of which are MITI's Electro-Technical Laboratory (ETL) and the NTT's Electrical Communication Laboratories (ECL) at four various locations.[372]

ICOT (Institute for New Generation Computer Technology)[373]

Established in April of 1982 under the directorship of Kazuhiro Fuchi, ICOT has approximately forty researchers assembled from the staffs of the seven corporate participants and the Japanese government. The member companies are Fujitsu, Hitachi, NEC, Sharp, Oki, Matsushita, Mitsubishi and Toshiba. The objective is the development of a total computer or computing system based on several revolutionary basic technologies, such as parallel processing, natural language processing, inference and knowledge bases. There are three research laboratories in operation under ICOT's leadership, and one department is devoted to research planning. Lab 1 conducts research into the hardware and architecture of parallel interface and knowledge-based machines. Lab 2 is devoted to software research. Lab 3 is responsible for research on experimental sequential inference machines. The total estimated budget figure for ICOT is approximately $500 million for its projected eight-year life span. Two million dollars was spent in 1982, $15 million in 1983, and $22 million in 1984. Of the total annual expenditures during the first three years, it has been reported that one-third was spent within ICOT, and the remaining two-thirds was subcontracted to ICOT's member companies. The director of the Esprit program has disputed this, stating that the breakdown is closer to 10 percent in-house and 90% industry.[374] Other sources indicate that all funding for the years 1981 through 1984 came from government sources.[375] ICOT functions in part as the central research house and part as a clearinghouse in the technology transfer mechanism. Industry researchers are rotated through ICOT on relatively short tours of two to three years.

There has been some criticism of U.S. cooperative ventures for supposedly having gotten off to a slow start. In particular, MCC has been singled out for admonishment.[376] If the example of ICOT is any standard to judge by, then the time required to organize MCC research efforts has been relatively rapid. Discussions in Japan among interested parties regarding collaborative action in ICOT began in 1978 and lasted for three years until a framework for cooperation could be agreed upon. It should be noted that ICOT is also not without its critics.[377]

The National High Speed Computer Program

This program was established to build a high-speed computer for computationally complex scientific and technological users. It is a nine-year effort that was started in 1981 and should be finished by 1990. The program is sponsored by MITI and administered by MITI's Agency of Industrial Science and Technology. The participating companies are Fujitsu, Hitachi, NEC, Toshiba, Mitsubishi, and Oki. MITI's ETL will also actively participate in the research. The goal is to develop a ten-gega flop machine to be used in scientific and technological applications. The Japanese government is funding the program entirely and no reimbursements from the participating companies are required.

The National Software Development Program

The first five-year program was initiated in 1976 as a Japanese effort to improve software productivity and production capability. The goal was to include automatic software generation so that software production could become less labor-intensive and less costly through the use of a modular approach for editing and software assembly. Again the program was sponsored by MITI. Seventeen private software companies participated in the program and formed the joint System Developing Corporation in April of 1976. MITI paid for the expenses and the participating companies were not required to repay MITI for research expenses. The total five-year budget was a little over $30 million. Out of this effort a National Software Technology Center (NSTC) was established, which is a permanent general purpose R&D facility for the use of software engineers. Although the first five-year program was not regarded as having been very successful, a second five-year plan to automate the production of software was announced at the ICOT conference, November 6 through 9, 1984. The five-year budget for this second effort was announced as $120 million.

The Next Generation Industries Program

This is a program with an overall objective to begin research on the revolutionary basic technologies essential to new industries in Japan, such as aerospace information, knowledge engineering, bio-industry, nuclear power, alternative energy sources, and exploitation of ocean resources. The program was initiated in 1981 and is expected to run ten years. Three areas will be emphasized in the various programs. One will be micro-technology, the second will be information technology, and the third will be composite technology, which consists of large, integrated, completely automated systems for use in hostile environments such as space or deep seas. Forty-one private companies are involved, but they are in a variety of different fields. Not all of the forty-one will be involved in microelectronics and computer technology.[378]

The New Functional Elements for Semiconductor Devices Project

This particular project has three goals: (1) develop extremely fine ladder-structured elements capable of very high computation speeds at room temperatures, (2) develop elements with three-dimensional structure in order to increase greatly the number of functions that can be combined on a single chip, and (3) develop the elements capable of functioning in space inside nuclear reactors, inside automobile engines, and in other hostile environments. Project duration is ten years, having commenced in 1980. Under the sponsorship of MITI, ten companies are participating: Fujitsu, Hitachi, Sumitomo, NEC, Oki, Toshiba, Mitsubishi, Sanyo, Sharp, and Matsushita. Total budget is estimated to be $113 million over the ten-year period. Although separately listed, this project is part of the next-generation industries program.

The Optical Measurement and Control Systems Project

The goal of this project is to design a complete system for high-quality, high-speed, remote monitoring control of large-scale industrial processes, using the optical technology for sensing and for transmission of large amounts of data without interference from electromagnetic induction. This program began in 1979 and is scheduled to run for eight years. It is sponsored and managed by MITI. The private participants are Fujitsu, Hitachi, NEC, Toshiba, Mitsubishi, Matsushita, Furukawa, Oki, and Sumitomo. The budget for the eight years is $81 million.

EUROPEAN PROGRAMS

Esprit (European Strategic Programme for Research and Development in Information Technology)

The Esprit program has been in existence since December of 1982 and was formed mainly because the leaders in the European information technology industry felt that there was an imminent danger that an independent European industry would disappear in the face of foreign competition. The program is designed to extend over ten years and is based on an initial five-year funding commitment. The research itself will not take place in one center, but rather it will be dispersed throughout several centers within the consortia. Because of political and geographic requirements, the research will be performed throughout Europe. The total cost of the program over the full ten years is expected to be $1.5 billion and will be divided equally between industry and the Commission of the European Communities (CEC).

By May 1, 1984, Esprit was halfway through the pilot phase, and a total of $23 million had been committed to thirty-six projects. In 1985 Esprit granted companies $126 million in matching grants to fund R&D projects, and the figure for 1986 was projected to increase to $150 million.[379]

The British Alvey Directorate

The Alvey Directorate was formed in May of 1983 in response to a set of recommendations by a committee chaired by Sir John Alvey, the senior director of technology for British Telecom, on how to respond to the challenge posed by the Japanese ICOT program.[380] In essence, the Alvey Directorate is a collaborative research program among industry, government, and the universities that will establish consortia to do research in six major areas: (1) VLSI/ CAD, (2) software engineering, (3) intelligent knowledge-base systems, (4) man-machine interface, (5) large-scale demonstrators and infrastructure, and (6) communications. The overall funding commitments have been made, and a total effort is expected to be conducted at a cost of $525 million over five years. The $75 million of the total that will go to university research will be fully paid for by the British government. The remaining $450 million will be split 60–40 by the government and industry, respectively. The general approach in setting up a research consortium calls for at least two industry partners working with at least one university or government laboratory.

The European Computer Research Center (ECRC)

The ECRC is a joint research venture between ICL of Great Britain, Compagnie de Machines Bull of France, and Siemens of West Germany, which was initiated in December of 1983 and began operations on January 1, 1984. Established to coordinate research activities at "a precompetitive level in the key area of knowledge processing," ECRC reportedly arose out of worries regarding the ability of the three participants to match the output of Japanese and United States research consortia.[381] According to some U.S. researchers, ECRC has experienced difficulties in getting good researchers and disagreements between the companies were reportedly to blame.[382] As of November 1984, ECRC had only recruited twelve researchers out of a total planned staff of fifty. It is operating under a five-year plan with an annual budget of $5 to $7 million per year. The research focus is decision-making by computers and is organized into five topics: (1) logic programming languages and high-level AI languages, (2) knowledge-based systems, with an emphasis on relational data basis, (3) advanced computer architectures, (4) human interface, and (5) expert systems tools. ECRC should be eligible for Esprit funding, and as a result it could be part of the Esprit effort. The participating companies will get free licenses to the products and systems developed, and licensing to nonparticipants will be considered on a case-by-case basis. Technology transfer will be effected through rotation of staff.

Eureka

The Eureka Project was announced by French President François Mitterand with great fanfare in April of 1985. Conceived as a pan-European effort to help close the technology gap between European companies and those in Japan and the United States, Eureka got off to a slow start because of vagueness and uncertainty regarding the organization's mission. By July of 1986, representatives from the nineteen participating companies had approved seventy-two research and development projects with budgets of over $2 billion. Essentially, Eureka is a source of funding for European companies conducting cooperative R&D projects favored by the organization. The research projects cover a wide range of technologies, from textile-manufacturing robots and sunflower seeds to semiconductor chips and lasers. Private companies submit R&D proposals to Eureka for approval. In order to qualify for Eureka funding a project must involve the collaboration of companies from at least two member countries. It is important to note that Eureka approval is not a guarantee of funding. The applying companies must first seek financial support directly from their respective governments. The prospects for Eureka's success are difficult to assess given the lack of consensus regarding the organization's purpose, but already at least one Eureka-funded project has floundered.[383]

Appendix 3: Federal Register Listing of Cooperative R&D Ventures under the National Cooperative Research Act of 1984

Guide to Citation:

Name of Venture (Other Name if Any) [Date of Notice in Federal Register, FRP = page in Federal Register]

    Parties to the venture.

1.   Adirondack Lakes Survey Corp. (ESEERCO) [2/8/85 FRP: 5543]

    New York State Department of Environmental Conservation
    Empire State Electric Energy Research Corporationn (ESEERCO)

        (ESEERCO members):
        Central Hudson Gas & Electric Corporation
        Consolidated Edison Co. of New York Inc.
        Long Island Lighting Co.
        New York State Electric & Gas Corporation
        Niagara Mohawk Power Corporation
        Orange and Rockland Utilities, Inc.
        Rochester Gas and Electric Corporation

2.   Agrigenetics [2/8/85 FRP: 5443] Agrigenetics Research Associates Limited: Agrigenetics Research Corporation American Cyanamid Co. [2/5/87 FRP: 3719-3720]

3.   Pine Oil Plant Research Venture:

    American Cyanamid Company
    Arizona Chemical Co.
    Dow Consumer Products, Inc.
    Hercules, Inc.
    Johnson Chemical Co., Inc.
    Lehn & Fink Products CorP.
    Procter & Gamble Co.
    SCM Organic Chemicals
    T&R Chemicals Inc.
    Union Camp Corporation

4.   Applied Information Technologies Corp. [10/9/85 FRP: 41232]

    Battelle Memorial Institute, The
    American Chemical Society
    CompuServe Incorporated
    Mead Data Central, Inc.
    Online Computer Library Center, Inc.

5.   ARCO Chemical Co. [8/28/86 FRP: 30724]

    ARCO Chemical Company, Division of Atlantic Richfield Company

Air Products and Chemicals, Inc.

6. Armco Inc., Bethlehem Steel Corp., Inland Steel Co., and Weirton Steel Corp.
    [6/12/86 FRP: 21426]

    Armco Inc.,
    Bethlehem Steel Corporation
    Inland Steel Company
    Weirton Steel Corporation

7. Automotive Polymer-Based Composites Joint Research and Development
    Partnership [8/4/88 FRP: 29396]

    Chrysler Corporation
    Ford Motor Company
    General Motors Corporation

8. Babcock and Wilcox Company [2/24/86 FRP: 46727]

    The Babcock & Wilcox Company
    Seitz-Filter-Werke, Theo & Geo Seitz GMBH und Co.,

9. Battelle Memorial Institute -- Optoelectronics Group Project [11/29/85 FRP:
    49141-49142]

    Allied Corporation
    Amp Incorporated
    Dukane Corporation
    Hewlett-Packard Company
    ITT Corporation
    Litton Systems, Inc.

10. B.F. Goodrich Company and European Vinyls Corp. [3/10/89 FRP: 10197]

    The B.F. Goodrich Company
    European Vinyls Corporation (Holdings) B.V.,

11. Bell Communications Research, Inc. (Ameritech) [2/13/87 FRP: 4670, 2/19/87
    FRP: 5241]

    Ameritech Services, Inc.
    Bell Atlantic Network Services, Inc.
    Bell Communications Research, Inc. (Bellcore)
    BellSouth Services Incorporated
    NYNEX Service Company
    Pacific Bell
    Southwestern Bell Telephone Company
    U S WEST, Inc.

12. Bell Communications Research, Inc. (Bellcore) [1/30/85 FRP: 4280]

    Ameritech Services, Inc.
    Bell Atlantic Management Services, Inc.
    BellSouth Services Incorporated
    NYNEX Service Company
    Pacific Bell
    Southwestern Bell Telephone Company

The Mountain States Telephone & Telegraph Company
Northwestern Bell Telephone Company
Pacific Northwest Bell Telephone Company

13. Bell Communications Research, Inc. (BNR) [6/15/89 FRP: 25509]

Bellcore
Bell-Northern Research Ltd. (BNR)

14. Bell Communications Research, Inc. (Fujitsu) [2/13/87 FRP: 4670, 11/16/88 FRP: 46127]

Bellcore
Fujitsu

15. Bell Communications Research, Inc. (GCT) [11/16/88 FRP: 46128]

Bellcore
GCT

16. Bell Communications Research, Inc. (Landis & Gyr) [9/15/88 FRP: 35935]

Bellcore
Landis & Gyr

17. Bell Communications Research, Inc. (Microwave Semiconductor Corporation) [7/13/87 FRP: 26190]

Bellcore
Mircowave Semiconductor Corporation (MSC)

18. Bell Communications Research, Inc. (NEC) [12/18/87 FRP: 48164]

Bellcore
NEC

19. Bell Communications Research, Inc. (NHK) [6/3/88 FRP: 20380-1]

Bellcore
NHK

20. Bell Communications Research, Inc. (PictureTel) [5/10/89 FRP: 20213]

Bellcore
PictureTel

21. Bell Communications Research, Inc. (Sarnoff) [6/3/88 FRP: 20381]

Bellcore
Sarnoff Research Center

22. Bell Communications Research, Inc. (SSI) [5/10/89 FRP: 20213-4]

Bellcore
SSI

23. Bell Communications Research, Inc. (Sumitomo) [4/6/88 FRP: 11352]

Bellcore
Sumitomo

24. Bell Communications Research, Inc. (TFL) [7/27/89 FRP: 31266]

Bellcore
TFL

25. Bell Communications Research, Inc. (Telettra) [9/15/88 FRP: 35935]

Bellcore
Telettra

26. Bell Communications Research, Inc. (TriQuint) [4/30/87 FRP: 15787]

Bellcore
TriQuint

27. Bell Communications Research, Inc. (Vitesse) [10/2/87 FRP: 37031]

Bellcore
Vitesse

28. Bell Communications Research, Inc. (VTC) [5/10/89 FRP: 20213]

Bellcore
VTC

29. Bell Communications Research, Inc. (ADC Telecommunications, Inc.) [9/5/85 FRP: 36162]

Bellcore
ADC Telecommunications, Inc. (former SRI)

30. Bell Communications Research, Inc. (Avantek, Inc.) [6/28/85 FRP: 26849]

Bellcore
Avantek, Inc.

31. Bell Communications Research, Inc. (HHI) [8/6/85 FRP: 31785]

Bellcore
Heinrich-Hertz-Institute Fur Nachrichtentechnik

32. Bell Communications Research, Inc. (Hitachi, Ltd.) [12/12/85 FRP: 50857]

Bellcore
Hitachi, Ltd.

33. Bell Communications Research, Inc. (Honeywell) [3/25/85 FRP: 11762]

Bellcore
Honeywell

34. Bellcore - Racal Data Communications [6/28/85 FRP: 26849]

Bellcore
Racal Data Communications

35.   Bellcore - U.S. Department of Army [6/28/85 FRP: 26850]

Bellcore
U.S. Department of Army - Electronics Technology and Devices Laboratory

36.   Berkeley Sensor and Actuator Center [12/15/87 FRP: 47642]

Allied Corporation
Baxter Healthcare Corp.
Borg-Warner Corporation
Ford Motor Company
General Motors
Honeywell, Inc.
Texas Instruments

37.   Bethlehem Steel Corporation & U.S. Steel Corporation [1/30/85 FRP: 4281]

Bethlehem Steel Corporation
United States Steel Corporation

38.   Biotechnology Research and Development Corp. [5/12/88 FRP: 16919,
11/4/88 FRP: 44679-80]

American Cyanamid Company
Amoco Technology Company
Ecogen Inc.
Hewlett-Packard Company
International Minerals & Chemical Corp.

39.   Cable Television Laboratories, Inc. (CableLabs) [9/7/88 FRP: 34593, 12/16/88
FRP: 50590-1, 3/1/89 FRP: 8608]

Adelphia Cable Communications
American Television & Communication Corporation
Armstrong Utilities, Inc.
Avenue TV Cable Service, Inc.
Benchmark Communications
Bismarck-Mandan Cable TV
Bluffton Cablevision Ltd.
Bresnan Communications Co.
C-TEC Cable Systems
Cable America Corporation
Cable TV Company
Cablevision Industries Inc.
Cablevision Systems Corporation
Cencom Cable Associates
Centel Cable Television Company
Chambers Communications Corporation
Coaxial Communications
Colony Communications, Inc.
Comcast Corporation
Consolidated Cable Properties, Inc.
Continental Cablevision, Inc.
Cox Cable Communications, Inc.

Cross Country Cable Inc.
Denver Technological Center
Douglas Communications Corporation II
Greater Media, Inc.
Guam Cable TV
Harron Communications
Helicon Corporation
Heritage Communications
Higgins Lake Cable, Inc.
Hornell Television Service, Inc.
Insight Communications Co.
J.S. Gans Cable TV
Jones Intercable Inc.
Karnack Corporation
Metrovision, Inc.
Monmouth Cablevision Assoc.
Multimedia Cablevision Inc.
New Channels Corporation
New World Stratovision
Newhouse Broadcasting Company
Paradigm Communications
Paragon Communications
Post Office Drawer A
Post-Newsweek Cable Inc.
Prime Cable Corp.
Rifkin & Associates Inc.
Rock Associates
Roger US Cablesystems Inc.
Rogers Cable TV Limited
Sammons Communications, Inc.
Star Cablevision Group
Susquehanna Cable Company
Tele-Communications Inc.
Tele-Media Corporation
TeleCable Corporation
The Cable Company
The Lenfest Group
Times Mirror Cable Television
TKR Cable Company
United Artists Cablesystems Corporation
United Cable Television Corporation
Valley Cable TV
Viacom Cable
Vision Cable Communications, Inc.
Warner Cable Communications Inc.
Western Communications Inc.
Westmarc

40. CAD Framework Initiative, Inc. [3/13/89 FRP: 10456, 4/20/89 FRP: 16013,
     6/22/89 FRP: 26265-66. 8/4/89 FRP: 32141]

     Corporate Members:

     Advanced Micro Devices, Inc.
     Alcatel NV
     Bull, S.A.
     CADENCE Design Systems, Inc.

Control Data Corp.
Daisy Systems Corp.
Digital Equipment Corporation
EDA Systems, Inc.
GE Aerospace
General Motors/Delco Electronics
Harris Semiconductor
Hewlett-Packard Company
Honeywell, Inc.
IMEC, VZW
Intergraph Corp.
International Computers Ltd.
Mentor Graphics Corporation
Microelectronics & Computer Technology Corporation
Motorola, Inc.
NCR Corp.
Nixdorf Computer AG
Object Design, Inc.
Objectivity, Inc.
Robert Bosch GbmH
SCME Foundation Centers for Micro-Electronics
SGS Thomson Microelectronics
Siemens AG
Sony Corporation
Sun Microsystems
Texas Instruments, Inc.
Valid Logic Systems, Inc.
VIEWLOGIC Systems, Inc.
VLSI Technology
Westinghouse Electric Corp.
IBM
Mitsubishi Electronic Corp.
Philips Research Laboratories
Plessey Semiconductors Ltd. Zycad Corp.

Associate Members:

Alan Ford
Arding Hsu
Bill Harding
Daniel Daly
David Jakopac
Delft University of Technology
Dyson Wilkes
Erwin Warshawsky
Frauhofer AIS
Gateway Design Automation Corp.
Gesellschaft Fur Mathematik and Datenverarbeitung mbH (GMD)
Hong-Tai Chou
Intel Corp.
Kenneth Bakalar
Marlene Kasmir
Mitch Morey
Moe Shahdad
PTT Research Neher Laboratories
Semiconductor Research Corporation
Timothy Andrews

41. Center for Advanced Television Studies (CATS) [2/1/8 FRP: 4819, 9/19/86, FRP: 33307]

   American Broadcasting Companies, Inc. (Capital Cities/ABC)
   Ampex Corporation
   Home Box Office, Inc.
   National Broadcasting Company, Inc.
   Public Broadcasting Service
   RCA Corporation (wholly owned subsidiary of GE)
   Tektronix Corporation
   Zenith Radio Corporation
   Eastman Kodak Company

42. Composite Materials Characterization, Inc. [1/15/88, FRP: 1074, 1/13/89, P1454]

   General Electric Company
   Grumman Aerospace Corporation
   Lockheed Corporation
   LTV Aerospace and Defense Company
   Rohr Industries, Inc.
   United Technologies Corporation, Sikorsky Aircraft Division The Dow Chemical Company

43. Computer Aided Manufacturing International, Inc. [1/24/85 FRP: 3425-6, 2/26/86 FRP: 6812-3, 5/4/87 FRP: 16321-2, 2/12/88 FRP: 4232-3, 2/6/89 FRP: 5693-4]

   (Industrial and Educational Members from Europe and Japan also.)

   Industrial Members (U.S.):

   Allied Aerospace
   Allied Signal Inc. Bendix Kansas City Division
   Arthur Andersen and Company
   AT&T
   Avery International
   Beckman Instruments Inc.
   Campbell Soup Company
   Carnation Company
   Caterpillar Tractor Company
   Cooper & Lybrand
   Dana Corporation
   Deere & Company CAM Systems Division
   Deloitte, Haskins & Sells
   Eastman Kodak Company
   Eaton Corporation
   Electronic Data Systems
   Ernst & Whinney
   General Dynamics/Fort Worth
   General Electric Company
   Grumman Corporation Grumman Aircraft Systems Division
   Hewlett-Packard Co.
   Honeywell Inc.
   Hughes Aircraft Company
   Johnson Controls, Inc.

Lockheed Missiles & Space Co., Inc.
Lockheed-Georgia Company
LTV Aerospace & Defense Co.
Management Science America
Martin Marietta Energy Systems, Inc.
McDonnell Douglas Corporation
Nabisco Brands, Inc.
Northern Telecom Ltd.
Northrop Aircraft Corporation
Parker Hannifin Corporation
Parker Bertea Aerospace
Price Waterhouse
Rockwell International
Sandia National Laboratories
        CAD Technical & Organizational Division
        Sheffield Measurement Division
Structural Dynamic Research Corp.
Texas Instruments Inc.
Textron Inc.
Proctor & Gamble Co.
U.S. Air Force, ASD/PMDI
U.S. Department of Energy
U.S. Navy Office of Naval Acquisition Support
United Technologies Research Center
United Technologies Corp. Pratt & Whitney Aircraft Group Hamilton Standard
Westinghouse Electric Corporation
Williams International

Educational Members (U.S.):

Arizona State University
California Polytechnic State University
Illinois Institute of Technology
Massachusetts Institute of Technology
North Carolina State University
Purdue University
North Texas State University
Oklahoma State University
University of California
University of Maryland
University of Massachusetts
University of New Hampshire
University of Southern California

44.   Corning Glass Works [7/15/87 FRP: 26580]

        Corning Glass Works
        Nippon Telegraph and Telephone

45.   Corporation for Open Systems International [6/11/86 FRP: 21260, 9/4/86 FRP:
      31735-6, 10/28/86 FRP: 39434, 2/13/87 FRP: 4671, 4/24/87 FRP: 13769,
      7/21/87 FRP: 27273-4, 10/7/87 FRP: 37539, 11/9/87 FRP: 43138, 12/4/87
      FRP: 46129-30, 2/15/87 FRP: 47642-3, 12/18/89 FRP: 48164, 2/19/88 FRP:
      5060, 3/8/88 FRP: 7411, 6/30/88 FRP: 24811, 11/25/88 FRP: 47773, 4/20/89
      FRP: 16013-14]

        3 Com Corporation

Air Force Communications – Computer Systems Integration Office
Amdahl Corporation
Apollo Computer Inc.
Apple Computer, Inc.
AT&T Inc.
Bechtel Power Corporation
Bell Atlantic
Bell Communications Research
Boeing Computer Services
Bridge Communications, Inc.
Burroughs Corporation
Central Computer and Telecommunications Agency
Citicorp Technology Office
Combustion Engineering
Concord Communications Inc.
Concurrent Computer Corp.
Control Data Corporation
Data Connection Ltd.
Data General Corp.
Defense Communications Agency
Dialcom Inc.
Digital Equipment Corporation
Eastman Kodak Company
General Motors Corporation - Advanced Engineering Staff
GSI Danet Inc.
Her Majesty's Treasury - British Government
Hewlett-Packard Inc.
Honeywell Bull
Hughes Aircraft Company
IDACOM
Intel Corporation
International Business Machines Corporation
Morgan Guaranty Trust Company
Motorola, Inc.
National Bureau of Standards
National Communications System
National Computing Center Ltd. (UK) - joint development agreement with COS
(May 1987)
National Semiconductor Corp. - National Advanced Systems Division
Naval Data Automation Command
NCR Corporation
Network Systems Corporation
Northern Telecom Inc.
NYNEX Corporation
Pacific Bell
Prime Computer Inc.
Rockwell International
Soft-Switch Inc.
Southwestern Bell Telephone Company
SPAG - (agreeement with COS for cross-distribution & licensing of each other's
            test products throughout Europe, N. and S. America)
Sun Microsystems Inc.
Sytek Incorporated
Tandem Computers Inc.
Texas Instruments, Inc.
Touch Communications Inc.
Ungermann-Bass

Unisys - Sperry Computer Systems
United States Army - Information Systems
Wang Laboratories, Inc.
Xerox Corporation

46.   CPW Technology [6/15/87, FRP: 22692]

Paramount Pictures Corp.
Columbia Pictures Industries, Inc.
Warner Bros. Inc.

47.   Dialkyl Project [8/15/88, FRP: 32480]

Lonza Inc.
Huntington Lab. Inc.
Mason Chemical Company
Scepan Company

48.   Eaton Corporation (Eaton) -- Fiat Veicoli/Industrialia, S.P.A. [1/4/85, FRP: 4918]

Eaton Corporation
Eaton Ltd.
Fiat Veicoli Industrialia S.P.A.

49.   Empire State Electric Energy Research Corp. (ESEERCO) [2/8/85, FRP: 5443-4]

Central Hudson Gas & Electric Corp.
Consolidated Edison Co. of NY Inc.
Long Island Lighting Co.
New York State Electric & Gas Corp.
Niagara Mohawk Power Corp.
Orange & Rockland Utilities Inc.
Rochester Gas & Electric Corp.

50.   Engine Manufacturers Association [7/17/86, FRP: 25956-7, 4/13/88, FRP: 12202]

Caterpillar Tractor Company
Cummins Engine Company, Inc.
Deere & Company
Detriot Diesel Allison Division of General Motors Corp.
Deutz Corporation
Ford Tractor Operations
Iveco Trucks of North America, Inc.
Mack Trucks, Inc.
Mercedes-Benz Truck Company, Inc.
Navistar International Corporation
Onan Corporation
Ontario Research Foundation
Perkins Engines, Inc.
Saab-Scania AB
Volvo Truck Corporation
White Engines, Inc.

51.   Exxon Production Research Company & Halliburton Services [1/17/85, FRP: 2632-3]

Exxon Production Research Company
Halliburton Services

52   Fabric Softener Quats Joint Venture [8/19/88, FRP: 31772]

Sherex Chemical Company
Capital City Products
Croda Inc.
Chemical Specialties Manufacturers Association

53.   Geothermal Drilling Organization [10/29/85, FRP: 43801-2]

California Energy Company
Chevron Resources Co.
Dailey Directional Services
Dresser Industries
Eastman Whipstock
Foamair Divsion of Pool Co.
Geothermal Resources Int. Inc.
H&H Oil Tool Co. Inc.
MCR Geothermal Corporation
Mono Power Company
NL Industries
Pajarito Enterprises
Republic Geothermal Inc.
Sandia National Lab
Steam Reserve Corp.
Union Geothermal Division

54.   Huntington Laboratories, Inc. (ADBAC QUAT Joint Venture) [10/7/86, FRP: 35706, 12/8/86, FRP: 45067]

Chemical Specialties Manufacturers Association
Economics Laboratory, Inc.
Ethyl Corporation
Huntington Laboratories, Inc.
Lonza, Inc.
Sherex Chemical Company, Inc.
Stepan Company

55.   Industrial Consortium for Research & Education [12/8/88, FRP: 49613, 1/31/89, FRP: 4920]

University of Illinois at Urbana-Champaign
Mobil Research & Development Corp.
Union Oil Company of California

56.   Industry-University Center for Glass Research [9/10/86, FRP: 32262-3, 3/19/87, FRP: 8661, 6/9/88, FRP: 21742]

AFG Industries Inc.
Alfred University
Aluminum Company of America
CertainTeed Corp.
Corning Glass Works
E.I. DuPont DeNemours, Inc.

Ford Motor Company
M & T Chemicals Inc.
Manville Building Materials Corp.
Owens-Illinois Inc.
PPG Industries Inc.
Specialty Products Company
U.S. Borax Research

57.   Industry/University Cooperative Research Center for Simulation and Design
      Optimization of Mechanical Systems [8/31/88, FRP: 33558-9]

Alliant Computer Systems
Apollo Computer Inc.
Boeing Computer Services
CADSI, Inc.
Case/IH
Caterpillar, Inc.
Contraves Goertz Group
CPC General Motors Corp.
Eastman Kodak Company
Evans & Sutherland
FMC Corporation
Intergraph Corporation
Silicon Graphics

58.   Institute for Manufacturing & Automation Research [6/30/88, FRP: 24811]

Hughes Aircraft Company
IBM Scientific Center
Northrop Corp.
Rockwell International Corp.
TRW Operations & Support Group
University of California, LA
University of Southern California
Xerox Corp.

59.   Intel Corporation/Xicor Corporation [12/12/85, FRP: 50864]

Intel Corporation
Xicor Corp.

60.   The International Energy Program; Amendment [3/22/88, FRP: 9382]

61.   International Diatomite Producers Association [7/14/88, FRP: 26687]

Ceca S.A.
Eagle-Picher Minerals, Inc.
Grefco, Inc.
Manville Corporation
Manville de France S.A./Manville Europe Corporation
Witco Corporation

62.   International Magnesium Development Corp. [6/30/86, FRP: 23609]

63.   International Partners in Glass Research [4/10/85, FRP: 14175, 1/6/87, FRP:
      468, 6/2/88, FRP: 20194]

ACI Ventures Inc.
Bayerische Falschen-Glashuettenwereke - Weigand & Soehne GmbH & Co.,
KG
Brockway Research Inc.
Emhart Glass Research, Inc.
Portion Research, Inc. - Consumers Glass Co. Ltd.,
Rockware Glass Limited
Yamamura Glass Co. Ltd.

64. Joint Venture of All-Terrain Vehicle Distributors; American Honda Motor Co. Inc.
     [10/14/87, FRP: 38157]

     American Honda Motor Co. Inc.
     Kawasaki Motors Corp.
     U.S.C.
     U.S. Suzuki Motor Corp.
     Yamaha Motor Corp., U.S.A.

65. Kaiser Aluminum & Chemical Corp. & Reynolds Metals Co. [5/13/85, FRP:
     20014]

     Kaiser Aluminum & Chemical Corp.
     Reynolds Metals Co.

66. Kean Manufacturing Corp. & Fabristeel Products, Inc. [1/28/86, FRP: 3519]

     Kean Manufacturing Corp.
     Fabristeel

67. KeraMont Research Corp. [4/3/86, FRP: 11489]

     Montedison S.p.A.
     Materials & Electrochemical Research Corp.
     KRC
     James C. Withers
     Rauof O. Loutfy
     Robert A. Mallia

68. Lehn & Fink Products Group for the Aerosol Classification Joint Venture
     [5/31/89, FRP: 23301]

     Amway Corporation
     Boyle-Midway Household Products Inc.
     Carter Wallace
     Chemical Specialties Manufacturers Association
     Chesebrough Ponds Inc.
     Chevron Chemical Company
     Diversified CPC International
     Dow Brands
     Drackett Company
     E.I. DuPont de Nemours & Co.
     Faultless Starch
     Gillette Company
     S.C. Johnson & Son Inc.
     Lehn & Fink Products Group
     Mennen Company
     Peterson/Puritan Inc.

Precision Valve Company
Proctor & Gamble Company
Scott's Liquid Gold Inc.
Seaquist Valve Company
Summit Valve Company

69.   Manville Corp. - Bird Inc. Roofing Division Agreement [7/18/88, FRP: 27087]

Manville Corp.
Bird Inc., Roofing Division

70.   Material Handling Research Center [9/11/87, FRP: 34432]

Adolph Coors Company
3M Company
AT&T Technologies
Boeing Commerical Airplane Company
Burlington Industries
Caterpiller Tractor Company
The Coca-Cola Company
Data General Corporation
Digital Equipment Corporation
E.I. DuPont deNemours & Co. Inc.
Eastman Kodak Company
Eaton Kenway
Ford Motor Company
General Dynamics Corporation
General Motors Corporation
Georgia Tech Research Corporation
Grumman Aerospace Corporation
IBM Corporation
Intech Systems
The Kroger Co.
Litton Unit Handling Systems, Inc.
Lockheed-Georgia Company
Logan/Figgie International
Lyon Metal Products, Inc.
Sears, Roebuck & Co.
SI Handling Systems Inc.
Stanley/Vidmar, Inc.
TRW, Inc.
Texas Instruments, Inc.
The Union Metal Manufacturing Company
Unisys Corporation
Westinghouse Electric Corporation
Xerox Corporation

71.   Measurement and Control Engineering Center [11/4/88, FRP: 44680]

Aluminum Company of America
Amoco Corporation
Celanese Corporation
DOW Chemical Company, U.S.A.
Martin Marietta Energy Systems
Eastman Kodak Company
Texas Instruments, Inc.

72.   Merrell Dow Pharmaceuticals Inc. (MDPI) [2/19/85, FRP: 7006-7]

        Merrell Dow Pharmaceuticals Inc.
        Hoffmann-La Roche Inc.

73.   Metal Casting Technology, Inc. [4/1/87, FRP: 10420-1]

        General Motors Corporation
        Hitchiner Manufacturing Co. Inc.

74.   Microelectronics and Computer Technology Corp. [1/17/85, FRP: 2633,
        4/23/85, FRP: 15989-90, 9/10/86, FRP: 32263, 12/8/86, FRP: 44131, 2/3/87,
        FRP: 3356, 3/19/87, FRP: 8661, 1/22/88, FRP: 1859, 3/29/88, FRP: 10159-60,
        9/22/88, FRP: 36910]

        Advanced Micro Devices, Inc.
        Bell Communications Research, Inc. (Bellcore):
             Bellcore Subsidiaries:
                 NYNEX Service Company
                 Bell Atlantic Management Services, Inc.
                 Ameritech Services, Inc.
                 BellSouth Services Inc.
                 The Mountain States Telephone & Telegraph Co.
                 Northwestern Bell Telephone Company
                 Pacific Northwest Bell Telephone Company
                 Southwestern Bell Telephone Company
                 The Pacific Telephone & Telegraph Company
                 Illinois Bell Telephone Company Inc.
                 Indiana Bell Telephone Company, Inc.
                 Michigan Bell Telephone Company
                 The Ohio Bell Telephone Company
                 Wisconsin Telephone Company
                 The Bell Telephone Company of Pennsylvania
                 The Diamond State Telephone Company
                 The Chesapeake & Potomac Telephone Company
                 The Chesapeake & Potomac Telephone Company of Maryland
                 The Chesapeake & Potomac Telephone Company of Virginia
                 The Chesapeake & Potomac Telephone Company of W. Virginia
                 New Jersey Bell Telephone Company
                 Southern Bell Telephone & Telegraph Company
                 South Central Bell Telephone Company
                 New England Telephone & Telegraph Company
                 New York Telephone Company
                 Bell Telephone Company of Nevada
        The Boeing Company
        Control Data Corporation
        Digital Equipment Corporation
        Eastman Kodak Company
        General Electric and each of its subsidiaries
        General Motors and each of its subsidiaries
        Harris Corporation
        Hewlett-Packard Company & each of its subsidiaries
        Minnesota Mining and Manufacturing Company
        Motorola, Inc.
        National Semiconductor Corporation
        NCR Corporation
        Rockwell International Corporation

United Technologies and each of its subsidiaries
Westinghouse Electric Corporation & each of its subsidiaries

75. Microelectronics Center of North Carolina [8/1/88, FRP: 28922-3]

Airco Industrial Gases
Cadence Design System Inc.
Digital Equipment Corp.
E.I. DuPont deNemours & Co. Inc.
General Signal Corporation
General Electric Company
International Business Machines
Megatest Corp.
Northern Telecom Inc.

76. The Industry/University Cooperative Research Center for Microwave/Millimeter-Wave Computer-Aided Design [5/31/88, FRP: 19830]

Ball Aerospace Systems Division
Boeing Electronics High Technology Center
Hewlett-Packard
Hughes Microwave Products Division
ITT Corporation/GaAs Technology Center
National Bureau of Standards
Teledyne MMIC
Texas Instruments/Equipment Group
TRW/Electronic Systems Group
U.S. Army - LABCOM
Westinghouse/Defense Electronics Center

77. Motor Vehicle Manufacturers Association (MVMA) -- Acid Rain [2/8/85, FRP: 5449]

Motor Vehicle Manufacturers Association of the U.S. Inc.
   MVMA Members:
      AM General Corporation, LTV Aerospace & Defense Company
      American Motors Corporation
      Ford Motor Company
      General Motors Corporation
      International Harvester Company
      M.A.N. Truck & Bus Corporation
      PACCAR Inc.
      Volkswagen of America, Inc.
      Volvo North America Corporation
American Petroleum Institute
Coordinating Research Council, Inc.

78. MVMA -- Aerosol Formation in the Atmosphere [2/8/85, FRP: 5549]

MVMA members (see 77)

79. MVMA -- Atmospheric Transformation of Nitrogenous, Oxidant and Organic Compounds [2/8/85, FRP: 5450]

MVMA members (see 77)

80. MVMA -- Benzene Emissions [2/8/85, FRP: 5448]

MVMA members (see 77)

81.   MVMA -- Combustion Research [2/8/85, FRP: 5446]

      MVMA members (see 77)
      United States Department of Energy

82.   MVMA -- Composition of Diesel Exhaust [2/8/85, FRP: 5444-5]

      MVMA members (see 77)

83.   MVMA -- Effects of Fuel and Engine Variables on Diesel Engine Emissions
      [2/5/85. FRP: 5445-6]

      MVMA members (see 77)

84.   MVMA -- Fate of Diesel Particulates in the Atmosphere [2/8/85, FRP: 5448]

      MVMA members (see 77)

85.   MVMA -- Fate of Polynuclear Aromatic Hydrocarbons in Exhaust Dilution
      Sampling Systems [2/8/85, FRP: 5447]

      MVMA members (see 77)

86.   MVMA -- Fluorocarbon 134a [7/30/87, FRP: 28494]

      MVMA members (see 77)

87.   MVMA -- Hose Connections [7/30/87, FRP: 28494]

      MVMA members (see 77)

88.   MVMA -- Long Range Transport of Air Pollutants [2/8/85, FRP: 5549-50]

      MVMA members (see 77)

89.   MVMA -- Motor Fuels Testing [2/8/85, FRP: 5447]

      MVMA members (see 77)

90.   MVMA -- National Gasoline & Diesel Fuel Survey [2/8/85, FRP: 5445]

      MVMA members (see 77)

91.   MVMA -- Test Methods for Unregulated Exhaust Emissions [2/8/85, FRP: 5444]

      MVMA members (see 77)

92.   MVMA -- Truck/Trailer Brake Research [2/8/85, FRP: 5450-1]

      MVMA members (see 77)
      American Trucking Associations, Inc.
      MVMA members (see 77)
      Canadian Trucking Association
      Truck/Trailer Manufacturers Association, Inc.

93.   MVMA -- Vehicle Side Impact Test Procedure [2/8/85, FRP: 5446]

      MVMA members (see 77)

94.   NAHB Research Foundation -- Smart Home Project [10/10/85, FRP: 41428-9,
      1/28/86, FRP: 3520, 5/16/86, FRP: 18049, 8/28/86, FRP: 30724-5, 1/1/5/87,
      FRP: 1673, 5/8/87, FRP: 17490, 7/30/87, FRP: 28494-5, 9/22/87, FRP: 35596-
      7, 1/5/88, FRP: 186-7, 3/21/88, FRP: 9154-5, 5/3/88, FRP: 15750-1, 12/8/88,
      FRP: 49614-5]

         AMP Inc.
         Apple Computer, Inc.
         Arco Solar, Inc.
         AT&T Technologies, Inc.
         Bell Northern Research Ltd.
         Bose Corporation
         BRIntec Corporation
         Broan Mfg. Co., Inc.
         Burndy Corporation
         Canada Wire & Cable Limited
         Carrier Corporation
         Challenger Electrical Equipment Corp.
         Dicon System Ltd.
         Dormont Manufacturing Company
         Dukane Corporation
         E.I. DuPont de Nemours & Company
         Emerson Electric co.
         Federal Pioneer Ltd.
         Gas Research Institute
         General Electric Company
         Honeywell Corporation
         Johnson Controls
         Kohler Company
         Landis & Gyr Metering, Inc.
         Lennox Industries, Inc.
         Molex Incorporated
         Multiplex Technology, Inc.
         NAHB Research Foundation, Inc.
         North American Philips Consumer Electronics Corp.
         Northern Telecom, Inc.
         Onan Corporation
         Robertshaw Controls Company
         Schlage Lock Company
         SCICON Systems Control, Inc.
         Scott Instruments Corporation
         Scovill Inc.
         Shell Chemical Company (Division of Shell Oil Company)
         Siemens Energy and Automation, Inc., Circuit Protection Division
         Slater Electric, Inc.
         Smart House Development Venture, Inc.
         Smart House, LP
         Sola Basic Industries, Inc.
         Southwire Company
         Square D Company
         Whirlpool Corporation
         The Wiremold Company

Advisors to the Venture:
  AgipPetroli
  Allegheny Power Service Corporation
  American Electric Power Service Corp.
  American Gas Association
  Arkla, Inc.
  Baltimore Gas & Electric Company
  Bell Canada
  Bell South Services
  Boston Edison Company
  Columbia Gas Distribution Companies
  Consolidated Natural Gas Company
  Consumers Gas Company, Ltd.
  Consumers Power Company
  Copper Development Association, Inc.
  Delmarva Power & Light Company
  Detroit Edison Company
  Duke Power Company
  Edison Electric Company
  Electric Power Research Institute
  Gas Research Institute
  Home Builders Institute
  Houston Electric Institute
  Houston Lighting & Power Company
  Hydro Quebec
  Illinois Consolidated Telephone Co.
  International Conference of Building Officials
  Kansas Gas & Electric Company
  Long Star Gas Company
  Michigan Consolidated Gas Company
  Minnesota Blue Flame Gas Association
  National Association of Home Builders
  National Cable Television Association
  National Joint Apprenticeship & Training Committee
  Northern Illinois Gas
  Oklahoma Gas & Electric Co.
  Oklahoma Natural Gas Company
  Ontario Hydro
  Pacific Gas & Electric Company
  Pacific Power & Light Company
  Paragon Design Resources W.S. Ltd.
  Portland General Electric Company
  Potomac Electric Power Company
  Professional Builder
  Southern California Edison Company
  Southwest Gas
  Southwestern Bell Telephone Company
  U.S. Dept. of Housing & Urban Development
  U.S. West
  Union Gas Ltd.
  Virginia Electric & Power Company
  Washington Gas Light Company
  Wisconsin Electric Power Company

95.   National Center for Advanced Technologies, Inc. [5/30/89, FRP: 22971-2]

Aerospace Industries Association of America, Inc.
Aerojet General
Aeronca, Inc.
Allied-Signal Aerospace Company
Aluminum Company of America
Agro-Tech Corporation
B.H. Aircraft Company, Inc.
The Boeing Company
Celion Carbon Fibers
Chrysler Technologies Corporation
Colt Industries, Inc.
E-Systems, Inc.
Fairchild Industries
FMC Corporation
General Dynamics Corporation
General Electric Company
General Motors Corporation
The B.F. Goodrich Company
Grumman Corporation
Harris Corporation
Heath Tecna Aerospace Company
Hercules Incorporated
Hexcel Corporation
Honeywell, Inc.
IBM Corporation, Systems Integration Division
The Interlake Corporation
ISC Defense & Space Groups, Inc.
ITT Defense Technology Corporation
Kaman Aerospace Corporation
Lear Astronics Corporation
Lockheed Corporation
The LTV Corporation
Lucas Western, Inc.
Martin Marietta Corporation
McDonnell Douglas Corporation
Morton Thiokol, Inc.
Northrop Corporation
Parker Hannifin Corporation
Pneumo Abex Corporation
Precision Castparts Corporation
Raytheon Company
Rockwell International Corporation
Rohr Industries, Inc.
SLI Avionics Corporation-Smiths Industries
Sundstrand Corporation
Teledyne CAE
Textron, Inc.
TRW, Inc.
United Technologies Corporation
Westinghouse Electric Corporation
Wyman-Gordon Company

96. National Center of Manufacturing Sciences [3/17/87, FRP: 8375, 6/2/88, FRP: 20194, 8/19/88, FRP: 31771-2, 11/4/88, FRP: 44680, 1/18/89, FRP: 2006. 4/13/89, FRP: 14878]

Adept Technolgies, Inc.

Advanced Controls, Inc.
Advanced Material Process Corporation
Advanced Technology Materials, Inc.
Aircraft Engines Engineering Division, General Electric Company
Airborne, Incorporated
Amphion, Inc.
Aries Technology, Inc.
American Telephone & Telegraph Co.
Automation Intelligence, Inc.
The Bodine Corporation
Bresson, Rupp, Lipa & Company
The Cincinnati Gilbert Machine Tool Company
Consilium, Inc.
Control Technology, Inc.
The Cross Co.
DeVlieg Machine Company
Digital Equipment Corporation
Drie Press Systems (an EFCO company)
Dravo Automation Sciences, Inc.
Extrude Hone Corporation
Fabreeka Products Company
Ford Motor Company
Gearhart Industries, Inc.
General Motors Corporation
Gilbert/Commonwealth, Inc. of Michigan
The Gleason Works
Hardinge Brothers, Inc.
Haworth, Inc.
Hougen Manufacturing Company, Inc.
Jufcor, Inc.
S.E. Huffman Corp.
Hurco Companies, Inc.
Kasper Machine Co.
Kayex Spitfire, a unit of General Signal Corporation
Kinefac Corporation
Kingsbury Machine Tool Corp.
H.R. Kraeger Machine Tool, Inc.
The M.D. Larkin Company
Lehr Precision, Inc.
Len Industries, Inc.
Litton Industrial Automation Systems, Inc.
Manuflex Corporation
Masco Machine, Inc.
Mattison Machine Works
Mayday Manufacturing Co.
Measurex Automation Systems, Inc.
Mechanical Technology, Incorporated
Medar, Inc.
Met-Coil Systems Corporation
Metal Improvement Company, Inc.
Microfab Technologies, Inc.
Modern Engineering Service Company
Moore Special Tool Co. Inc.
Murdock Engineering Company
The National Machinery Company
Newcor Bay City, Division of Newcor, Inc.
Oracle, Inc.

Parker-Majestic, Inc.
Perceptron, Inc.
Plainfield Tool and Engineering Inc. (d/b/a/ Plainfield Stamping - Illinois
    Incorporated)
Prime Technology, Inc.
Radian Corporation
R & B Machine Tool Company
Recognition Equipment Incorporated
RF Monolithics, Inc.
Rockwell International Corporation
Savoir
Sheffield Machine Tool Company
SpeedFam Corporation
Sybase, Inc.
The Taft-Pierce Manufacturing Company
Technology Integration, Inc.
Teledyne Inc.
Texas Instruments Incorporated
Transform Logic Corporation
Turchan Enterprises, Inc.
United Technologies Corporation
Valisys Corporation
The Vulcan Tool Company
Walker Magnetics Group, Inc.
The Warner & Swasey Co.
Weldon Machine Tool, Inc.
Weyburn Bartel, Inc.
Wizdom Systems, Inc.

97. National Forest Products Association (NFPA) [10/30/87, FRP: 41786, 8/4/88,
     FRP: 29396, 10/13/88, FRP: 40140]

Alpine Engineered Product, Inc.
American Institute of Timber Construction
American Plywood Association
Boise Cascade Corporation
California Lumber Inspection Service
Canadian Wood Council
Fabricated Wood Components, Inc.
Gang-Nail Systems, Inc.
Mitek Wood Products, Inc.
MSR Lumber Producers Council
National Forest Products Association
Northeastern Lumber Manufacturers Association
Pacific Lumber Manufacturers Association
Southern Forest Products Association
Southern Pine Inspection Bureau
Standard Structures Inc.
Timber Products Inspection, Inc.
Truss Joist Corporation
Truss Plate Institute
Truswal Systems Corporation
West Coast Lumber Inspection Bureau
Western Wood Products Association
Weyerhaeuser Building Systems, Inc.
Willametie Industries, Inc.

98. Norton-TRW Ceramics [1/28/86, FRP: 3519-20]

Norton Company
TRW Inc.

99. Omega Marine Services International, Inc. (OMSI) [3/1/89, FRP: 8606-7]

Amoco Production Company
BP-Exploration
Occidental International Exploration & Production Co.
Exxon Production Research Company
Conoco Inc.
Chevron Corporation
Shell Oil Company
Mobil Research & Development Corporation
National Institute of Standards & Technology on behalf of the Naval Civil
    Engineering Lab. and the Minerals Management Service

100. Oncogen Limited (Bristol-Myers Co.) [4/30/85, FRP: 18326]

General Partners:
    Wallingford Research, Inc.
    Cancer Research, Inc.
    Sygenic Company
Limited Partner:
    ONKEM Limited Partnership

101. Open Software Foundation, Inc. [9/7/88, FRP: 34594, 11/25/88, FRP: 4773,
2/23/89, FRP: 7893-4]

Voting Members:
    Apollo Computer, Inc.
    Groupe Bull SA
    Digital Equipment Corporation
    Hitachi Ltd.
    Hewlett-Packard Company
    International Business Machines Corporation
    Siemens AG
    High Technology Investments, Inc. – subsidiary of Nixdorf Corporation,
    N.V. Philips' Gloeilampenfabrieken
Non-voting members:
    88 Open Consortium Ltd. - Textronics, Inc.
    Addamax Corporation
    Adobe Systems, Inc.
    Advanced Micro Devices
    Altos Computer Systems
    Booz, Allen & Hamilton Inc.
    Canon Inc.
    Carnegie Mellon University
    Centrum vorr Wiscunde en Informatica (CWI)
    Chalmers University of Technology
    Compagnie Europpene des Techniques de L'Ingenierie Assistee (CETIA)
    Computer Consoles
    Concurrent Computer Corporation
    Convex Computer Corporation
    Cornell University
    CSK Corporation

Data General Corp.
Data Logic Ltd.
DECUS U.S. Chapter (DEC User Group)
Dell Computer Corporation
Ecole Nationale Supenseure d'Ingenieers - Electricienf de Grenoble
   (E.N.S.I.E.G.)
EDUCOM
GKSS Forschungszentrum Geesthacht GmbH
GM/EDS C4 Program
HCR Corporation
Informix Software, Inc.
Institut d'Informatique et de Mathematiques Appliquees de Grenoble
   (IMAG)
Institut National de Recherche en Informatique et en Automatique   (INRIA)
Institute for Information Industry
Intel Corporation
Interactive Systems Corporation
Interfirm Graphics Systems
Intergraph
Kendall Square Research Corp.
Lachman Associates, Inc.
Landmark Graphics
Locus Computing Corporation
Mentor Graphics Corporation
MICOM-Interlan, Inc.
Micro Focus
MIPS Computer Systems
Mitre Corporation
NASA/Goddard Space Flight Center
National Institute for Higher Education
National Semiconductor Corp.
Norsk Data A.S.
Omron Tateishi Electronics Comp.
Oracle Corporation
Pacific Bell
Phoenix Technologies Ltd.
Project Athena, MIT
Relational Technology
RIAC NASA Ames Research Center
S.I.A. V.le Certosa
Samsung Group
Sequent Computer Systems, Inc.
Shell International
Softsiel Corp.
Software AG, Darmstadt D-6100
Stanford University
Stratus Computer, Inc.
Swedish Telecom Group
Synthesis Software Solutions, Inc.
Tecsiel S.p.A., a wholly owned subsidiary of Softsiel Corp.
Texas Instruments
Tolerant Systems
Toshiba America Inc.
University of Guelph
University of Maryland
University of Michigan
University of Southern California

University of Texas
Wang
Xerox Corporation

102. OSI/Network Management Forum [12/8/88, FRP: 49615, 1/26/89, FRP: 3870, 4/25/89, FRP: 17834-5, 8/4/89, FRP: 32141]

Voting Members:
Amdahl Corporation
Applied Computering Devices, Inc.
British Telecommunications PLC
Digital Communication Associations Inc.
France Telecom, Direction Generale
Gandalf Data Ltd
GEC Plessey Telecommunications Ltd.
General Datacomm, Inc.
Hewlett-Packard Company
MCI Telecommunications
McDonnell Douglas Network Systems Company
Microtel Limited
Netlabs
Nippon Telegraph and Telephone
Northern Telecom Inc.
Tandem Computers, Inc.
Televerket
STC Telecommunications
Societa Finanziaria Telefonia
Stratus Computer, Inc.
Teknedron Communications Systems Inc.
Telecom Canada
UNISYS Networks
Ungermann-Bass, Incorporated
Associate Members:
Alcatel N.V.
Avant-Garde Computing Inc.
Bull S.A.
Cable & Wireless PLC
Case Communications Ltd.
Computrol, A division of Modcomp, an AEG company
Contel Technology Center
CNCP Telecommunications
Data General Corporation
Dynatech Communications
Ericsson Business Communication AB
Fujitsu America, Inc.
Gartner Group
Ing. C. Olivetti & C.S.p.A.
Hekimian Laboratories, Inc.
Infotron Systems Corporation
Interlan, Inc.
Kokusai Denshin Denwa Co. Ltd.
NCR Corporation
NEC America, Inc.
Network Equipment Technologies
Newbridge Networks Corporation
Nixdorf Computer Engineering Corporation
Novell Inc.

OKI Electric Industry Co. Ltd.
Paradyne Corporation
Philips Telecommunications & Data Systems
Prime Computer, Inc.
Protocols Standards and Communications (PSC) Inc.
Racal-Milgo
Racal-Milgo, Ltd.
Retix
Siemens AG
Sirti S.P.A.
Spider Systems Ltd.
Synoptics Communications, Inc.
Systems Reliablity PLC
Tech Nel Data Products Ltd.
Telenet Communications Corp.
Telindus N.V.
Vance Systems Inc.
Zellweger Telecommunications

103. Pacific Bell and Integrated Network Corp. [7/1/87, FRP: 24542]

Pacific Bell
Integrated Network Corp.

104. PDES, Inc. [10/14/88, FRP: 40282-3, 3/21/89, FRP: 11580, 7/18/89, FRP: 30116]

The Boeing Company
Computervision Corp.
Digital Equipment Corp.
FMC Corporation
General Dynamics Corporation
General Electric Company
General Motors Corporation
Grumman Corporation
Honeywell Inc.
IBM
Lockheed Corporation
LTV Corporation
Martin Marietta Corp.
McDonnell Douglas Corporation
Newport News Shipbuilding & Drydock Co. Westinghouse Electric Corp.
Northrop Corporation
Rockwell International Corporation

105. Petroleum Environmental Research Forum [3/14/86, FRP: 8903, 6/9/86, FRP: 20897-8, 6/19/86, FRP: 22365, 7/17/86, FRP: 25957, 3/1/89, FRP: 8607, 4/20/89, FRP: 16014]

Amerada Hess Corporation
Amoco Oil Company
Ashland Oil Inc.
Atlantic Richfield Company
BP America
Chevron Research Co.
Conoco Inc.
Exxon Research & Engineering Co.

Kerr-McGee Corporation
Koch Refining company
Marathon Oil Company
Mobil Research & Development Corp.
Murphy Oil USA, Inc.
Pennzoil Company
Phillips Petroleum Company
Shell Development Company
Sun Company Inc.
Texaco Refining & Marketing Inc.
Union Oil Company of California

106. Petroleum Environmental Research Forum (86-05) [3/25/87, FRP: 9554]

Chevron Research Company
Exxon Research and Engineering Company
Texaco Refining and Market Inc.

107. Petroleum Environmental Research Forum (86-06)   [3/25/87, FRP: 9554-5]

Amoco Oil Company
Chevron Research Company
Murphy Oil U.S.A. Inc.
Sun Refining and Marketing Company
Texaco Refining and Marketing Inc.
Union Oil Company of California

108. Petroleum Environmental Research Forum (86-09) [3/25/87, FRP: 9554,
2/12/88, FRP: 4233]

Amoco Oil Company
Atlantic Richfield Company
Chevron Research Company
Exxon Research & Engineering Company
The Standard Oil Company
Texaco Refining and Marketing Inc.
Union Oil Company of California

109. Petroleum Environmental Research Forum (87-04) [5/1/89, FRP: 18607]

Amoco Oil Company
BP America
Shell Oil Company
Chevron Research Company
Radian Corporation

110. Petroleum Environmental Research Forum (87-05) [12/30/88, FRP: 53079]

Amoco Oil Company
Chevron Research Company
Conoco Inc.
Mobil Research & Development Corporation

111. Petroleum Environmental Research Forum "Premix Surface Combustion PSC
Burner Demostration Program" [6/3/88, FRP: 20385]

Atlantic Richfield Company

Chevron U.S.A. Inc.
Union Oil Company of California

112. Plastics Recycling Foundation, Inc. [5/21/85, FRP: 20954, 10/9/85, FRP: 41232]

Allegheny Leeter-Eater
Allied Corporation
Bev-Pak
Brockway, Inc.
Coca-Cola Bottling Company of New York
Coca-Cola USA
Conair, Inc.
Continental Plastic Containers
Eastman Chemical Products, Inc.
E.I. duPont de Nemours & Company
Hoover Universal, Inc.
Occidental Chemical Corporation
Nelmor Company
Owens Illinois, Inc.
Rohm and Haas Company
The Seven-Up Company
Sewell Plastics
The Society of the Plastics Industry, Inc.
Sundor Brands
Union Carbide Corporation
U.S. Industrial Chemicals Company
Van Dorn Plastic Machinery Company

Notes

1. A study conducted by Coopers & Lybrand and Yankelovich, Skelly and White, Inc. in which 38 collaborative ventures were examined found that over 68 percent fell short of the partners' expectations. See *Collaborative Ventures: A Pragmatic Approach to Business Expansion in the Eighties* (Coopers & Lybrand, 1984), p. 10. A recent example of disappointment in cooperative action is the failure of U.S. Memories. Robert D. Hof, "This Will Surely Come Back to Haunt Us," *Business Week*, January 29, 1990, pp. 72–73.

2. Kathryn Rudie Harrigan, *Strategies for Joint Ventures* (Lexington Books, 1985), p. 1.

3. Coopers & Lybrand et al., *Collaborative Ventures*.

4. Secretariat, *Trends in Collective Industrial Research* (Delft, Netherlands: Six Countries Programme on Aspects of Government Policies Toward Technological Innovations, November 1979).

5. *National Cooperative Research Act of 1984* (Public Law 98–462), 15 U.S.C. §4301 (1984). See also Note, "Joint Research Ventures Under the Antitrust Laws," 39 *George Washington Law Review* 1112 (1971).

6. Robert Pitofsky, "A Framework for Antitrust Analysis of Joint Ventures," 54 *Antitrust L.J.* 893, 894 (1985).

7. Hugo E. R. Uyterhoeven, "Foreign Entry and Joint Ventures," unpublished DBA thesis, Harvard Business School, 1963. See also Karen Kraus Bivens and Enid Baird Lovell, *Joint Ventures with Foreign Partners* (National Industrial Conference Board, 1966), and Raymond Vernon and Louis T. Wells, Jr., *Manager in the International Economy* (Prentice-Hall, 1976). In accord is Harrigan, *Strategies*, p. 13.

8. Douglas W. Hill, *Co-operative Research in Industry* (Hutchinson's Scientific and Technical Publications, 1946).

9. For example, exploration and exploitation of the North Slope oil fields in Alaska involved a number of cooperative ventures to spread risk and accumulate the vast resources required.

10. The New United Motor Manufacturing Co. (NUMMI) owned 50/50 by Toyota and General Motors.

11. IBM's joint venture with Rohm eventually led to IBM's 100 percent owner-ship of Rohm. In the other, IBM acquired a 20-percent interest in Intel. IBM has also entered into strategic alliances with Siemens, Mitel (abrogated in 1983), British Telecom, Mitsubishi, MCI, and Stet/Italtel.

12. See, e.g., United States v. Automobile Mfgs. Assn., 1969 Trade Cases ¶72,907 (C.D. Cal 1969), also popularly known as the Smog Conspiracy Case, and United States v. Manufacturers Aircraft Assn., 5 Trade Reg. Rep. ¶45,072 (S.D.N.Y. 1972). A more detailed discussion regarding the Smog Conspiracy case and related legal considerations is contained in chapter three.

13. The Microelectronics and Computer Technology Corporation, Harvard Business School Case Service (383–067); The Chemical Industry Institute of Toxicology, Harvard Business School Case Service (382–167 and 385–061), and The American Industrial Health Council, Harvard Business School Case Service (383–047).

14. Chester Barnard, *The Functions of the Executive* (Harvard University Press, 1938, 1968).

15. Harrigan, *Strategies*, p. 1.

16. For examples see Donald A. Hay and Derek J. Morris, *Industrial Economics: Theory and Evidence* (Oxford University Press, 1979), pp. 143–80, in which the authors discuss the economics of interfirm cooperation from "quasi-agreements" (cooperation without specific collusion) to formal cartels; and F. M. Scherer, *Industrial Market Structure and Economic Performance* (Rand McNally College Publishing, 1970), pp. 158–82.

17. See chapter 3 and the economic theories underlying domestic competition policy and the antitrust laws.

18. William G. Shepherd, *The Economics of Industrial Organization* (Prentice-Hall, 1979), p. 305, note 9. See also Richard M. Cyert and James G. March, *A Behavior Theory of the Firm* (Prentice-Hall, 1963), p. 120.

19. Bengt Högberg, *Interfirm Cooperation and Strategic Development* (BAS, Stockholm, 1977), pp. 6–8.

20. Scherer, *Industrial Market Structure*, pp. 116–17.

21. For an overview of the field see John W. Pratt and Richard J. Zeckhauser, eds., *Principals and Agents: The Structure of Business*, (Harvard Business School Press, 1985). This book is the result of a research colloquium held at the Harvard Business School on the occasion of the seventy-fifth anniversary of the school's founding.

22. It is important to note that the agency-principal relationship in the economics literature is not the same as that found in the legal literature. The former is more inclusive and less subject to rigid characterizations. Under the law, agency is a fiduciary relationship that has four elements: (1) parties competent to act as principal and agent, (2) who mutually agree (3) that the agent will act for or on the principal's behalf, and (4) will be subject to the principal's direction and control. *Restatement of the Law of Agency*, Second, §1e (American Law Institute).

23. Pratt and Zeckhauser, eds., *Principals and Agents*, pp. 2–3.

24. Ibid., p. 3.

25. Ibid., p. 5.

26. "In a business organization the coalition members include managers, workers, stockholders, suppliers, customers, lawyers, tax collectors, regulatory agencies, etc." and, "Drawing the boundaries of an organizational coalition once and for all is impossible." Cyert and March, *Behavior Theory*, p. 27.

27. Ibid., p. 120.

28. Ibid.

29. Ibid., p. 119.

30. Cyert and March cite the following for this assessment: D. B. Truman, *The Governmental Process* (Knopf, 1951), A. D. Kaplan, J. B. Dirlam, and R. F. Lanzillotti, *Pricing in Big Business* (Brookings Institute, 1958), and P. Selznick, *TVA and the Grass Roots* (University of California Press, 1949). Ibid., p. 28.

31. For example, some authors argue that the "more similar the co-venturers objectives . . . the better the chances for success." Richard Young and Standish Bradford, Jr., *Joint Ventures: Planning & Action*, (Financial Executives Research Foundation, 1977), p. 8.

32. Cyert and March, *Behavior Therapy*, p. 28.

33. James D. Thompson, *Organizations in Action* (McGraw-Hill, 1967), pp. 35–36.

34. According to Thompson there are three types of organizational interdependence: pooled, sequential, and reciprocal. To each he assigned an appropriate coordinating process: pooled — standardization, sequential — planning, and reciprocal — mutual adjustment. Ibid., p. 64–65.

35. John von Neumann and Oskar Morgenstern, *Theory of Games and Economics Behavior* (Princeton University Press, 1944).

36. Battle of the Sexes is the name generally applied to a particular two-person, non-zero-sum game. The game often appears in the following descriptive form: A husband and wife must decide whether they go to the ballet or a prizefight. Although the husband would prefer to go to the fight with his wife, he would prefer to go the ballet with her rather than go to the fight alone. The wife's preferences are similar but reversed.

37. "Colonel Blotto" is the label used in connection with a class of games in which the participants are required to allocate resources at their disposal. In that the game is often described in terms of a colonel or general deploying troops, the military name has become the most widely recognized.

38. The Prisoner's Dilemma is discussed in the following text.

39. Thomas C. Schelling, *The Strategy of Conflict*, (Harvard University Press, 1960).

40. See, for example, L. G. Telser, *Competition, Collusion, and Game Theory* (Aldine-Atherton, 1972), and D. K. Osborne, "Cartel Problems," *American Economic Review*, 66:835–44 (1976).

41. This part of the "history" of the Prisoner's Dilemma appears in Robert Axelrod, *The Evolution of Cooperation* (Basic Books, 1984), p. 216, note 2. One of the earliest published version of the game appears in Merrill M. Flood, "Some Experimental Games," *Rand Memorandum*, RM-789-2 (1952).

42. William D. Hamilton, "The Evolution of Altruistic Behavior," *American Naturalist*, 97:354–56 (1963). Later expanded upon in a jointly authored article, Robert Axelrod and William D. Hamilton, "The Evolution of Cooperation," *Science*, 211:1390–96 (1981).

43. William Riker and Steve J. Brams, "The Paradox of Vote Trading," *American Political Science Review*, 67:1235–47 (1973).

44. Paul Samuelson, *Economics* (McGraw-Hill, 1973).

45. Robert Axelrod, *The Evolution of Cooperation (Basic Books, 1984).*

46. Evidence of this attitude can be seen in the decisions actually made by the member companies of MCC. See chapter 5.

47. Michael Aiken and Jerald Hage, "Organizational Interdependence and Intraorganizational Structure," *American Sociological Review*, 33:912–929 (1968).

48. Stanley E. Boyle, "An Estimate of the Number and Distribution of Domestic Joint Subsidiaries," *Antitrust Law & Economics Review*, 1:81–92 (1968).

49. James D. Hlavacek, Brian H. Dovey, and John J. Biondo, "Tie Small Business Technology to Marketing Power," *Harvard Business Review*, 55(1):106–16 (Jan.–Feb. 1977). In accord with Hlavacek, Dovey, and Biondo's argument that disparate relative firm size can be advantageous in a cooperative venture are Berg and Friedman, "Joint Ventures in American Industry," *Mergers and Acquisitions* (Fall 1978), p. 17. On the other hand, there are authors who argue that joint venture success is better served by partners of more equal size or resources. Young and Bradford, *Planning & Action*, p. 8., and Stephen E. Roulac, "Structuring the Joint Venture," *Mergers & Acquisitions* (Spring 1980), p. 7.

50. Ibid., p. 109.

51. Jeffrey Pfeffer and Phillip Nowak, "Patterns of Joint Venture Activity – Implications for Antitrust Policy," *Antitrust Bulletin*, 21(2):315–39 (1976).

52. Anders Edström, "Acquisition and Joint Venture Behavior of Swedish Manufacturing Firms," *Scandinavian Journal of Economics*, Vol. 3 (1976).

53. Daniel R. Fusfeld, "Joint Subsidiaries in the Iron and Steel Industry," *American Economic Review*, 48:578–587 (1958).

54. Pfeffer and Nowak, "Patterns."

55. W. J. Mead, "Competitive Significance of Joint Ventures," *Antitrust Bulletin*, 12:819–49 (1967).

56. Sanford V. Berg and Philip Friedman, "Joint Ventures in American Industry," *Mergers and Acquisitions* (Summer 1978), p. 38.

57. Harrigan, *Strategies*, p. 13 (emphasis hers).

58. John M. Stopford and Louis T. Wells, Jr., *Managing the Multinational Enterprise* (Basic Books, 1972).

59. Lawrence G. Franko, *Joint Venture Survival in Multinational Corporations* (Praeger Publishers, 1971).

60. Stopford and Wells, *Multinational Enterprise*, p. 123.

61. Franko, *Survival*, p. 20.

62. Ibid., p. 142–46.

63. Karen J. Hladik, *International Joint Ventures* (Lexington Books, 1985).

64. Benjamin Gomes-Casseres, "Multinational Ownership Strategies", unpublished doctoral dissertation, Harvard Graduate School of Business Administration (1985).

65. This "lack of success" for joint ventures has been commented upon by: Edgar Herzfeld, *Joint Ventures* (Jordan & Sons, 1983), p. 23; Management Monograph, *Recent Experience in Establishing Joint Ventures* (Business International, 1972), p. 2; Sanford Berg and Philip Friedman, "Joint Ventures in American Industry," *Mergers and Acquisitions*, (second of three articles, Fall 1978), p. 17. In accord is the study conducted by the accounting firm of Coopers & Lybrand on joint ventures.

66. Harrigan, *Strategies*, p. 14.

67. For example, Herzfeld, *Joint Ventures*, p. 23.

68. For example, Sanford Berg, Jerome Duncan, and Philip Friedman, *Joint Venture Strategies and Corporate Innovation* (Oelgeschlageer, Gunn & Hain, 1982),

p. 72. The authors, whose research is based on a survey/questionnaire of 650 domestic joint ventures with follow-up interviews of a smaller number of executives, discovered that joint ventures were viewed as a "last resort."

69. Young and Bradford, *Planning & Action*, p. 8.

70. Ibid.

71. Business International Management Monograph No. 54, *Recent Experience in Establishing Joint Ventures* (Business International Corporation, 1972), p. 2.

72. Herzfeld, *Joint Ventures*, pp. 26–27.

73. Management Monograph No. 54, *Recent Experience*, p. 3.

74. The four are: (1) Make available diverse resources and minimize risk, (2) increase options, (3) circumvent capital crisis, and (4) permit project-specific financing. Roulac, "Structuring," p. 5.

75. Berg and Friedman "Ventures in Industry" (Summer 1978), p. 39.

76. Berg, Duncan, and Friedman, *Strategies and Innovation*, p. 93.

77. Coopers & Lybrand et al., *Collaborative Ventures*, p. 3.

78. Ibid.

79. Ibid., p. 4.

80. Management Monograph No. 54, *Recent Experience*, p. 3.

81. Harrigan, *Strategies*, p. 2.

82. Herzfeld, *Joint Ventures*, p. 7.

83. Wolfgang G. Friedman and George Kalmanoff, eds., *Joint International Business Ventures* (Columbia University Press, 1961). To Friedman and Kalmanoff the central concept in the joint international business venture is that of partnership. Furthermore, this partnership has two sides — technical and emotional. The technical side is a joining of contributions; the emotional side is a feeling of united or cooperative effort. Some cooperative ventures, particularly those in military hardware development, may not have the government as an active partner, but the government is a significant influence. For a discussion of the issues facing these joint ventures see Milton S. Hochmuth, "The Effect of Structure on Strategy: The Government Sponsored Multinational Joint Venture", unpublished doctoral dissertation, Harvard Business School (1972).

84. Berg and Friedman, "Ventures in Industry," (Summer, Fall, and Winter 1978), also Berg, Duncan, & Friedman, *Strategies and Innovation*.

85. Berg and Friedman, "Ventures in Industry" (Summer 1978), p. 34.

86. Richard J. Thompson, "Competitive Effects of Joint Ventures in the Chemical Industry", unpublished doctoral dissertation, University of Massachusetts at Amherst (1970).

87. Berg and Friedman, "Ventures in Industry" (Summer 1978), p. 34.

88. Harrigan, *Strategies*, p. 3.

89. Ibid., p. 2.

90. Roulac, "Structuring", p. 5.

91. Berg, Duncan and Friedman, *Strategies and Innovation*, pp. 16–18.

92. Harrigan, *Strategies*, p. 8. The database cited by Harrigan is from Jerome Lawson Duncan, Jr., "The Causes and Effects of Domestic Joint Venture Activity", unpublished doctoral dissertation, University of Florida (1980).

93. See discussion, Harrigan, *Strategies*, pp. 27–28.

94. See for example Stopford and Wells, *Multinational Enterprise*, and Franko, *Survival*.

95. Differences in the motivations for foreign joint ventures may be one reason for treating them as a special subset of interfirm cooperation. For example, according to one study, foreign joint ventures are primarily formed for defensive reasons "as a response to nationalism." This, of course, would not be true of cooperative ventures between two domestic companies. Management Monograph No. 54, *Recent Experience*, p. 3.

96. Young and Bradford, *Planning & Action*, p. 12.

97. Management Monograph No. 54, *Recent Experience*.

98. David A. Ricks, Marilyn Y.C. Fu, and Jeffrey S. Arpan, *International Business Blunders* (Grid, 1974), p. 39.

99. Young and Bradford, *Planning & Action*, p. 12.

100. Ibid.

101. Herzfeld, *Ventures*, p. 7. Although the author would include less permanent forms of cooperation he would exclude short-term arrangements such as underwriting groups from the ranks of true joint ventures.

102. The football analogy is particularly apt given the history of antitrust and football. For example, NCAA v. The Board of Regents of Oklahoma et al., 52 U.S.L.W. 4928 (1984), North American Soccer League v. National Football League, 670 F.2d 1249 (2d Cir.), cert. denied, 459 U.S. 1074 (1982), and United States v. National Football League, 196 F.Supp. 445 (E.D.Pa 1961).

103. Just to cite one of the most popular works in this vein, consider Michael E. Porter, *Competitive Strategy* (Free Press, 1980). Business schools have also given attention to the role of competitive forces on business organizations by offering courses such as "Industry and Competitor Analysis" as key elements of graduate business education.

104. For a summary overview of the applicable antitrust laws see Appendix 1.

105. United States v. Topco Associates, Inc., 405 U.S. 596, 610 (1972).

106. Adam Smith, *An Inquiry into the Nature and Causes of the Wealth of Nations* (1776).

107. Earl W. Kinter, *The Legislative History of the Federal Antitrust Laws and Related Statutes* (The MacMillan Company, 1978), p. 60.

108. 15 U.S.C.A., §§1–3.

109. 15 U.S.C.A. §§13, 14, 18 and 45.

110. United States v. Trenton Potteries Company, 273 U.S. 392, 397 (1927).

111. For a discussion of this issue see, J. L. Bower and E. A. Rhenman, "Benevolent Cartels", 85 Harvard Business Review 124 (July-August 1985).

112. Tag Mfrs. Institute v. FTC, 174 F.2d 452 (1st Cir. 1949).

113. E.g., United States v. Concentrated Phosphate Export Associations, Inc., 393 U.S. 199 (1968).

114. United States v. Morgan, 118 F.Supp. 621 (S.D.N.Y. 1953).

115. Compare United States v. International Boxing Club of New York, Inc., 348 U.S. 236 (1955) with United States v. Guerlain, Inc., 155 F.Supp. 77 (S.D.N.Y. 1957), vacated mem. 358 U.S. 915 (1958).

116. United States v. Aluminum Company of America, 148 F.2d 416, 429 (2d Cir. 1945).

117. Sugar Institute, Inc. v. United States, 297 U.S. 553 (1936). The concept of "fair" competition is embodied in Section 5 of the Federal Trade Commission Act and interjects some notion of competition by certain standards rather than an all-out,

unrestrained, dog-eat-dog competition. For a discussion of competitive fairness see Federal Trade Commission v. Sperry & Hutchinson Co., 405 U.S. 233 (1972).

118. 166 U.S. 290 (1897).

119. 21 Cong. Rec. 2457 (1890).

120. A. D. Neale, *The Antitrust Laws of the U.S.A.*, p. 14 fn. 2.

121. 21 Cong. Rec. at 5956 (1890). See also, William L. Letwin, "Congress and the Sherman Antitrust Law: 1887–1890", 23 U. Chicago Law Review 221, 257 (Winter 1956).

122. Standard Oil Co. of N.J. v. United States, 221 U.S. 1, 89 (1911).

123. 221 U.S. 1 at 58–60.

124. United States v. Trans-Missouri Freight Association, 166 U.S. 290 (1897).

125. Earl W. Kinter, *An Antitrust Primer* (The MacMillan Company, 1973), p. 21.

126. A. D. Neale, *The Antitrust Laws of the U.S.A.*, p. 39.

127. United States v. Socony-Vacuum Company, 310 U.S. 150 (1940).

128. 310 U.S. 150, 224–25 fn. 59 (1940).

129. For examples of the latter, see American Column and Lumber Company v. United States, 257 U.S. 377 (1921), United States v. American Linseed Oil Company, 262 U.S. 371 (1923) and Sugar Institute, Inc. v. United States, 297 U.S. 553 (1936). For an example of the former see, Maple Flooring Manufacturers' Association v. United States, 268 U.S. 563 (1925).

130. 196 U.S. 375, 400 (1905).

131. 101 Fed. Supp. 856 (DC Minn. 1951).

132. 101 Fed. Supp. 856, 868 (DC Minn. 1951).

133. 15 U.S.C.A. §§61–65 (1973).

134. 15 U.S.C.A. §§638(d)(3) (1964).

135. 15 U.S.C.A. §§4301–4305.

136. 333 U.S. 287, 310 (1948).

137. Chicago Board of Trade v. United States, 246 U.S. 231, 238 (1918).

138. Joseph F. Brodley, "The Legal Status of Joint Ventures under the Antitrust Laws: A Summary Assessment", 21 *Antitrust Bulletin* 453, (1976).

139. Ibid., p. 454.

140. Joseph Taubman, "What Constitutes a Joint Venture?," 41 *Cornell L. Quarterly* 640, 641 (1957).

141. Gerhard A. Gesell, "Joint Ventures in Light of Recent Antitrust Developments: Joint Ventures and the Prosecutor," 10 *Antitrust Bulletin* 31 (1965).

142. 394 U.S. 131 (1969).

143. 405 U.S. 596 (1972).

144. Timken Roller Bearing Co. v. United States, 341 U.S. 593, 597–8 (1951).

145. 194 F.2d 89 (4th Cir. 1952).

146. For a discussion of this issue, see Donald F. Turner, "Patents, Antitrust and Innovation," 28 *Univ. of Pittsburgh L. Rev.* 151 (1966). For a criticism of how effective antitrust policy and enforcement may be in this regard, see Douglas H. Ginsberg, "Antitrust, Uncertainty, and Technological Innovation," *The Antitrust Bulletin* 635 (Winter 1979).

147. 98th Congress 2d Session House of Representatives Report 98–656 and 98th Congress 2d Session Senate Report 98–247, which both note that the Justice Department has never mounted a challenge to a pure R&D joint venture. A similar claim was also made by Assistant Attorney General for Antitrust Douglas Ginsberg during a speech made at the Harvard Business School, April 1986.

148. Terrence F. MacLaren and Walter G. Marple, Jr.; *Licensing in Foreign and Domestic Operations — Joint Ventures*, Clark Boardman Company, Ltd., Vol. 4 at 5–5, (1985).

149. United States v. Motor Vehicle Manufacturers Association , et al., U.S. District Court, Central District of California, Civil Action No. 69–75–JWC (November 9, 1981).

150. 50 Federal Register, No. 27, 5444–50 (Feb. 8, 1985).

151. In February of 1982 a number of computer and computer component manufacturers met in Orlando, Florida, to discuss the possibility of forming a cooperative R&D venture. Out of this and subsequent meetings the Microelectronics and Computer Technology Corporation (popularly referred to as MCC) was formed.

152. Letter from Joseph M. Alioto to MCC member company executives and Senator Howard Metzenbaum, July 27, 1983.

153. Ibid., p. 3.

154. H.R. 1952, H.R. 33.93, S. 568, S. 1383.

155. Opening Remarks of Congressman Doug Walgren, Chairman, House Subcommittee on Science, Research, and Technology, U.S. House of Representatives, July 12, 1983.

156. Statement of Congressman Ed Zschau before the House Subcommittee on Science, Research, and Technology, July 12, 1983.

157. H.R. 5041 and S. 1841.

158. Memorandum of the Commission on the Action Programme for the Second Stage, Com. (62) 300, (October 24, 1962).

159. Treaty Establishing the European Economic Community [hereafter Treaty of Rome], March 25, 1957, 1 Common Mkt. Rep. (CCH).

160. Treaty of Rome, Article 86.

161. Van Themaat, *Competition and Restrictive Trade Practices in the European Economic Community* (The Federal Bar Association, 1960), p. 114.

162. Hawk, *Joint Ventures Under EEC Competition Rules*, "Private Investors Abroad — Problems and Solutions in International Business," (1980).

163. For example, in the European Economic Commission's Sixth Report on Competition Policy (April 1977) the following was set forth regarding the assessment of joint ventures: "From the decisions taken by the Commission so far, the following conclusions can be drawn: the Commission will refuse to grant exemptions under Article 85(3) wherever the formation of a joint venture does not offer substantial economic benefits and wherever there is a chance that competition in the relevant market may be appreciable reduced."

164. General Motors Corp. and Toyota Motor Corp., FTC File No. 8210159. Statement of Chairman Miller and Commissioners Douglas and Calvani, 48 Fed. Reg. 57, 314 (1983).

165. Shiteki dokusen no kinshi oyobi kōsei torihiki no kakuho ni kansuru hōritsu (Act concerning Prohibition of Private Monopoly and Maintenance of Fair Trade), Law No. 54 of 1947 (hereafter the Antimonopoly Law).

166. K. Haitani, *The Japanese Economic System* (1976), p. 131.

167. Note, "Trustbusting in Japan," 94 Harv. L. Rev. 1064, 1066 (1981).

168. Law No. 259 of 1953.

169. Akinori Uesugi, "Japanese Antimonopoly Policy — Its Past and Future," 50 Antitrust L.J. 709 (1981).

170. After the war Mitsubishi Trading had been split into 139 companies. By 1954 Mitsubishi Corporation, anchored by a bank, had recovered much of its former prominence. Ibid., p. 711.

171. 94 Harv. L. Rev. at 1071 (1981).

172. Seichi Yoshikawa, "Fair Trade Commission vs. MITI: History of the Conflicts Between the Antimonopoly Policy and the Industrial Policy in the Post War Period of Japan," 15 Case W. Res. J. Int'l. L. 489 (1983).

173. Sekiyu Renmei hoka 2 mei (Petroleum Association of Japan and 2 others v. Japan), Tokyo High Court September 26, 1980. 983 Hanrei jiho 22, 985 Hanrei jiho 3. For a detailed discussion of the evolution of Japanese antitrust policy following the Petroleum Cartel case, see J. Mark Ramseyer, "Japanese Antitrust Enforcement After the Oil Embargo," 31 Am.J.Comp.L. 395 (1983).

174. "The biggest stumbling block to R&D collaboration has been the U.S. antitrust legislation." William P. Dunk and Courtney W. Beinhorn, "Making R&D Dollars Work Harder," *High Technology*, April 1984, p. 69. "U.S. Industry has long been wary of joint research ventures because of their ambiguous legal status under the antitrust laws." Jonathan B. Tucker, "R&D Consortia: Can U.S. Industry Beat the Japanese at Their Own Game?" *High Technology*, Special Report. "For companies even to consider pooling research efforts in the past was considered anticompetitive." Robert L. Simison, "Quiet War Rages on Technology's Front Line," *Wall Street Journal*, December 24, 1985, p. 4. "Antitrust laws and Justice Department guidelines on compliance currently require lengthy and complex analyses – and even then, in virtually every situation, legal opinions have varying degrees of ambiguity. This tends to discourage cooperation." William Norris, "Keeping America First," *Datamation*, September 1982, p. 287.

175. Most notably the passage of NCRA in 1984 but also in the active promotion of interfirm cooperation in certain sections of government such as the Department of Commerce and the Department of Defense. See for example "Electronic Warfare 1984 Part 2: Getting It Together," *Aviation Week and Space Technology*, April 23, 1984, pp. 73–132; and, Evert Clark, "American Can Beat Anyone in High Tech. Just Ask Bruce Merrifield," *Business Week*, April 7, 1986, pp. 94–96.

176. Robert J. Conrads, partner of McKinsey & Co., as reported in "Reshaping the Computer Industry," *Business Week*, July 16, 1984, p. 85.

177. The term "strategic alliance" has also been used to describe this new-found interest in collaboration. Jonathan B. Levine and John A. Byrne, "Corporate Odd Couples," *Business Week*, July 21, 1986, p. 100.

178. "U.S. Electronics Firms Form Venture to Stem Challenge by Japanese," *Wall Street Journal*, August 26, 1982, p. 26. "America's Riposte," *The Economist*, March 6, 1982, pp. 95–96. "How to Expand R&D Cooperation," *Business Week*, April 11, 1983, p. 21. "U.S. Entering Race for Supercomputer," *Chicago Tribune*, Jan. 22, 1984, p. 1. "Competition Means U.S. Cooperation," *Database Monthly*, Feb. 1984.

179. Barnard, *Executive*, Harvard University Press, 1938, 1968.

180. For example, Kenneth R. Andrews, *The Concept of Corporate Strategy* (Richard D. Irwin, Inc., 1980), pp. 5, 11–14. In accord, Joseph L. Bower, *The Two Faces of Management*, Houghton Mifflin Company, 1983, p. 121.

181. Barnard, *Executive*, p. 73.

182. Ibid., p. 82.

183. Ibid., p. 217.

184. The bulk of the data contained in this chapter came directly from interviews and surveys of MCC personnel, the participating companies and the individuals associated with the organization's creation and development. In particular, the cooperation of Admiral Inman with the author is deeply appreciated.

185. The R&D focus of MCC also serves to distinguish it from past foreign joint ventures, in that one author who studied domestic-foreign joint ventures noted a lack of collaborative R&D in these cooperative undertakings. Hladik, *International Joint Ventures*, pp. 7–8.

186. For a more detailed discussion of the National Cooperative Research Act of 1984 see chapter 3 and Appendix 1.

187. As evidence of this new corporate confidence is the fact that following the passage of NCRA over forty cooperative R&D ventures were quickly registered with the Department of Justice and the FTC. The number is currently over one hundred and they are listed in Appendix 3.

188. MCC officials have already reported that they have received a number of inquiries from companies planning to set up similar cooperative efforts. MCC is even considering hosting a conference on the establishment and management of MCC-type collaborative ventures.

189. See Appendix 2 for a description of Japanese and European cooperative efforts in microelectronics and computer technology.

190. The original proposed name of the venture was to be the Microelectronics and Computer Enterprises. Later the word Technology was added to indicate the involvement of non-computer companies. The name became the Microelectronics and Computer Technology Corporation when the enterprise became incorporated in 1982. The initials MCC rather than MCTC were adopted to avoid confusion with another organization using the latter set.

191. "The Japanese Threat – Challenge and Response," MCC-prepared video-tape, October 6, 1982. Also, "MCC – A Government Perspective," MCC-prepared videotape, November 4, 1982.

192. "The Japanese Threat – Challenge and Response," MCC-prepared video-tape, October 6, 1982.

193. Transcript of Norris's remarks made at Orlando, Florida, meeting, February 19, 1982, p. 1.

194. Ibid., p. 2 (emphasis his).

195. Unless otherwise indicated, the sources of the information regarding the events prior to MCC's incorporation in late 1982 are MCC member company executives who were involved at the time. Some of these member company executives later became executives of MCC.

196. MCC Business Plan, July 1, 1982, pp. 3, 32.

197. "Management Bob Price," Robert M. Price, later became chairman and chief executive of Control Data Corporation, succeeding William Norris.

198. For example, see the introduction to *Washington Post* reporter Philip J. Hilts's interview with Admiral Inman appearing *Omni Magazine*, 1984, p. 100. Also, "U.S. Intelligence Agencies 'Still Suffering from Scars' ", *U.S. News & World Report*, December 20, 1982, pp. 37–38, editorial, "Inman Is Out, C.I.A. and F.B.I. Vie to Spy," *The Nation*, May 8, 1982. Michael Schrage, "Adm. Inman In Command at Consortium," *Washington Post*, July 28, 1985, p. D1.

199. The Business Plan, prepared largely by CDC employees on loan, specifically recognized this concern: "MCC will not be dominated by a single participant (or small group of participants)." *MCC Business Plan*, July 1, 1982, p. 29.

200. This person was George Black, who was RCA's vice president for industrial relations and was selected as MCC first vice president for personnel.

201. Diane E. Downing, "Thinking for the Future: The Promise of MCC," *Austin Magazine*, August 1983, pp. 105–10.

202. Letter from Del Asmussen on behalf of MCC to John H. Gray, Manager of Economic Development of the Austin Chamber of Commerce, April 18, 1983.

203. The site selection criteria drawn up for MCC specifically required the presence of a leading university.

204. MCC Memorandum, "Executive Summary: The Texas Incentive for Austin," 1983.

205. Management Monograph No. 54, *Recent Experience*, p. 3.

206. Interview with William Norris conducted by the author.

207. Evert Clark, "American Can Beat Anyone in High Tech. Just Ask Bruce Merrifield," *Business Week*, April 7, 1986, pp. 94–96

208. Ibid.

209. For a description of Japanese and European cooperative ventures in the microelectronics and computer technology field see Appendix 2.

210. According to the MCC bylaws, firms not "domiciled in the United States and ultimately controlled and substantially owned by citizens of the United States" are not eligible for MCC membership. This exclusivity was modified in the wake of the Canada-US free trade agreement in 1989 to include Canadian firms. Public sector entities are not specifically excluded from membership by the bylaws, but the bylaws permit the board of directors to establish other admission criteria not explicitly stated. At this time the board of directors has chosen to exclude government participation. MCC Bylaws, adopted Dec. 7, 1982, as amended as of June 4, 1986, Article IV, Section 9.

211. The number of participating companies in MCC has fluctuated over the years. Although MCC had twenty-one member companies for a period from the end of 1984 through 1986, the identity of the twenty-one changed during that period, with Westinghouse purchasing Mostek's membership in June 1986 and Hewlett-Packard purchasing BMC's in November 1986. The shareholding membership fell to a low of nineteen in 1988. By mid-1990 the twenty-one shareholders were Advanced Micro Devices; Bellcore; Boeing; Cadence Design Systems, Inc; Control Data Corporation; Digital Equipment Corporation; Eastman Kodak; General Electric; Harris; Hewlett-Packard; Honeywell; Hughes Aircraft; Lockheed; Martin Marietta; 3M; Motorola; National Semiconductor; NCR; Northern Telecom; Rockwell International, and Westinghouse.

212. The acronym originally stood for: Burroughs, Univac (later Sperry), NCR, Control Data and Honeywell. Univac later became Sperry and is now part of Unisys following the Sperry-Burroughs merger.

213. "Honeywell's New Thrust," *Business Week*, December 1, 1986, p. 40.

214. United Press International, "Digital withdraws from two research projects," Dateline: Austin, Texas: Jan. 31, 1989.

215. In accordance with MCC bylaws, Lockheed gave the required one-year notice of its intention to leave MCC at the end of 1987. After subsequent negotiations Lockheed decided to remain a shareholder.

216. At the end of 1986 Allied-Signal announced its intention to leave MCC.

217. See chapter seven for a detailed discussion of the MCC communication system and strategy.

218. "MCC Technology Program Personnel Selection, Retention & Motivation," Internal MCC Policy Document, November 4, 1982.

219. For a discussion of the recruiting problem as an example of the Prisoner's Dilemma see chapter 2.

220. Kevin Kelly, "A High-Tech Think Tank Thinks Big Bucks," *Business Week*, September 25, 1989, p. 222–26.

221. David H. Freedman, "Common Sense and the Computer," *Discover*, August 1990, p. 65.

222. Although broad authority was given to the individual program directors it was not a "give and forget" type. Inman made it clear that the program directors had an important obligation to review and plan in coordination with the other programs and in consultation with the executive committee. Memorandum from Inman to MCC vice presidents, November 23, 1983. The details of these obligations are set forth in *The MCC Authorities Guide*, November 18, 1983.

223. One recent article made note of Inman's hands-off policy, stating that during Inman's Navy days, he "once created a team that fell apart when he left." Inman did not want that to happen at MCC. Otis Port and Every Clark, "Is Bobby Inman's Baby Strong Enough to Go It Alone?" *Business Week*, September 22, 1986, p. 31.

224. Donna K. H. Walters, "High-tech Consortium Enters Critical Phase With New Chief," *Los Angeles Times*, July 6, 1987, Part 4, p. 1.

225. Andrew Pollack, "Ousted U.S. Research Leader to Join Computer Consortium," *The New York Times*, July 4, 1990, Section 2, p. 44.

226. "Fields takes over as MCC president," UPI Newswire, July 10, 1990.

227. Money; Business Roundup, *The Washington Times*, July 10, 1990, p. C1.

228. Unless otherwise noted, much of the information contained in this chapter was obtained by the author from interviews with CIIT and industry officials.

229. For a discussion of CIIT's formation see "The Chemical Industry Institute of Toxicology," Harvard Business School Case Study 382–167 (1982) prepared by the author under the supervision of Professor Joseph L. Bower.

230. For another example, see Thomas J. Bray, "Protecting the Health of Du Pont Employees Is a Costly Proposition," *Wall Street Journal*, June 28, 1976, p. 1.

231. "Chemical Companies Team Up for Early Warning on 'more VCMs' " *Chemical Week*, January 29, 1975, pp. 44–45.

232. To gain a sense of the controversy surrounding vinyl chloride see: Ralph L. Cherry, "VCM's Labor and Management In Confrontation at Hearings on 'Viable' Industry Standards," *Chemical Marketing Reporter*, July 1, 1974, p. 1, 38; Patrick P. McCurdy, "We're In This Together," *Chemical Week*, July 3, 1974, p. 5; "How They Found the Vinyl-Cancer Link," *Chemical Week*, July 17, 1974, pp. 30–32; "Vinyl Chloride Controversy Lends New Urgency to Interest in Toxic Chemicals Legislation," *Chemical Marketing Reporter*, August 26, 1974, pp. 5, 25; "Vinyl Chloride Exposure Set at One Part per Million—SPI Sues to Reverse Ruling," *Chemical Marketing Reporter*, October 7, 1974, p. 1; and "High Court Takes Two Lines in VCM and Taconite Rulings," *Chemical Marketing Reporter*, April 7, 1975, pp. 7, 32.

233. *CIIT 1980 Annual Report*.

234. "People: He's Leading Industry Search for Better Methods to Pinpoint Chemical Hazards," *Chemical Week*, March 17, 1976, p. 48.

235. For a discussion of CIIT's early years, see "CIIT Moves to a Home of Its Own," *Chemical Week*, July 25, 1979.

236. The shortage of skilled toxicologists was particularly acute following the passage of the Toxic Substances Control Act. "Will There Be Enough Toxicologists?" *Chemical Week*, November 17, 1976, pp. 38–39. According to one article at the time an unfilled demand for over one thousand trained toxicologist existed. "Wanted 1,000 Toxicologists," *Chemical Week*, September 21, 1977, p. 51.

237. *CIIT Operating Policies*, 1980.

238. "Filling in Toxicology Gaps," *Chemical Week*, November 17, 1976, pp. 36–37.

239. For a discussion of the formaldehyde issue as it developed in the late 1970s see "Formaldehyde Under Fire," *Chemical Marketing Reporter*, October 22, 1979, pp. 3, 61.

240. Patrick P. McCurdy, "CIIT: Happy 10th Birthday—and More," *Chemical Week*, June 27, 1984.

241. Patrick P. McCurdy, "CIIT: Not for Spectators," *Chemical Week*, July 30, 1986, p. 3. It should be noted that these thirty-four companies represented nearly one-third of annual U.S. chemical shipments and included all ten top chemical producers as well as 80 percent of the top twenty.

242. David Rotman, "Seeking New Ways to Assess Toxic Chemicals," *Chemical Week*, January 18, 1989, p. 52.

243. Peter H. Lewis, "Are U.S. Companies Learning to Share?" *New York Times*, February 7, 1988, E9.

244. Gary Hector, "The U.S. Chipmakers' Shaky Comeback," *Fortune*, June 20, 1988, p. 64.

245. Ibid., p. 59.

246. Letter from Robert Noyce, president of Sematech and founder of Intel, to John N. Ols, Jr., U.S. General Accounting Office, September 22, 1989.

247. J. Raloff, "DOD is Asked to Aid Semiconductor Firms," *Science News*, February 21, 1987, p. 117.

248. Jeffrey Bairstow, "Can the U.S. Semiconductor Industry be Saved?" *High Technology*, May 1987, p. 34.

249. Robert B. Reich, "The Quiet Path to Technological Preeminence," *Scientific American*, October 1989, vol. 261, number 4, pp. 41–47.

250. Richard Brandt, Jonathan Levine, and Robert D. Hof, "The Future of Silicon Valley," *Business Week*, February 5, 1990, p. 54. Peter Waldman and Brenton R. Schlender, "Falling Chips: Is a big federal role the way to revitalize semiconductor firms?" *Wall Street Journal*, February 17, 1987, p.1. "Pentagon task force to offer $2b survival plan for US chip industry," *The Boston Globe*, January 8, 1987, p. 34. "The High Tech Commodity," *The Economist*, November 22, 1986, p. 88. John W. Wilson, "Is it too late to save the U.S. semiconductor industry?" *Business Week*, August 18, 1986, p. 62. "A Cartel to stop America's chip makers feeling dumped upon," *The Economist*, March 22, 1986, p. 69.

251. For the history of MCC see chapter 5.

252. The name Sematech is derived from SEmiconductor MAnufacturing TECHnology.

253. SIA also established the Semiconductor Research Corporation, headed by Larry W. Sumney, a former defense official. SRC operates as a clearinghouse for research funding for institutions and corporations.

254. Richard Brandt and Otis Port, "Silicon Valley Unfurls a Flag: 'Don't Tread on Me,' " *Business Week*, August, 31, 1987, p. 62.

255. Ibid.

256. Lewis, "Are U.S. Companies Learning to Share?," p. E9.

257. Dorinda G. Dallmeyer, "National Security and the Semiconductor Industry," *Technology Review*, November/December 1987, pp. 47–55.

258. Hector, "The U.S. Chipmakers' Shaky Comeback," p. 62.

259. Ibid.

260. Ibid.

261. Noyce's sudden and unexpected death on June 3, 1990, forced the consortium into a search for a new leader. Although it was recognized that finding someone with Noyce's unique blend of managerial skill and vision, his loss was not seen as crippling to the organization since he had been planning to retire later in 1990. The one role where Noyce would be missed was in his lobbying abilities for increased government support. "Noyce Death Won't Panic Sematech," *Inside R&D*, June 13, 1990, Volume 19, Number 24, p. 2. Sematech selected William J. Spencer, an industry outsider, as new chief in October 1990.

262. Smith, *Wealth of Nations*, p. 248.

263. Ibid.

264. Otis Port, Thane Peterson, and Robert D. Hof, "Hands Across the Chipmaking Chasm," *Business Week*, July 3, 1989, pp. 28–29.

265. Naomi Freundlich, ed., "Western Chipmakers Form a Superteam to Take on Japan," *Business Week*, June 26, 1989, p. 158.

266. Statements of John M. Ols, Jr., Director of Housing and Community Development Issues for the United States General Accounting Office, before the House Subcommittee on Transportation, Aviation, and Materials and the House Subcommittee on Science, Space, and Technology, November 8, 1989, p. 2.

267. The industry members of Sematech are: Advanced Micro Devices, Inc.; AT&T; Digital Equipment Corporation; Harris Corporation; Hewlett-Packard Company; Intel Corporation; IBM; LSI Logic Corporation; Micron Technology, Inc.; Motorola, Inc.; National Semiconductor Corporation; NCR Corporation; Rockwell International Corporation; and Texas Instruments, Inc.

268. Budget Director Richard Darman and Michael J. Boskin, chairman of the Council of Economic Advisers, oppose Defense Department support of consortia with commercial spin-offs on the grounds that they represent the Pentagon practicing industrial policy.

269. John Carey, "Will the White House Torpedo America, Inc.?" *Business Week*, November 27, 1989, p. 80.

270. Bob Davis, "Sematech Funds Don't Face Cut, Bush Aide Says," *Wall Street Journal*, November 20, 1989, B4.

271. Richard A. Shaffer, "The Chip Consortium Debate: Let a Thousand Companies Fight," *New York Times*, July 9, 1989, F2.

272. United States General Accounting Office, "The SEMATECH Consortium's Start-up Activities," *Report to Congressional Requesters*, GAO/RCED–90–37, November 1989, p. 3.

273. Ibid., p. 4.

274. Smith, *Wealth of Nations*, p. 254.

275. Ibid., p. 252.

276. Ibid., p. 246.

277. The number of assignees per member company ranges from three to twenty-seven.

278. General Accounting Office, "SEMATECH Start-up," p. 35.

279. See discussion of this issue in chapter 5.

280. GAO, "SEMATECH Start-up," p. 2.

281. Ibid., p. 6.

282. Ibid., p. 5.

283. Ibid., p. 38.

284. In its proposal, Texas, in conjunction with the University of Texas at Austin, agreed to: (1) provide a four-acre site, including a five-story office building and a warehouse, in southeast Austin; (2) renovate and furnish the office building; (3) construct a central utility building; (4) partially renovate the warehouse into a semiconductor fabrication facility; and (5) pay issuance costs and first-year interest on construction bonds. The City of Austin provided electrical power facilities, utility connections, and building and development fee abatements.

285. Brandt and Port, "Silicon Valley Unfurls a Flag," p. 62.

286. General Accounting Office, "SEMATECH Start-up," p. 35.

287. Ibid., p. 5.

288. Smith, *Wealth of Nations*, p. 248.

289. Ibid., p. 254.

290. Reich, "Technological Preeminence," p. 45.

291. Although there is consideration within the government of extending cooperative permissiveness beyond R&D activities to manufacturing, approved legislation similar to the National Cooperative Research Act of 1984 is still absent.

292. Robert N. Noyce, "Cooperation Is the Best Way to Beat Japan," *New York Times*, July 9, 1989, F2.

293. Smith, *Wealth of Nations*, p. 246.

294. G. Christian Hill and Michael W. Miller, "Computer Firms Make Bold Pitch to Retake Market Lost to Japan," *Wall Street Journal*, June 22, 1989, p. 1.

295. Hector, "The U.S. Chipmakers' Shaky Comeback," p. 64.

296. Hill and Miller, "Computer Firms," p. 1.

297. Jane Fitz Simon, "High-tech Firms Form Joint Venture to Make Chips in US," *Boston Globe*, June 22, 1989, p. 35.

298. Lawrence Edelman, "US Memories Out To Prove Its Worth," *Boston Globe*, October 29, 1989, p. A1.

299. "America's Chipmakers: Memory Games," *The Economist*, October 26, 1989, p. 74.

300. Ibid., p. 72. Edelman, "US Memories" p. A1.

301. Individual company investment was expected to range from $5 million to $50 million apiece.

302. "Reports Say US Microchip Consortium Expected to Fold," *Boston Globe*, January 15, 1990, p. 11.

303. Stephen Kreider Yoder, "U.S. Memories to Abandon Bid for Chip Venture," *Wall Street Journal*, January 15, 1990, p. B4.

304. Hof, "This Will Surely Come Back," p. 73.

305. Editorial, "The Sad Death of a Consortium," *Business Week*, January 29, 1990, p. 106. Hof, "This Will Surely Come Back," pp. 72–73. Stephen Kreider Yoder, "Lessons Linger as U.S. Memories Fails," *Wall Street Journal*, January 16, 1990, p. B1.

306. Hof, "This Will Surely Come Back," p. 72.

307. Ibid.

308. Peter Dworkin, "Will Corporate Myopia Mean Goodbye, U.S. Chips?" *U.S. News & World Report*, December 18, 1989, p. 38.

309. Stephen Kreider Yoder, "Collapse Spells Victory for Foe of Consortium," *Wall Street Journal*, January 16, 1990, p. B9.

310. Stephen Kreider Yoder, "Lessons Linger ," p. B9.

311. Clifford Barney, "R&D Co-op Gets Set to Open Up Shop," *Electronics*, March 24, 1983. "Inman's Innovation," *The National Journal*, March 5, 1983. David Warsh, "High-Tech Gets Even Smarter," *Boston Globe*, April 10, 1983.

312. "Why MCC Picked Austin," *High Tech Facilities*, November 1983, pp. H27–H31. Jeffrey M. Guinn, "Consortium Is Gambling All Its Chips," *Fort Worth Star-Telegram*, June 26, 1983, pp. 1, 8. William H. Gregory, "Recruiting High Technology," *Aviation Week & Space Technology*, February 27, 1984, p. 11. Harry Hurt III, "Birth of a New Frontier," *Texas Monthly*, April 1984, pp. 132–35, 238–47. "Austin Discards Its Dungarees," *The Economist*, May 26, 1984, p. 34. "Austin, Texas: On a High-Tech High," *Fortune*, October 15, 1984, pp. 164–71.

313. "High-Tech Companies Team Up in the R&D Race," *Business Week*, August 15, 1983, pp. 94–95. Karen Blumenthal, "High-Tech Consortium Growing," *Dallas Morning News*, October 11, 1983, pp. 1D, 3D. "Inman: The Man in the Driver's Seat," *The Chronicle*, February 1984, p. 5.

314. Fifth *MCC Draft Policy on Protection of Proprietary and Confidential Information*, October 8, 1984.

315. David E. Sanger, "Computer Consortium Lags: Rivalries Split U.S. Project," *The New York Times*, September 5, 1984, D1, D5.

316. This information was eventually disclosed to the press by a member company. Clinton Wilder, "The MCC Payoff," *Computerworld*, June 10, 1985, pp. ID9–ID14.

317. MCC ByLaws, December 7, 1982, as amended as of June 4, 1986, Article X, Section 55.

318. In late 1986, Texas Instruments again evaluated membership when they were considering purchasing Gould's position in MCC.

319. *Cray Research, Inc.*, Harvard Business School Case Service 385–011, p. 16.

320. MCC ByLaws, December 7, 1982, as amended as of June 4, 1986, Article X, Section 58.

321. Such a endeavor was undertaken by MCC in 1985 "Technology Transfer Readiness Evaluation," 1985 internal MCC document prepared by Richard L. Gerstner, director of the associates program of MCC.

322. See discussion in chapter 2.

323. Barnard, *Executive*. Kenneth R. Andrews, *The Concept of Corporate Strategy* (Richard D. Irwin, Inc., 1980), pp. 5, 11–14. Benton E. Gup, "Begin Strategic Planning by Asking Three Questions," *Managerial Planning*, November–December 1979, pp. 28–31.

324. See chapter 5 for more detail on Norris's ideas on the purpose of MCC.

325. The original notion was that technology created by MCC would be assembled into a Standard Technology Package (STP) that would then be transferred to the contributing shareholder companies. As MCC evolved, the transfer of technology began to occur in a more continuous, rather than discrete, manner.

326. For example, (1) limitation of investment, limitation of risk, (2) overcoming nationalistic prejudice, and (3) merging skills and strengths: Herzfeld, *Ventures*, pp. 26–27. (1) Make available diverse resources and minimize risk, (2) increase options,

(3) circumvent capital crisis, and (4) permit project-specific financing: Roulac, "Structuring," p. 5. (1) Risk avoidance, (2) knowledge acquisition, and (3) market power creation: Berg, Duncan, & Friedman, *Strategies and Innovation*, p. 93. (1) Complementary strengths, (2) shared resources, (3) joining a winning team, and (4) sharing risk: Coopers & Lybrand et al., *Collaborative Ventures*, p. 3.

327. Ibid.

328. For a discussion of comparable Japanese cooperative ventures see Appendix 1.

329. For a more detailed discussion of CIIT see chapter 6.

330. The Semiconductor Research Corporation (SRC), originally named the Semiconductor Research Cooperative, was formed in 1982 by eleven companies to jointly conduct research and development, mostly by means of research contracts and grants. For a more detailed discussion of CIIT see chapter 7.

331. The Council for Chemical Research (CCR) was formed by the chemical industry to encourage, through university grants, the graduate training of chemists in areas of importance to the sponsors.

332. The Health Effects Institute was formed in 1980 by the major automobile manufacturers to coordinate researching into the pollution effects of the internal combustion engine. An earlier effort by the industry to collaborate in this area ended in a government antitrust attack. See the discussion regarding the Smog Conspiracy in chapter 3.

333. Even AT&T has sought out partners for strategic alliances. In 1983 AT&T sent shock waves through the telecommunications industry when it announced that it was forming a joint venture with Philips. The industry's fears appear to have been exaggerated. "The Big Order Still Eludes AT&T-Philips Venture," *Electronics*, October 28, 1985, pp. 38–39.

334. This was cited by the automobile manufacturers as one of the reasons for their ill-fated collaboration in pollution control devices. See discussion of the Smog Conspiracy in chapter 3.

335. For a discussion of the Smog Conspiracy case see chapter 3.

336. The Health Effects Institute is an independent, nonprofit organization funded not only by the automobile manufacturers but also by the federal government.

337. The Kodak-Matsushita cooperation involves electronic video equipment. The GM-Toyota collaboration involves compact automobiles.

338. The GM-Toyota joint venture, known as New United Motor Manufacturing Inc. or NUMMI, is reportedly twice as productive in assembling automobiles as the GM norm. *Business Week*, October 6, 1986, p. 61.

339. Harrigan, *Strategies*, pp. 144–150.

340. One might argue that the presence of multiple governments, not unlike the presence of multiple private firms in MCC, has made purpose definition and formulation more difficult in European collaborative ventures such as Esprit. For a discussion of Esprit and other foreign cooperative ventures, both Japanese and European, see Appendix 1.

341. The government's annual $100 million commitment to Sematech has recently been called into question. Dworkin, "Goodbye, U.S. chips?" pp. 36–38

342. MCC Shareholder Survey conducted by the author, Section VII, Questions 1 through 4.

343. See Appendix 1 for descriptions of Japanese (and European) examples of interfirm cooperation in microelectronics and computer technology.

344. It should be noted, though, that the government is explicitly recognized in the original MCC Business Plan as a significant "stakeholder," along with the member companies' customers, suppliers and vendors, and shareholders and investors. MCC Business Plan, July 1, 1982, p. 12.

345. The MCC shareholder companies surveyed accounted for nearly $37.7 billion of the $152.7 billion in U.S. defense contracts awarded in 1985, nearly 24 percent of the total.

346. The member companies selected retired Admiral Bobby Ray Inman, former NSA head and former deputy director of the CIA. MCC was Admiral Inman's first nonpublic position.

347. This theme has been elaborated upon by Joseph L. Bower and Eric Rhenman in "Benevolent Cartels," *Harvard Business Review*, July-August 1985, p. 124.

348. MCC Shareholder Survey conducted by the author, Section V, Question 2.

349. MCC Shareholder Survey conducted by the author, Section VI, Questions 1 through 5.

350. Draft of the Minutes of the Regular Meeting of the Board of Directors of MCC, June 4, 1986, p. 13. At the September 3, 1986, board meeting, the issue of MCC permanence was discussed but was overshadowed by the announcement of Inman's resignation.

351. See for example Sanger, "Computer Consortium Lags," pp. D1–D4; or more recently, David E. Sanger, "Inman to Resign at MCC," *New York Times*, September 5, 1986, pp. D1–D7.

352. At the June 4, 1986, board of directors meeting Admiral Inman noted that he and Mr. Howard, Motorola's representative on the board, had received indications that government support for the proposed manufacturing technology program that failed to gain shareholder support. Admiral Inman noted that the original MCC Business Plan, while prohibiting government equity participant, did not preclude government financial participation in a particular research program. Draft Minutes of the Regular Meeting of the Board of Directors, June 4, 1986, p. 11.

353. The decision to seek IR&D approval was not unanimous among the MCC member companies.

354. For example, the early difficulties in staffing, the long process of setting up an administrative structure, and the decision to go cafeteria-style on program participation. See discussion in chapter 5.

355. Given the reported difficulties with interfirm cooperation and the percentage of failures this wariness is not unexpected.

356. Simison, "Quiet War," p. 4. Harry Marshall, "The Best is Yet to Come," *Modern Machine Shop Monthly*, February 1984. James Coates, "U.S. Entering Race for Supercomputer," *Chicago Tribune*, January 22, 1984, p. 1. Diane E. Downing, "Thinking for the Future: The Promise of MCC," *Austin Magazine*, August 1983, pp. 105–10. Norris, "Keeping America First," pp. 282–87. "America's Riposte," pp. 95–96.

357. "Computer Czar Sets Talk," *San Antonio Light*, Dec. 29, 1983.

358. "The High-tech Commodity," *The Economist*, November 22, 1986, pp. 88–89.

359. See chapter 3.

360. Thomas M. Jorde, "Remarks on Acceptable Cooperation Among Competitors in the Face of Growing International Competition," *Antitrust Law Journal*, Vol. 58, No. 2, August 1989, p. 519.

361. Of course, Section 5 of the Federal Trade Commission Act [15 U.S.C.A. §45 (1976)] is also relevant in that it encompasses the referenced provisions of the Sherman and Clayton Acts.

362. The Act of July 2, 1890. 15 U.S.C. §1 (1976).

363. See discussion in Chapter 3.

364. The Act of July 2, 1890. 15 U.S.C. §2.

365. The Act of October 15, 1914. 15 U.S.C. §18 (1980).

366. 98th Congress 2d Session House of Representatives Report 98–656.

367. 98th Congress 2d Session Senate Report 98–247.

368. National Cooperative Research Act of 1984, §3. P.L. 98–462, 98 Stat. 1815 (1984), 15 U.S.C.A. §§4301–4305.

369. The Act contains six sections. As mentioned above, Section 3 specifies that the rule of reason shall apply to joint R&D ventures which are defined in Section 2. Section 4 reduces liability exposure to actual damages (in contrast to triple damages). Section 5 allows for a prevailing litigant to obtain costs and reasonable attorney's fees, subject to certain conditions and qualifications. Section 6 enumerates the procedures required for disclosure to antitrust enforcement agencies. For a detailed discussion of the Act, see Charles F. Rule, "The Administration's Views on Joint Ventures," 54 *Antitrust L.J.* 1121 (1985).

370. Unless otherwise stated, the source of the information contained in this appendix are documents prepared by MCC's International Liaison Office (ILO), which monitors research and development activities in foreign countries, as well as from interviews with Ted Ralston, MCC director of the ILO.

371. To cite one possible measure of success, the project applied for 1,000 patents. William G. Ouchi, "Political and Economic Teamwork: The Development of the Microelectronics Industry of Japan," *California Management Review* Vol. 26 No. 4 (Summer 1984), p. 26.

372. "Report on International Developments in Microelectronics and Computer Technology Research," prepared by MCC's International Liaison Office, (May 1, 1984).

373. For additional information regarding ICOT, see Edward A. Feigenbaum and Pamela McCorduck, *The Fifth Generation; Artificial Intelligence and Japan's Computer Challenge to the World* (Addison-Wesley, 1983) and Robert Haavind, "Playing to Win A New Generation," *High Technology*, August 1985, pp. 63–66.

374. *International Liaison Office (ILO) Newsletter*, Number 2, internal publication of MCC, December 7, 1984.

375. Ouchi, "Political and Economic Teamwork," pp. 28–29.

376. David Sanger, "Computer Consortium Lags," *New York Times*, September 5, 1984, pp. D1–D4. Against this position is J. Robert Lineback, "MCC: The Research Co-op's Surprising Fast Start," *Electronics*, December 16, 1985, pp. 49–51.

377. See for example the comments of Robert Dewar, professor of computer science at New York University, who claims that the project is "glossy and general and devoid of technical content" and is "grounded on uncritical acceptance of a number of pragmatically dubious avant-garde concepts." *Fortune Magazine*, Oct. 4, 1982, p. 88.

378. For additional information, see Special Report, "Where Japan Has A Research Edge," *Business Week*, March 14, 1983, p. 116.

379. Joyce Heard, "IBM Finds A Club That Doesn't Want It As A Member," *Business Week*, February 11, 1985, pp. 42–44.

380. For additional information, see "Fifth Generation Computers: The Race Is Still Open," *The Economist*, November 17, 1984, pp. 88–93.

381. Paul Tate, "An Eye on AI," *Datamation*, Vol. 30, January 1984, p. 54.

382. *ILO Newsletter*. Apparently part of the difficulties among the participants was attributable to the decision to locate ECRC in Munich. It was feared that this location would favor Siemens over the other members.

383. The attempt by Italy's Olivetti and Britain's Acorn to develop trans-European educational computers failed due to a lack of standards. "Eureka!" *The Economist*, July 5, 1986, pp. 16–17.

Selected Bibliography

BOOKS

Barnard, Chester. *The Functions of the Executive*. Cambridge, MA: Harvard University Press, 1938, 1968.

Berg, Sanford, Jerome Duncan, & Philip Friedman. *Joint Venture Strategies and Corporate Innovation*. Cambridge, MA: Oelgeschlageer, Gunn & Hain, 1982.

Dertouzos, Michael L., Richard Lester, and Richard M. Solow. *Made in America: Regaining the Productive Edge*. Cambridge, MA: The MIT Press, 1989.

Franko, Lawrence G. *Joint Venture Survival in Multinational Corporations*. New York: Praeger Publishers, 1971.

Harrigan, Kathryn Rudie. *Strategies for Joint Ventures*. Lexington, MA: Lexington Books, 1985.

Herzfeld, Edgar. *Joint Ventures*. Bristol: Jordan & Sons, 1983.

Hladik, Karen J. *International Joint Ventures*. Lexington, MA: Lexington Books, 1985.

Högberg, Bengt. *Interfirm Cooperation and Strategic Development*. Stockholm: BAS, 1977.

Kinter, Earl W. *The Legislative History of the Federal Antitrust Laws and Related Statutes*. New York: The MacMillan Company, 1978.

Link, Albert N. and Laura L. Bauer. *Cooperative Research in U.S. Manufacturing: Assessing Policy Initiatives and Corporate Strategies*. Lexington, MA: Lexington Books, 1989.

MacLaren, Terrence F. and Walter G. Marple, Jr. *Licensing in Foreign and Domestic Operations — Joint Ventures*. Vol. 4. New York: Clark Boardman, 1985.

Schelling, Thomas C. *The Strategy of Conflict*. Cambridge, MA: Harvard University Press, 1960.

Stopford, John M. and Louis T. Wells, Jr. *Managing the Multinational Enterprise*. New York: Basic Books, 1972.

Telser, Lester G. *A Theory of Efficient Cooperation and Competition*. Cambridge: Cambridge University Press, 1987.

Vernon, Raymond, and Louis T. Wells, Jr. *Manager in the International Economy*.
    Prentice-Hall, 1976.
von Neumann, John, and Oskar Morgenstern. *Theory of Games and Economics
    Behavior*. Princeton, NJ: Princeton University Press, 1944.

MONOGRAPHS

Coopers & Lybrand/Yankelovich, Skelly and White, Inc. *Collaborative Ventures: A
    Pragmatic Approach to the Business Expansion in the Eighties*. New York:
    Coopers & Lybrand, 1984.
Young, Richard and Standish Bradford, Jr. *Joint Ventures: Planning & Action*. New
    York: Financial Executives Research Foundation, 1977.

ARTICLES

Berg, Sanford, and Philip Friedman. "Joint Ventures in American Industry," *Mergers
    and Acquisitions* (Fall 1978).
Bower, Joseph L., and Eric A. Rhenman. "Benevolent Cartels." 85 *Harvard Business
    Review* 124 (July–August 1985).
Brodley, Joseph F. "The Legal Status of Joint Ventures under the Antitrust Laws: A
    Summary Assessment." 21 *Antitrust Bulletin* 453 (1976).
Letwin, William L. "Congress and the Sherman Antitrust Law: 1887–1890," 23 *U.
    Chicago Law Review* 221, 257 (Winter 1956).
Pfeffer, Jeffrey, and Phillip Nowak. "Patterns of Joint Venture Activity — Implications
    for Antitrust Policy," *Antitrust Bulletin*, 21(2):315–39 (1976).
Pitofsky, Robert. "A Framework for Antitrust Analysis of Joint Ventures." 54 *Antitrust
    L.J.* 893, 894 (1985).
Roulac, Stephen E. "Structuring the Joint Venture." *Mergers & Acquisitions* (Spring
    1980).
Taubman, Joseph. "What Constitutes a Joint Venture?" 41 *Cornell L. Quarterly* 640,
    641 (1957).

Index

ABOUT THE AUTHOR

WILLIAM J. MURPHY earned both his masters and doctorate degrees at the Harvard Business School and is currently a Professor of Law at the Franklin Pierce Law Center in Concord, New Hampshire. He is a founding partner of Frankel, Murphy & Ogden, a law firm specializing in intellectual property matters.